Psychology and
Child Custody Determinations

Children and the Law

General Editors:
Gary B. Melton
Lois A. Weithorn

Consulting Editors:
Thomas Grisso
Gerald P. Koocher
Robert H. Mnookin
Walter J. Wadlington

Psychology and Child Custody Determinations

Knowledge, Roles, and Expertise

Edited by Lois A. Weithorn

University of Nebraska Press
Lincoln and London

The paper in this book meets the minimum requirements of American
National Standard for Information Sciences—Permanence of Paper for
Printed Library Materials, ANSI Z39.48-1984.

Library of Congress Cataloging-in-Publication Data

Psychology and child custody determinations.

   (Children and the law)
   Includes indexes.
     1. Custody of children—United States.   2. Divorce suits—United
States.   3. Children of divorced parents—United States—Psychology.
I. Weithorn, Lois A., 1953–   . II. Series.
KF547.P78   1987   346.7301'7   86-25071
                      347.30617
ISBN 0-8032-4732-X (alk. paper)

Second printing: 1990

Contents

Preface

The Goals of This Book

The American Psychological Association's Ethics Committee and its members (e.g., Hall & Hare-Mustin, 1983; Keith-Spiegel & Koocher, 1985; Ochroch, 1982), legal scholars (Mnookin, 1975; Okpaku, 1976), and experts in psycholegal assessment (Grisso, 1986; Melton, Petrila, Poythress, & Slobogin, in press) have leveled sharp criticism at psychological consultants in divorce custody cases. In general, these rebukes cite a long list of deficiencies and abuses in professional practice, including inadequate familiarity with applicable legal standards and procedures; use of inappropriate psychological assessment techniques; presentation of opinions based on partial or irrelevant data; overreaching by exceeding the limitations of psychological knowledge in expert testimony and offering opinions on matters of law; loss of objectivity through inappropriate engagement in the adversary process; and failure to recognize the boundaries and parameters of confidentiality in the custody context.

The Division of Child, Youth, and Family Services (Division 37) of the American Psychological Association (APA), in response to these criticisms, established a Committee on Child Custody. The American Psychology-Law Society (the Division of Law and Psychology or Division 41 of APA) joined Division 37 in cosponsoring the committee's efforts. This book is the product of these interdivisional efforts. Although the sponsoring divisions have encouraged and supported this product, the opinions expressed here are those of the authors and do not represent an official APA or division position.

The title of this book, *Psychology and Child Custody Determinations: Knowledge, Roles, and Expertise,* reflects our goals in publishing it. In reviewing the state of scientific *knowledge* pertinent to the court's inquiries in divorce custody cases, the boundaries of our clinical *expertise,* and the conflicts inherent in particular *roles,* we have tried to identify the *strengths* of psychology and its potential contributions to legal resolution of custody disputes together with the *limitations* that we believe necessarily must constrain psychological forays into divorce custody cases. An overall theme of this book is the message that, above all, humility and caution must characterize the involvement of psychologists in custody cases. There is much we do not know, such as what is "best" for children. Our assessment tools are limited: they can neither predict the future nor substitute for the wisdom of the court. The dangers of missteps and oversteps can be dramatic because of the consequences of the court's adjudication on the participants' lives.

In planning this book, we made certain choices about its scope. We decided to focus on psychological consultation in *divorce* custody cases rather than on such consultation in child custody cases generally or in the child protection context in which some custody cases arise. Our decision was motivated by two factors. First, the committee judged that the divergence of issues in the divorce context as contrasted with the child protective custody context was sufficient to warrant treatment in separate volumes. Second, given that the resources of the committee permitted examination of only one of these contexts at present, we allowed our concern about the extent of criticism of psychological participation in divorce custody cases to guide our choice of emphasis. Although we do not discuss in any depth the scientific literature or professional issues relevant to psychological testimony in child abuse or neglect cases, in chapter 1 we have presented a brief overview of relevant legal concepts. Our purpose in doing so is to introduce the range of postures in which child custody cases may be presented to the courts and to distinguish for our readers the circumstances characterizing the private dispute settlement functions, as contrasted with the child protective functions, of the court in child custody adjudications (Mnookin, 1975).

The committee also determined that this book would not be a "handbook" or "how to" guide for clinicians participating in child custody evaluations. Again, considering the nature of the criticism cited above, we decided to retain a more theoretical perspective, reviewing the scientific basis for courtroom participation and related clinical and professional issues.

To further the goals of the Child Custody Committee of the Task Force on Legal Issues, this book has been structured in the following manner. Chapters 1 and 2 discuss the legal context of child custody cases. In chapter 1, Wyer, Gaylord, and Grove introduce the legal concepts and processes that define custody adjudication. In so doing, they highlight the broad judicial discretion resulting from the "best interests" standard and emphasize the subjectivity and unpredictability that sometimes characterize adjudications of custody in divorce. Scott and Emery, in chapter 2, present an analysis of the functioning of the adversary legal system in custody cases, in theory and in reality. They identify some of the possible effects of the divorce custody adjudication process for families, particularly children. They delineate some of the hopes and challenges of divorce mediation, an alternative to custody litigation.

Chapters 3 and 4 review the state of scientific knowledge in psychology relevant to child custody adjudication. Rohman, Sales, and Lou (chap. 3) focus on the "best interests" standard, reviewing applicable case and statutory law. As they enumerate those "factors" that courts have considered relevant to adjudication of children's best interests, they review the state of psychological knowledge pertaining to each factor. This comprehensive review underscores the limits and strengths of our current data base as it relates to those variables typically considered by the courts in custody cases. In a related and equally comprehensive literature review, Felner and Terre (chap. 4) examine the state of scientific knowledge about the effects of various custodial arrangements on children's psychological adaptation following divorce. Felner and Terre address pointedly the debate over the alleged superiority of joint custody as a placement alternative, and their arguments are firmly rooted in the research data. Both chapter 3 and chapter 4 highlight what we do and do not know about what appears to be good for children of divorce.

Chapters 5 and 6 focus on professional issues. Weithorn and Grisso, in chapter 5, examine in depth some of the more common problems characterizing psychological participation in custody cases and suggest principles and procedures that psychologists might observe so as to promote more competent and relevant custody evaluations. Finally, in chapter 6, I review some of the ethical issues that arise in relation to psychologists' testimony in divorce custody cases. The goal of this chapter is to highlight and address potential problems.

We hope that this book will instill caution in psychologists who consider venturing into the courtroom to participate in divorce custody cases. In reviewing the state of our psychological knowledge, the boundaries of our psychological expertise, and the dangers of particular roles undertaken by psychologists, we have tried to underscore the limitations of such psychological forays. Whereas the contributions of psychology to the adjudicatory process can at times be of great assistance to the courts, psychologists also must be loyal to their rigorous scientific, professional, and ethical traditions, particularly to the extent that these traditions require humility.

References

Grisso, T. (1986). *Evaluating competencies: Forensic assessments and instruments.* New York: Plenum.

Hall, J. E., & Hare-Mustin, R. T. (1983). Sanctions and the diversity of ethical complaints against psychologists. *American Psychologist, 38,* 714–729.

Keith-Spiegel, P., & Koocher, G. P. (1985). *Ethics in psychology.* New York: Random House.

Melton, G. B., Petrila, J., Poythress, N. G., Jr., & Slobogin, C. (In press). *Psychological evaluations for the court: A handbook for mental health professionals and lawyers.* New York: Guilford Press.

Mnookin, R. H. (1975). Child-custody adjudication: Judicial functions in the face of indeterminancy. *Law and Contemporary Problems, 39,* 226–293.

Ochroch, R. (1982). *Ethical pitfalls in child custody evaluations.* Paper presented at the American Psychological Association Convention, Washington, D.C.

Okpaku, S. (1976). Psychology: Impediment or aid in child custody cases? *Rutgers Law Review, 29,* 1117–1153.

Acknowledgments

In 1981 the president of the Division of Child, Youth, and Family Services, then Carolyn Schroeder, established a Task Force on Legal Issues in that division. Chaired by Gary B. Melton and with the membership of Gerald P. Koocher and Lois A. Weithorn, the task force directed its efforts toward conceptualizing and coordinating projects focusing on four current topics relating to children and the law: adolescent abortion, civil commitment of minors, informed consent for treatment and research involving children, and child custody. These four topics were selected because the task force members felt that in each area a particular piece of work would meet an important need in the field of psychology. In the area of child custody, we determined it was important that we address the concerns within the profession as to the appropriate role of psychology in the courtroom in child custody cases. Appreciation is expressed to Carolyn Schroeder and to succeeding presidents of the APA Division of Child, Youth, and Family Services—that is, Gerald P. Koocher, Donald K. Routh, and Diane Willis—and to the division's Executive Committee members, for their support of this project. We acknowledge also the participation of the Division of Psychology and Law of APA, which cosponsored the efforts of the task force.

The planning of this book was assisted by the other members of the task force, who also served as members of the Committee on Child Custody: Gary B. Melton and Gerald P. Koocher. Gary B. Melton, also a senior editor of the monograph series sponsored by Division of Child, Youth, and Family Services, of which this book is a part, provided invaluable assistance at each step of its preparation, writing, and editing. The contributors to this volume also served as committee members. The helpful comments and suggestions of many APA members who attended discussions of this book's prospectus and progress at recent conventions of the American Psychological Association are gratefully acknowledged. The response from APA members eager to contribute to the task force efforts was overwhelming. I regret that it was not possible to involve all of the more than 60 persons who volunteered their efforts.

My own involvement in the child custody area has developed in part from my work with the University of Virginia's Institute of Law, Psychiatry, and Public Policy and particularly with the Institute's Center for the Study of Children and the Law. Richard J. Bonnie, director of the Institute, and John Monahan, associate director, have supported and promoted the activities of the Center. The Center provides a collegial atmosphere in which faculty members of the Department of Psychology and School of Law at the University of Virginia can work together on problems of mutual interest concerning children and the law. Among the programs of the Center is a didactic-clinical course on psychology, children, and the law, cotaught by Elizabeth Scott and myself in recent years (and before that by Elizabeth Scott and Gary Melton). I thank the participants in the Center for their helpful input in the planning and preparation of this book and for reading earlier versions of several of the chapters: Mark Aber, Richard Balnave, Robert Emery, N. Dickon Reppucci, Elizabeth Scott, Walter Wadlington, and Janet Warren.

I also express appreciation to recent members of the APA Ethics Committee, on which I served from 1983 to 1985. Several members of the committee, notably Robyn M. Dawes, Karen S. Kitchener, and Philip S. Pierce, also contributed their comments on earlier versions of some of the manuscripts.

Finally I owe much gratitude to Debbie Mundie and Louise Spangler, whose diligent efforts provided the secretarial support for this book.

Lois A. Weithorn

PART I.

The Legal Context

1.

The Legal Context of
Child Custody Evaluations

Melissa M. Wyer, Shelley J. Gaylord,
and Elizabeth T. Grove

The legal concept of custody defines the rights and responsibilities of parents (or those given the authority of parents) relative to their children. Parents are given responsibility for the care and
protection of their children and are empowered with concomitant rights
and authority *(American Jurisprudence,* 1984). These rights and responsibilities extend to a broad range of routine and special decisionmaking contexts regarding, for example, children's health, education,
and religion. In normal circumstances a child is in the custody of his or
her biological parents in that the legal relationship is typically defined
by the biological relationship. It is only in atypical circumstances (e.g.,
adoption, legal intervention into family affairs, divorce) that this natural arrangement is altered.

Mnookin (1975) has pointed out that the courts may serve either of
two functions in resolving disputes about child custody: *private dispute
settlement* and *child protection.* In the former case the legal system in-
tervenes to settle a private dispute between parents. In such instances both parents may be fit, but divorce requires a restructuring of
parental rights and responsibilities in relation to the child(ren). If the
parents can agree to a restructuring arrangement, which they do in

the overwhelming proportion of divorce custody cases, there is no dispute for the court to settle. However, if the parents are unable to reach such an agreement, the court must step in and determine the relative allocation of decision making authority and physical contact each parent will have vis-à-vis each child. Whereas there may be other instances of private dispute settlement (e.g., a dispute between a child's maternal and paternal grandparents after the death of both parents), divorce custody disputes constitute the overwhelming majority of private dispute custody cases. As we will review below, the trend in divorce actions is for the courts to apply a "best interests of the child" standard in determining this restructuring of rights and responsibilities (Guernsey, 1981; Rohman, Sales, & Lou, this volume, chap. 3).

In contrast to divorce custody cases, the court may also act to resolve custodial disputes that arise when the state seeks to protect a child from allegedly inadequate or harmful parental conduct. There is typically a presumption of parental fitness and a strong legal tradition of respect for the privacy of the family (Thomas, 1972). Therefore state intervention in the private affairs of the family through adjudication of alterations in custodial rights and responsibilities, including possible removal of a child from a parental home, often conflicts with the state's interest in preserving family autonomy.

In either the divorce or the child protection context, state statutes vary in how much guidance they provide jurists on the standards and criteria to be used in custody adjudications. In that such standards typically are broad and therefore discretionary, it has been commented that custody adjudications often require somewhat subjective value judgments on what arrangements and circumstances will promote a particular child's best interests (Lindsey, 1985; Mnookin, 1975). For example, statute does not guide the judge in deciding which of two fit divorcing parents is a superior caretaker where the primary differences between the parents are matters of parenting style (i.e., one is a stricter disciplinarian, one is more expressive of affection), or of notions about how to raise a child (i.e., one favors religious education, one favors secular education). Thus, in resolving custodial disputes between such fit parents, a judge must necessarily call upon his or her culturally determined notions about what type of upbringing might be best for a child.

Dispute resolution in child abuse and neglect cases is no less thorny. Distinctions between acceptable corporal punishment and physical abuse, for example, are often difficult to make, and the threshold between them may be a product of one's cultural and social perspectives. Whereas it may be clear to most observers that an unfed, unclothed, and otherwise uncared for or abandoned child has been neglected, there are many cases that are less clear. Is a latchkey child neglected if routinely left at home alone from 3:00 until a parent comes home from work at 5:30? Is a child neglected in an otherwise loving but impoverished home where no one can afford a diet that is adequate nutritionally? Such judgments are subjective, and different jurists may judge them differently.

It is not surprising that judges may turn to the expertise of psychology when adjudicating some custodial disputes. Clearly, in that custodial determinations hinge on notions of what will best promote the well-being of a child, and because notions of parenting capacity and a child's needs are at issue, psychological knowledge may be of use. As chapter 5 (Weithorn & Grisso) will underscore, however, it is important that psychologists recognize the limitations of their current knowledge base and their assessment techniques when consulting with the court in a custody case. In particular, they must ensure that they do not go beyond what the science of psychology can offer and do not rely instead on their own culturally determined values about child rearing when providing expert testimony.

This chapter introduces basic law and legal standards relevant to custody determinations in the contexts of divorce and child protection proceedings. Whereas the rest of this book will focus exclusively on divorce custody cases, here we will also review basic concepts attendant to child protection cases so as to inform our readers of the distinctions between these two primary instances in which custody disputes occur.

Custody Law in Divorce: An Overview

The tremendous rise in the divorce rate reflects the large number of couples seeking a change in their family structure. In 1982, 1.17 million marriages terminated in divorce and over 2 million adults and 1.1 million children were affected (National Center, 1985). Dissolution of marriage proceedings produce most child custody disputes requiring adjudication (Mnookin, 1975).

Custody disputes arise upon a change in the marital relationship, as when two parents establish separate households. Courts may address disputed custody questions before a divorce, as at the time of separation, upon the dissolution of the marriage, or at any time thereafter (Clark, 1968). A custody decree is typically modified only when circumstances have substantially changed since the entry of the dissolution decree and when those circumstances were not anticipated by the trial court (e.g., Cole, 1984; *In re Marriage of Mikelson*, 1980).

Historical Background

Divorce custody law is related to the process of divorce, and so a brief review of the evolution of divorce law will be presented here. In common law marriage was favored, and divorce was granted only in limited circumstances, upon a showing of *fault* as evaluated by contemporary social mores. The common grounds for a claim of misconduct were adultery, physical cruelty, or desertion (Goldzband, 1982). These were later expanded by statute to include such specific characteristics as habitual intemperance or habitual use of illegal drugs (*Delaware Code Annotated*, 1981). The grounds asserted for a fault-based divorce have been thought to influence the custody determination (Freed & Foster, 1981) in that the emphasis on punishing misconduct led to a favoring of the "innocent" party.

There has been a trend toward minimizing fault-based decrees. Every state except South Dakota has some form of no-fault grounds for divorce (Freed & Foster, 1984). For example, testimony relating to misconduct is inadmissible in California (*California Civil Code*, 1983a) except as it relates to child custody. With the trend toward limiting fault-based divorces, situations are often described by statute as "irretrievable breakdown," "incompatibility," or "mutual consent" (Freed & Foster, 1984), and a reduction in the necessary separation period often is stipulated in states requiring such a period (Freed & Foster, 1981). While the punitive element has not disappeared from divorce law, the trend has been to increase the availability of dissolution decrees based on consent.

Child Custody

At early common law the sex of the parent was the sole criterion in determining a child custody award (Schiller, 1977). The father had exclusive rights to the child, as a chattel, based on his obligation to protect and financially support the minor (*King v. DeMannville*, 1804). This absolute control stemmed from ancient Rome, where a father could sell his children or condemn them to death (Roth, 1977). Treating the child as the father's chattel was occasionally defended on the grounds that the husband was the decision maker and legal entity for the couple upon marriage (e.g., *Bryant v. Dukehart*, 1922). The paternal preference rule of England was reflected in the United States in the 19th century (Derdeyn, 1976) and was set aside only in cases of gross paternal misconduct or potential harm to the child (Barker & Hamman, 1979; e.g., *Miner v. Miner*, 1849).

An emerging legal view during the late 19th and early 20th centuries was that children were not chattels but intelligent, moral human beings (e.g., *Sowders v. Sowders*, 1941). In 1881 Justice Brewer (*Chapsky v. Wood*) rejected the right of the parent as primary and emphasized instead the best interests of the child. Justice Cardozo echoed this idea on behalf of the New York State Supreme Court (*Finlay v. Finlay*, 1925), stating that the judge should act as a prudent parent and do what is best for the child. The common-law paternal presumption was thus replaced by a new emphasis on the child's welfare. By 1900, 14 states had enacted statutes modifying the paternal presumption rule (Roth, 1977).

The courts subsequently established a presumption in favor of the mother as custodian, if she was fit, during her children's early years (Barker & Hamman, 1979; Roth, 1977). The presumption that "a mother is the natural custodian of a child of tender years" (*B v. B*, 1978, p. 251) was based on the rationale that the father was unable to provide "that tender care which nature requires, and which it is the peculiar province of a mother to supply" (*Miner v. Miner*, 1849, p. 49). The mother was found to be the best provider of attention (*Johnson v. Johnson*, 1946), devotion (*Barth v. Barth*, 1949), and love during the period of nurture (*Jenkins v. Jenkins*, 1921). Young children of both sexes and minor girls of any age were traditionally awarded to the mother, while adolescent boys were frequently awarded to the father (Okpaku, 1976). The tender years presumption was often conditioned on an assumption of maternal fitness for child rearing (e.g., *Loebenberg v. Loebenberg*, 1956), thus placing the burden of proof on the father to show that the mother was unfit. Proof of unfitness in a custody proceeding is separate from proof of misconduct in a divorce action, although the same information (e.g., adultery) has been used to show lack of concern for a child (e.g., *Commonwealth ex rel. Bordelmay v. Bordelmay*, 1963). To deem a parent "fit" the court must find that parent capable of providing an environment that will enhance the child's growth and development (Barker & Hamman, 1979).

More recently we have seen the emergence of a more flexible standard favoring neither parent on the basis of sex and elevating the interests of the child. General acceptance of the tender years presumption has eroded somewhat, and its current application is limited. It has been attacked on the basis of the unconstitutionality of a sex-based presumption (e.g., *B v. B*, 1978). However, the latter argument has been rejected by some courts as emphasizing the interests of the *parents* rather than the best interests of the child in deciding custody (Roth, 1977). To the extent that the tender years presumption was based on a notion of the mother as full-time caretaker, it has been suggested that the doctrine's decline has paralleled the rise in the number of working women (Schiller, 1977). There remain only a small number of statutes that express a maternal preference, and there is an increasing number of awards to fathers (Freed & Foster, 1984). A number of jurisdictions specify a preference for neither parent on the basis of sex (e.g., *California Civil Code*, 1983b; *Virginia Code Annotated*, 1984). However, the maternal preference may still be used as a "tie breaker" when all other factors are equal (e.g., *Kirstukas v. Kirstukas*, 1972) and occasionally may be a factor in the best interests equation. At present, courts more carefully delineate the specific reasons why an award to a mother is in the child's best interests (e.g., *Kauffman v. Kauffman*, 1975), in that courts have been charged to examine the best interests of the particular children and not to presume that either parent would be a better custodian (e.g., *Scolman v. Scolman*, 1975).

Current Law

Generally neither parent is now presumed to have a superior right to the child. Rather, the prevalent standard requires a determination of what will most effectively enhance the growth and development of the child from a physical, emotional, and moral standpoint (Guernsey, 1981). Most state statutes provide no specific criteria for determining the best interests of the child (e.g., *New York Domestic Relations Law,*

1981), and those that do suggest criteria fail to specify how to evaluate each criterion and their relative weights, which leaves the court with substantial discretion (Mnookin, 1975). This amorphous standard attracts criticism for encouraging individualized determinations based largely on a judge's subjective impressions of the parties.

> The role of the trial court is to determine the best interests of the child based on the adversarial presentation of evidence. The lives and personalities of at least two adults and one child are telescoped and presented to him in a few hours. From this capsule presentation he must decide where lie the best interests of the child or, very often, which parent will harm the child the least. The judge's verdict is distilled from the hardest kind of fact finding. *From sharply disputed evidence, he must predict the future conduct of parents on his appraisal of their past conduct.* [italics added] (Botein, 1952, p. 424).

Reliance upon a judge's subjective impression of the parties may arise less often when one party exposes the child to a risk of immediate harm and the other party has a suitable relationship with the child and presents no risk. There seems to be at least minimal consensus about what is "bad" for a child, though judges are given almost no direction, together with broad discretion in determining what will promote a child's best interests (Mnookin, 1975).

It has been noted that "the handling of the matter of the disposition of a human life can both reflect that society as well as act back upon it" (Fanshel, 1957, p. 80). At present, determining the best interests of a child often means choosing the least detrimental alternative based on a subjective evaluation of circumstances and a prediction of future conduct. Although predicting outcomes is difficult and the probability of each is hard to estimate, there remains the question of what set of values to use in determining the best interests. These individualized determinations often address such value-laden questions as whether intellectual stimulation is more desirable for a child than security and stability (e.g., *Painter v. Bannister,* 1966). Justice White stated in *Stanley v. Illinois* (1977) that "procedure by presumption is always cheaper and easier than individualized determinations" (p. 656).

The decision of the trial court is rarely disturbed in child custody proceedings because it is largely based on factual findings (e.g., *Fle-*

harty v. Fleharty, 1979). The trial court hears the oral testimony of witnesses and is considered best situated to evaluate that evidence; thus its decision is overturned only in cases of abuse of judicial discretion (e.g., *Dalton v. Dalton,* 1974). Because the best interests standard provides broad discretion to trial judges, it limits appellate review.

Factors Considered by the Court

Chapter 3 (Rohman et al.) will review in greater depth the legal and psychological issues pertinent to those factors considered by the court in determining the best interests of children in custody cases. We shall review some of these factors briefly here as well. Determinations are based on case law and statutes guided by the Uniform Marriage and Divorce Act (1973) (hereafter UMDA). The UMDA is a model act that has been endorsed by the American Bar Association (1974), and all or parts of it have been adopted in many jurisdictions. Section 402 of the UMDA states that in determining the best interests of the child the court shall consider all relevant factors including:

(1) the wishes of the child's parent or parents as to his custody;
(2) the wishes of the child as to his custodian;
(3) the interaction and interrelationship of the child with his parent or parents, his siblings, and any other person who may significantly affect the child's best interest;
(4) the child's adjustment to his home, school, and community; and
(5) the mental and physical health of all individuals involved. The court shall not consider conduct of a proposed custodian that does not affect this relationship to the child.

The act does suggest that the court first examine all relevant factors, and it lists several that have been commonly weighed. Each of these factors, the vestiges of the tender years doctrine, and factors relating to parental fitness receive different emphasis in different jurisdictions.

The child's relationship to each member of the family is of primary importance and often includes discussion of the child's age, sex (Roth, 1977), and existing emotional ties (*Michigan Statutes Annotated,* 1974). A few jurisdictions have added statutory sections suggesting specific consideration of the potential for violence or threat of violence by a parent (*Illinois Annotated Statutes,* 1979). Several factors considered relate to the child's existing adjustment within environments such as the school and peer contexts.

In considering the child within his or her environment, many courts emphasize the desirability of maintaining continuity. This may include continuity by the primary caretaker (Okpaku, 1976) or preference for the parent who will provide access to siblings and the noncustodial parent (*California Civil Code*, 1979; *Carpenter v. Carpenter*, 1979). National interest in ensuring a more stable environment for these children can be seen in the almost unanimous adoption by states of the Uniform Child Custody Jurisdiction Act (1968). The act was designed to deter child abductions and promote interstate cooperation in adjudicating custody questions.

The wishes of the parents are obviously important in child placement (UMDA, 1973). Promulgation of the best interests standard and increasing concern over the absence of objective criteria also have promoted consideration of the child's custodial preference. At least 30 state statutes and the UMDA have recognized the child's wishes as a factor (Freed & Foster, 1984). Consensus is lacking, however, in the weight given the preference. Consideration often depends upon the age and maturity level of the child, the strength of the preference, and a comparison of preferences between siblings (Podell, Peck, & First, 1972). Several jurisdictions have an age minimum for consideration, typically 12 or 14, and in Georgia the wish of a minor who is at least 14 is controlling, pending a finding of parental fitness (*Georgia Code Annotated*, 1984). The weight given a stated preference has been held to be greater when other factors are equal (e.g., *Sharp v. Sharp*, 1973). Some concern has arisen that children's preferences may be coached by parents (Seigel & Hurley, 1977), or that "true preferences" are not achieved by current methods of investigation (*Nehra v. Uhlar*, 1977).

Parental fitness. The best interests standard suggests that the conduct of a parent should *not* bear on custody unless it impinges upon the child's welfare. Parental conduct, however, has often been used as a determinant of parental fitness, that is, the ability to rear the child competently (Derdeyn, 1976). Arguments have been raised that parental constitutional rights (e.g., privacy, freedom of association) are violated by this reliance on parental behavior, and yet parental conduct has repeatedly been cited (Badal, 1976).

Sexual behavior. Parents' sexual behavior is frequently cited as a factor in custody determinations. Evidence of nonmarital sexual behavior such as cohabitation or adultery has been used to presume or simply to show a direct adverse effect on the child (Lauerman, 1977). Both of these have been used under the best interests umbrella. A mother's relationship with a lover has been presumed to affect her children adversely (e.g., *Pfeiffer v. Pfeiffer,* 1974), but recently it has more appropriately been examined to see if it had an effect on the child and whether any effect was adverse (e.g., *Cleeton v. Cleeton,* 1979). Certain circumstances such as the notorious quality of a parent's sexual relationship (*Parker v. Parker,* 1974), the existence of more than one lover (*In re Marriage of Bowen,* 1974), and the sharing of a residence (*Jacobsen v. Jacobsen,* 1981) have been held to be aggravating factors. Other factors have been held to mitigate an adverse effect on the child, such as marriage to the lover, short duration of the relationship (*Cooley v. Cooley,* 1970), the termination of a relationship (*Huey v. Huey,* 1975), or the expressed willingness to terminate the relationship for the children's sake (*Doe v. Doe,* 1981).

A substantial number of cases turning on nonmarital sexual conduct involve lesbian mothers. It has been suggested that our knowledge of the outcome of these cases is limited because many are privately settled based on the history of denial of custody to homosexual parents (Weitzman, 1981). Sexual preference has alternatively been equated with parental unfitness, weighed as a factor in the best interests balancing, declared irrelevant without a showing of adverse effect on the children (e.g., *Bezio v. Patenaude,* 1980), and ignored as irrelevant (Badal, 1976). An increasing number of lesbian mothers are being allowed to retain custody (e.g., *Doe v. Doe,* 1981), although some of these awards are made on condition that the couple not reside together (Clemens, 1984).

Religious preference. Courts will not disqualify a parent based on religious beliefs but will consider the preference in determining the child's best interests. Religious orientation has been held to be appropriately considered when a parent's practices could endanger a child's physical welfare, as in a snake-handling ceremony (e.g., *Harris v. Harris,* 1977), or could endanger a child's emotional welfare (e.g., as if a parent withdraws affection from a child for disobedience to the church (*Burnham v. Burnham*, 1981). Religious behavior also has been considered as it relates to the needs of the child. While one parent's devout practice as compared with the other party's passive orientation has been held an impermissible factor (e.g., *Bonjour v. Bonjour*, 1979), the geographical availability of religious training and the child's preference have been held appropriate factors (Mangrum, 1981). While religious preference has been consistently held not to be a controlling factor, it is explicitly included in the best interests equation by at least six state statutes (Note, 1984).

Race. In the past, varying weights were assigned to racial differences between the two parties to a proceeding and between a parent and a third party in custody determinations. In cases of the dissolution of a miscegenous marriage or the dissolution of a marriage involving non-marital sexual behavior with a member of another race (e.g., Jonas, 1984), race itself was consistently held not to be a controlling factor. Such cases were often remanded to the trial court for further consideration of all relevant factors (Schiller, 1977), although the instructions often were silent on whether race can be considered at all (e.g., *Beazley v. Davis*, 1976). More recently, the Supreme Court has held that race simply cannot be considered (*Palmore v. Sidoti*, 1984).

Physical and emotional condition of a parent. A parent's physical and emotional condition is considered relevant. The UMDA 402(5) (1973) states that the physical and mental health of all parties shall be considered. The few cases on the issue of parental physical handicap have held that a condition such as epilepsy should not be overemphasized in a determination (e.g., *Moye v. Moye*, 1981). Paralysis has been held not to render a parent automatically unfit, but it was a basis for examination of the adjustment of the whole family (e.g., *In re Marriage of Carney*, 1979).

The emotional health of the parent is to be considered (Schiller, 1977), although a clear definition of stability is lacking. Evidence of suicide attempts and repeated hospitalization (e.g., *Larson v. Larson*, 1966) has been used to suggest instability. While a parent's financial condition is not to be determinative, mental state, in combination with an inability to provide financially for children, has been held sufficient to deny custody (e.g., *Calhoun v. Calhoun,* 1977). Courts rely heavily on expert testimony on this issue, especially in assessing the effect of parents' health on children (e.g., *Ridgeway v. Ridgeway,* 1980).

Summary

The vagueness of the best interests of the child standard affords broad discretion to trial courts and limits appellate review. The heavily factual nature of the standard requires case-by-case determination and allows little purely legal precedent to develop. Thus prospective litigants cannot easily predict what courts will decide. This lack of predictability has been criticized as the cause for an increase in custody litigation (Mnookin, 1975). While it may be a reasonable criticism, there is no guarantee that greater predictability would discourage litigation, particularly in such an emotionally charged area. Finally, predictability alone is not valuable. Experience has amply demonstrated that if presumptions are to be useful in the custody context, they must be both accurate and flexible.

Custody Law in Child Protection: An Overview

In the recent Supreme Court case of *Parham v. J. R.,* (1979), Justice Burger stated for the majority, "[H]istorically [the law] has recognized that natural bonds of affection lead parents to act in the best interests of their children" (p. 602). Yet Justice Burger immediately qualified that statement: "As with so many other legal presumptions, experience and reality rebut what the law accepts as a starting point; the incidence of child neglect and abuse cases attest to this" (*Parham v. J. R.,* 1979, p. 602). Indeed, the nearly one million cases of child abuse and neglect reported annually bear out this observation only too well (Butz, 1982).

Parents have historically had extensive rights over their children. As noted above, historically children were viewed as chattels or possessions of their parents. Parents had virtual carte blanche to do as they pleased with their children (Semler, 1979). This right was manifested in the extreme by the parents' practice of infanticide and in the lesser sense by the use of severe corporal punishment (Thomas, 1972).

Defining "Abuse" and "Neglect"

The terms "abuse" and "neglect" have been used interchangeably to signify mistreatment of the child. However, the terms signify two distinct sets of behaviors. Midonick (1972) described these terms as follows: "'Neglect' and 'abuse' generally involve 'fault' on the part of the parents; 'abuse' usually refers to willful injuries to the child, while 'neglect' refers to inadequate parental care."

It is possible to separate certain incidents that are more in line conceptually with either "abuse" or "neglect." The typical "battered child" with broken bones and extensive bruises comes under the rubric of abuse (Katz, Ambrosino, McGrath, & Sawitsky, 1977). On the other hand, "failure to provide necessities, such as food, proper care and support, clothing, shelter, education, and medical attention" fits into the concept of neglect (Gordon, 1979, p. 127). Abandonment is also conceptualized as neglect.

As a practical matter, however, the line between abuse and neglect is often blurred. Many states use a common description for both terms. For example, Montana (*Montana General Code Annotated,* 1979) defines an "abused or neglected child" as "a child whose normal physical or mental health is harmed or threatened with harm by the acts or omissions of his parent or other person responsible for his welfare." "Harm" then includes sexual assault, causing failure to thrive, inflicting injury, and abandonment. Thus it is probably easier to think of "neglect" and "abuse" in terms of the categories common to most state statutes: "nonaccidental physical injury; sexual molestation; emotional abuse or mental injury; and neglect" (meaning omissions in care or abandonment).

Finally, one area of abuse and neglect laws that has received much attention is emotional injury. Many states were reluctant to include this form of harm in their laws. The general apprehension centered on the fact that emotional injury cannot be observed and is hard to prove. Yet states have recognized the need to prevent such injury, and many have included emotional harm in their statutes.

Custody in Abuse and Neglect: A Historical Overview

The Supreme Court has repeatedly upheld parental rights in cases involving child rearing and family autonomy (Butz, 1982). Yet as we became more aware of the prevalence of child abuse and neglect in this country, it became apparent that parental rights were not absolute. The first reported child abuse case arose in 1874 when concerned citizens protested the brutal treatment of 10-year-old Mary Ellen Wilson by her foster mother (Katz et al., 1977). The foster mother was ultimately found guilty of assault and battery (Thomas, 1972). The case also resulted in the formation of the New York Society for the Prevention of Cruelty to Children (Thomas, 1972) as well as passage of Protective Services and Cruelty to Children Criminal Acts (Katz et al., 1977).

The next noteworthy event occurred in 1962 when five leading physicians published their findings of a pattern of unexplained injuries in certain children (McCoid, 1965). Their article provided thorough treatment of the topic of child abuse and coined the phrase that was to become synonymous with child abuse: "the battered child syndrome."

The publication gave impetus to statutes across the country requiring that abuse be reported and that state action be taken to aid the child. States justified their right to act on the child's behalf under the state power of *parens patriae*. In practical terms this doctrine means that a "state will protect all who cannot protect themselves" (Schwartz & Hirsh, 1982). Hence, under the doctrine of *parens patriae* states have the power to intervene between abusing parents and their children in order to protect the latter. Whereas each state writes its own child abuse statutes, generalizations can be made about the evolution of state statutes nationwide. For example, the states' initial reaction to child abuse was to prosecute cases through the criminal justice system (Mondale, 1978). Yet this response was ultimately viewed as counterproductive for child and parent alike. Instead, states began to take a more positive approach to child abuse cases by stressing rehabilitation over punishment (Cozzola, 1980). Thus, though criminal sanctions still exist, the major emphasis is now on civil actions on behalf of the child.

As states began enacting far-reaching statutes, the goal under the *parens patriae* doctrine was to act in "the child's best interests" (Cozzola, 1980). The term reflects not only a goal but a standard for deciding what action to take on a child's behalf. Yet the "best interests" standard has drawn criticism, faulted for being "a vague and illusory concept that varies in meaning from case to case, depending on the context in which it is applied" (Butz, 1982, p. 1227).

Several alternatives that have been suggested depart dramatically from the "best interests of the child" standard. For example, Goldstein, Freud, and Solnit (1973, 1979) advocate using the "least detrimental available alternative" when deciding when and how to intervene on a child's behalf. The Juvenile Justice Standards also set the threshold for state intervention higher than the best interests standard by requiring a showing of "substantial risk" of harm or "imminent" danger to the child (IJA-ABA Joint Commission, 1981) before removing the child from the parents' custody.

Custody in Abuse and Neglect: Questions Before the Court

As noted above, in abuse and neglect cases the court attempts to balance its *parens patriae* power to protect the child and promote the child's well-being against traditional legal protections for the integrity and privacy of the family. Therefore the court is required to make a determination as to what level of "imperfection" in a home situation is sufficient to lead to interference in the family, that is, what the threshold is between what is tolerable and intolerable to a child given societal standards. Weithorn and Grisso (chap. 5 below) point out that the ultimate, somewhat subjective judgment on these matters is a social and legal, not a psychological matter. Such decisions may be guided by psychological knowledge and testimony, which elucidate facts, circumstances, and psychological relationships inherent in a situation, but the final decision should not be usurped by psychologists.

Typically, in an abuse or neglect case the questions before the court, for which psychological testimony may provide important elucidating—though certainly not dispositive—data, are: (*a*) Has abuse or neglect, as defined by state statute, actually occurred? If so, (*b*) Is it in the child's best interests to be removed from the home temporarily? (*c*) What types of interventions and supports can be provided to the parent(s) so as to begin to remediate those deficiencies/problems that may have led to the inadequate/harmful home situation? (*d*) If an alternative placement is recommended, are there any particular placements (i.e., extended family members), or *types* of placements that would be in the child's best interests? and (*e*) What should be the nature and frequency of visitation between the offending parent and the child?

Conclusion

In either the divorce or the child protection context, child custody decisions draw upon the values of the society. The process of establishing criteria for such determinations is still evolving. Historically, the courts were guided by relatively clear presumptions favoring the granting of custody to one parent over another. It is only in recent years that the neutral "best interests of the child" standard has been adopted. This standard has alternately been applauded for its "child-centered" focus, its flexibility, and its minimal a priori bias relative to the parties and criticized for its vagueness and indeterminacy. The vagueness and indeterminacy of this standard often stimulate judges to look to the expertise of psychologists and others to assist in these determinations. Subsequent chapters in this volume will address the state of our psychological knowledge and expertise relative to such custody consultation.

References

American Jurisprudence (Second, Supplement). Sections 25–38 (1984).

B v. B, 242 S.E.2d 248 (W.Va. 1978).

Badal, C. M. (1976). Child custody: Best interests of children vs. constitutional rights of parents. *Dickinson Law Review, 81,* 733–754.

Barker, L., & Hamman, C. L. (1979). The best interests of the child in child custody controversies between natural parents: Interpretations and trends. *Washburn Law Journal, 18,* 482–498.

Barth v. Barth, 150 Neb. 591, 35 N.W.2d 509 (1949).

Beazley v. Davis, 92 Nev. 81, 545 P.2d 206 (1976).

Bezio v. Patenaude, 381 Mass. 562, 410 N.E.2d 560 (1975).

Bonjour v. Bonjour, 592 P.2d 1233 (Alaska 1979).

Botein, B. (1952). *Trial judge.* New York: Simon and Schuster.

Bryant v. Dukehart, 109 Ore. 359, 210 P. 454 (1922).

2.

Child Custody Dispute Resolution:

The Adversarial System and Divorce Mediation

Elizabeth S. Scott and Robert Emery

Observers have commented on the irony of resolving child custody disputes through the adversary system (Emery, 1983; Watson, 1969). While the objective of the law is to resolve the custody issue in a manner that will be in the child's best interests, the legal process may have a destructive impact on both child and parents (Ellsworth & Levy, 1969). Many participants regard child custody disputes negatively. Some mental health professionals who are involved as expert consultants are horrified by the acrimonious exchange and the minimal attention given to its effect on the child (Derdeyn, 1975). Many lawyers and judges also find custody disputes among the most distasteful of legal confrontations (Landsman & Minow, 1978). Perhaps even more significant, many parents who have gone through divorce report dissatisfaction with the legal system and describe negative effects on their postdivorce adjustment (Spanier & Anderson, 1979).

Several aspects of the full-blown custody battle may evoke criticism. Attorneys employed by the parents may focus their energies single-mindedly on winning custody for their clients, regardless of

Preparation of portions of this chapter was supported by the William T. Grant Foundation.

whether such efforts promote the child's welfare (Brown, 1984). Private investigators may be hired and neighbors, friends, and teachers interviewed to build the case. Divorcing spouses, who before the onset of marital strife would have readily acknowledged that their children had two competent parents, suddenly attempt to prove otherwise. Any behavior, habit, or character trait that reflects positively on one parent or negatively on the other may be raised in the courtroom if it can be remotely linked to parenting skills or the parent-child relationship (Mnookin, 1975; Scott & Derdeyn, 1984). Attorneys representing husband and wife may advise their clients not to communicate with each other. Negotiations in an adversarial setting may involve a significant amount of strategic bargaining (Mnookin & Kornhauser, 1979). One parent may threaten litigation of the custody issue to achieve a favorable outcome in the support and property settlement, whether or not custody is actually desired.

In general, the traditional legal process of resolving custody disputes holds the potential to exacerbate hostilities between the parents, which may have a harmful effect on the child. There is a substantial empirical evidence of the harmful impact on children's adjustment of conflict between their parents (Ellison, 1983; Emery, 1982; Rutter, 1981). The frequently observed detrimental effects of divorce have been linked to this conflict by many researchers (Emery, 1982; Hetherington, Cox, & Cox, 1978). It seems likely that aside from the destructive impact of the divorce itself, the legal process by which it is achieved can exact significant psychological costs from the family (Spanier & Anderson, 1979).

The adversary system is not universally condemned as a mechanism for resolving custody disputes. Some observers have suggested that criticism of the adversary process is unfounded and that indeed this type of dispute-resolution mechanism may offer benefits to the child (Melton & Lind, 1982). They argue that children who participate actively may have a sense of having a voice in the decision and thus derive satisfaction. Such speculation remains hypothetical at this point, however.

This chapter examines the adversarial process and its unique and difficult application to child custody decisions. We shall explore several recent developments within the system itself that represent attempts to mitigate the destructive impact of the custody battle as well as looking at possible benefits of the system. Prominent among these developments are the expanded role of the child's attorney, the guardian *ad litem,* the increased use of mental health consultation, and a growing emphasis in the law on the child's preference as an important consideration in the custody decision. Finally, we will examine a new method of resolving custody disputes—divorce mediation. This alternative to resolution of the custody dispute through adversarial negotiation and adjudication has been hailed by many as the most promising development in child custody dispute resolution in recent years.

The Adversary System as a Model for Resolving Child Custody Disputes

The adversary system has been well established in Anglo-American law for hundreds of years. There are two basic characteristics of this dispute resolution model: the decision maker is a neutral party not involved in the dispute (the judge), and the evidence about the dispute that the judge considers is controlled and developed by the disputing parties themselves (Thibault & Walker, 1978). These characteristics have several implications for the process. Each litigant, through an attorney, attempts to present all the evidence favorable to his or her side of the case and unfavorable to the opponent's. There is no incentive on either side to present an objective account to the judge and usually no other means by which such an account is presented. The judge does not have authority, in general, to direct independently that certain evidence be presented or witnesses called, as would be the case under an inquisitorial model of dispute resolution. In theory, since the opponents will present very different evidence, most relevant facts should emerge in the process. Since both sides are allowed to present their versions of the dispute, it is often said that the adversary system is more concerned with justice between the parties than with truth (Thibault & Walker, 1978). Adjudication through this process is designed to produce a "winner" and a "loser." After hearing each side's evidence, the judge announces the verdict, holding for the plaintiff or the defendant.

Thibault and Walker have produced substantial research findings suggesting that litigants derive more satisfaction from an adversary proceeding than from other mechanisms for dispute resolution (Thibault & Walker, 1975, 1978; Walker, La Tour, Lind, & Thibault, 1974). Through experiments utilizing students as disputants, these researchers found that the subjects preferred adversary procedures because they allowed the individuals to control presentation of evidence and argument. This resulted in a greater sense that the proceeding was fair, even for those who were unsuccessful in the dispute.

Melton and Lind (1982) contend that the Thibault and Walker research is applicable to custody proceedings and that children therefore may benefit from having the custody decision made through an adversary process. They assume that the child's attorney, the guardian *ad litem,* acts as an advocate for the child's wishes in the proceeding and, based on this assumption, posit that the child may obtain satisfaction from process control in the manner observed by Thibault and Walker. In essence, they argue that the child who participates actively will "have his/her day in court" and may thus feel that the decision reached is fair. Melton and Lind (1982) also point out that the child who is the subject of a custody dispute will derive security from knowing that both parents are willing to fight for custody. They caution against hastily embracing reforms based on inadequate empirical support.

The disadvantages of the adversary system in this context should not be exaggerated. For children whose attorneys act as advocates and who wish to participate actively in the proceeding, the adversary process may indeed offer some benefits. This may be particularly true for some older children, but there is no research generally supporting the adversary process as a superior method of conflict resolution in custody suits. The notion that children generally want to participate in the dispute or that they experience satisfaction from having done so has not been studied. Furthermore, no research suggests that guardians *ad litem* view themselves as advocates for the child's wishes; a paternalistic role is probably more common (Landsman & Minow, 1978). This is certainly true when younger children are involved.

Several characteristics of custody disputes distinguish them from other types of litigation; therefore the application of the Thibault and Walker findings may be inappropriate, particularly regarding the children. First and most important, the child is not a litigant disputing a claim but the subject of the dispute. Other differences that distinguish custody disputes include the past relationships of the individuals involved; the nature of the inquiry; the postdispute interactions, mandated by the relationships among the participants; and the fact that the legal objective of the custody decision is to promote the welfare of a nonlitigating third party, the child. Resolving custody through the adversary process may heighten hostility between the parties; this hostility may have a lasting damaging effect on both parents and their children.

Few other legal confrontations involve the emotional intensity of a custody dispute. In most litigation the adversaries are strangers, business associates, or acquaintances. The divorcing couple's prior intimate relationship exaggerates from the outset the potential for hostility. Because of the prior relationship, each parent may know particularly hurtful and damaging facts about the other (Mnookin, 1975). Further, the subject of the dispute, the custody of their child, may be crucially important to each parent. Generally, only in criminal adjudications of very serious offenses do the stakes have such personal importance.

The nature of the inquiry in custody disputes further heightens the tendency to promote hostility (Scott & Derdeyn, 1984). Most litigation focuses on some event in the past and is directed toward determining which litigant's account is accurate (Mnookin, 1975). In making a custody decision, by contrast, the judge looks to the future in an attempt to discern whether the mother or the father will be the better parent. Further, custody adjudication focuses on the personal qualities of the parents. Each parent's efforts to persuade the judge that he or she is the better custodian may involve presenting evidence about the character, habits, life-style, and moral fitness of the former spouse. While in theory only evidence relating to an individual's capacity as a parent is relevant, any character deficiency or behavior that the judge is likely to view negatively often will be exposed. If the father's attorney concludes that a judge will disapprove of the mother's sexual activities, evidence of her behavior will probably be introduced in the custody proceedings (*McCreery v. McCreery,* 1977). In fact, no other form of litigation involves the same broad inquiry into the quality of an individual's character as does a custody dispute (Mnookin, 1975).

This expanded inquiry is promoted by the best interests of the child standard, which dominates custody law today. Under this standard, the judge has broad discretion to weigh any factor that may be relevant in determining which parent's custody will promote the child's welfare. Some laws direct that the judge consider specific factors such as the parents' fitness, stability, moral character, and relationship with the child, which parent is primary caretaker, which parent can best meet the child's needs, the child's preference, and other factors that may be important (*Michigan Statutes Annotated*, 1984; see also chap. 3).

Although state law may provide guidelines, in making the custody decision the judge is free to consider almost any factor she or he deems important to the child's welfare; possibly the only exception is the race of a parent or step-parent (*Palmore v. Sidoti*, 1984). Thus such factors as a parent's sexual behavior, life-style, community standing, or religious practice may be taken into account by a judge who finds them important to the custody decision (*Painter v. Bannister*, 1966). The determination of which parent's custody is in the best interest of the child may reflect the values of the judge.

Until recently, most states followed the "tender years presumption" in resolving custody disputes, awarding custody to the mother if she was fit (Derdeyn, 1976; Klaff, 1982). The tender years presumption has received substantial criticism as being unfair to fathers and a distortion of modern social realities in its assumption that the mother automatically is the more important parent (Roth, 1977). Nonetheless, this legal rule had the advantage of narrowing the inquiry somewhat in comparison with the best interests standard. Under some versions of the rule, the only relevant inquiry concerned the mother's fitness. If she was fit, she was awarded custody (*Whatley v. Whatley*, 1975). More important, the tender years presumption may have discouraged litigation and threats of litigation. Fathers would be less inclined to pursue custody under a legal rule that strongly favored mothers, and therefore agreements regarding custody arrangements might be more readily reached (Mnookin & Kornhauser, 1979; Scott & Derdeyn, 1984).

The effect of submitting the custody dispute to the adversary process is often increased conflict between the parents (Spanier & Anderson, 1979). Many divorcing parents have stated in retrospect that their interaction with attorneys and with the legal process was detrimental to their relationship (Pearson & Thoennes, 1982a). This is particularly disturbing since, unlike other litigants, the combatants in a divorce suit have a continuing relationship where children are involved. It is well established that the extent to which the parents' postdivorce relationship is acrimonious or harmonious may have an important effect on the child's welfare and adjustment (Emery, Hetherington, &

DiLalla, 1985; Hetherington et al., 1978). That many couples continue to have conflict regarding their children is reflected in the substantial percentage of families that return to court to relitigate custody and visitation (Westman, Cline, Swift, & Kramer, 1970).

High levels of conflict between parents have been associated with antisocial behavior, poor academic performance, and other problems of adjustment in children in both intact and divorced homes (Emery et al., 1985; Rutter, 1971). To the extent that the adversary process promotes conflict, it seems to be detrimental to children in divorce. The correlation between the legal proceeding, parental conflict, and children's postdivorce adjustment is a virtually unexplored research area.

The Role of the Parents' Attorneys in the Process

Attorneys are often held responsible by their clients and others for the destructive effects of the adversary process in divorce proceedings (Spanier & Anderson, 1979). To some extent criticisms of attorneys may be due to misunderstanding about their legitimate role in the system or to observation of incompetent attorneys. In part, however, the criticism reflects a fundamental challenge to the traditional role of attorneys, however responsibly carried out (Milne, 1978; Coogler, 1977).

The professional duty of the attorney is to represent his or her client and to promote the client's position in any way that is lawful. Canon 7 of the *Canon of Professional Ethics* directs attorneys to represent their clients "zealously within the bounds of the law" (American Bar Association, 1969a). While frivolous lawsuits are ethically proscribed, if a client's case has legal merit it is not the attorney's role to make a judgment about the rightness of the client's position. The attorney's job is to analyze the strengths and weaknesses of the position and to present it to the judge in a manner that emphasizes the former and minimizes the latter (Lambe, 1983). While good legal representation involves careful objective assessment of all aspects of a dispute, neutrality has no part in the attorney's role.

In a custody dispute, once an attorney has undertaken to represent a parent, a professional obligation arises to pursue the client's objective zealously. An attorney who feels strongly that his or her client should not have custody might appropriately refer the individual to another lawyer. In representing a parent, the attorney's first obligation is *not* to protect the child's best interests but to pursue the parent's objectives. In a litigated case, the goal of the attorney will be to marshal any available evidence to persuade the judge that giving custody to the attorney's client will be in the child's best interests. Thus, many attorneys view presentation of evidence about the character and habits of the other client as a necessary if unfortunate part of effective representation.

Although the attorney has an obligation to represent his or her client zealously, consideration of the child's welfare is not foreclosed. An important part of the attorney's role is to be a counselor and advisor to the client. Encouraging the client to avoid a bitter adjudication may be appropriate. The attorney may advise a client against pursuing a custody suit if the other parent seems likely to be favored or if a negotiated settlement that is fair to both parties seems feasible (Weitzman & Dixon, 1979). Attorneys frequently remind their clients of the detrimental effects to themselves and their children of protracted legal confrontation. They also may appropriately remind clients of the controlling legal standard—protection of the welfare of the child—and may urge them to act in accordance with this standard (Fain, 1967). However, one study reported that only 19% of attorneys attempted to dissuade their clients from seeking custody either when they thought the parent was being vindictive or when they believed the client would not be the better parent (Weitzman & Dixon, 1979).

It is generally estimated that 90% of divorces are settled by agreement through negotiation rather than through a formal court hearing, although as many as one-third of all divorces involving children result in a postdissolution custody or visitation hearing (Foster & Freed, 1973). Thus most families do not experience the full impact of the adversary process. However, custody negotiations are greatly influenced by the adversarial context in which they occur. Adversarial negotiations often take place in an atmosphere only slightly less hostile than that of litigation. Each attorney attempts to reach an agreement that achieves his or her client's goals as fully as possible. Parties seeking to obtain an advantage in the financial settlement may use the threat of litigation strategically (Mnookin & Kornhauser, 1979). Each side attempts to gather and use information that will promote its advantage. Sometimes the divorcing parents are instructed by their attorneys not to talk to each other for fear that a concession will result or damaging information will be disclosed. Thus in negotiation as well as adjudication each disputing parent, through his or her attorney, may be acting to promote his or her own objectives, and the child's interests may be forgotten.

The maneuvering of divorce negotiations may be acrimonious and may discourage a satisfactory working relationship between the parties afterward. Thus it is not surprising that a less adversarial approach to divorce dispute resolution has been sought. Divorce mediation, discussed below, has emerged as an approach that encourages the divorcing couple to work together toward a resolution satisfactory to both of them.

If the parent insists on pursuing custody and litigating the issue, the attorney's obligation is to provide the best representation possible. In fact, failure to pursue a client's interests aggressively in a divorce suit has been the basis of a malpractice claim (*Schneider v. Richardson,* 1979). There is substantial anecdotal evidence that many attorneys do not adhere to the ethical mandate to "treat with consideration all persons involved in the legal process and . . . avoid the infliction of needless harm"; (American Bar Association, 1969b). The following attorney's account conforms to a widely held stereotype of the divorce lawyer. "As I walk through the door of my office heading for the courtroom, I know that I am walking to a case where there will be no compromises, no conciliations, no good feelings to balance the bad. This will be an all out confrontation, a real tooth and nail fight. I love it" (Coogler, 1977, p. 2).

Reform Efforts Within the Adversary Process

Recently there have been several promising legal developments that may promote more reasoned custody decisions focusing on the child's welfare. These developments include the increased use of guardians *ad litem* (attorneys for the child), greater involvement of mental health consultants acting as "friends of the court" to assist the judge in decision making, and growing emphasis on the child's preference regarding his or her custodian as an important factor. All these developments are designed to modify the process from a battle waged by opposing attorneys on behalf of the parents to a more rational process that one hopes may ameliorate some of the destructive effects of the adversary encounter.

The Guardian ad Litem

Many judges routinely appoint guardians *ad litem* in contested custody cases. The various functions of the child's attorney may include investigating the case, presenting and cross-examining witnesses, soliciting and advocating the child's views, and counseling the parents to avoid litigation (Landsman & Minow, 1978; Wallace, 1982). There is substantial debate about the appropriate role of the guardian *ad litem*. Some observers believe this attorney should be an advocate for the child's wishes (Bersoff, 1976–1977; Inker & Perretta, 1971); others support a more traditional approach and see guardians *ad litem* as paternalistic protectors of the child's welfare (Kay & Segal, 1974). In either role, the child's attorney may serve an important function in focusing the proceedings on the child's interests and in limiting the adversarial quality of the conflict (Foster & Freed, 1972; Goldstein, Freud, & Solnit, 1979; Ramsey, 1983). For this reason many observers have recommended that the child have a right to legal representation when custody is at issue (Foster & Freed, 1972; Inker & Perretta, 1971; IJA-ABA, 1980).

An important function of the guardian *ad litem* is to perform an independent investigation (Wallace, 1982). The attorney for each parent will present in court evidence about the family situation that is most favorable to his or her client. While in theory the adversary process should disclose most relevant information, it may well be that some witnesses will not be heard by the judge because they present a mixed picture containing both positive and negative evidence regarding each parent. Only the guardian *ad litem* is in a position to perform a thorough objective investigation. The guardian *ad litem* may interview neighbors, teachers, and friends of the family and attempt to present an objective comprehensive picture. At a minimum, the guardian *ad litem* serves to reduce the distortion that may result from the introduction of evidence by the two parents.

A role sometimes advocated for the guardian *ad litem* is that of mediator and counselor to the parents (Landsman & Minow, 1978). Again, because of the special position of this attorney, he or she may be able to counsel the parents and encourage them to reach an agreement regarding custody without going to trial. In this role the guardian *ad litem* could serve a function similar to that of a divorce mediator.

Because the role of the guardian *ad litem* involves mediation and counseling, it has been suggested that the child's representative need not be an attorney. Programs in some jurisdictions with nonattorney guardians *ad litem* report successful results. However, if the dispute goes to court, legal training may be important for effective representation. One positive response has been a program to train attorneys in child development and other nonlegal aspects of the guardian *ad litem* role (McFarland, 1984).

Whether or not they are attorneys, guardians *ad litem* are potentially a positive force in custody dispute resolutions. The greatest restriction on their effectiveness may be a financial one. In many states guardians *ad litem* receive such minimal statutory fees that many attorneys perform the role only perfunctorily. Some new statutes reflect efforts at fair compensation for the child's attorney that may lead to more effective representation.

There is substantial controversy over whether the guardian *ad litem* should be an advocate for the child's wishes or adopt a paternalistic stance (IJA-ABA, 1980; Long, 1983). The traditional and still widely shared view is that the guardian *ad litem* should investigate and discern the child's best interests and promote those interests to the judge. The primary benefit of the guardian *ad litem* in this view is to ensure that an objective and complete account is presented to the judge and that the child's welfare remains the focus of the dispute.

One criticism of the traditional approach is that it contemplates a role for the attorney that duplicates that of the judge, who is responsible to protect the child's welfare in the dispute (Mlyniec, 1977–1978). However, the guardian *ad litem* is in a far better position to develop evidence and to investigate the case. Unless there is a guardian *ad litem*, the judge will have only the information presented by the contesting parties and thus may have limited ability to protect the child's interests. Further, the guardian's counseling the parents, protecting the child from coercion, communicating with the child before the hearing, and acting on the child's behalf in the court proceedings, may be extremely valuable functions that cannot be fulfilled by the judge (Landsman & Minow, 1978). It has been pointed out that by the time the judge sees the family the parents have become very polarized and their stances have hardened (Child Custody Commission, 1984).

For younger children, a paternalistic approach by the guardian *ad litem* may be the only practical one and may substantially benefit the child. However, a growing number of observers have criticized this approach for older children who may well be capable to decide with which parent they wish to live. Some proponents of an advocacy approach believe that the attorney's role in negotiations and in court should be to achieve whatever result the child client wants in terms of custody and visitation, regardless of the attorney's own views of the child's best interests (Bersoff, 1976–1977). Others suggest that a guardian *ad litem* be appointed *only* if the child has a preference (Mlyniec, 1977–1978). An advocacy role for the child's attorney is consistent with the growing trend toward recognizing the child's preference in the custody dispute.

Even if the child's attorney does not see his or her role as primarily an advocate for the child's wishes, the child's preferences, concerns, and fears are important considerations for the judge in most cases. Thus one of the most important roles of the guardian *ad litem* is to communicate with the child and attempt to understand his or her perspective on the custody dispute. The attorney for a parent is poorly suited to explore the child's concerns objectively and may exert subtle or overt pressure on the child to favor the parent he or she represents. The guardian *ad litem* not only can ensure that the child's preferences and feelings about custody are heard and taken into account but may insulate the child from the coercive efforts of the parents' attorneys and even of the parents themselves. In most cases the parents and their attorneys will be significantly motivated to cooperate with and avoid alienating the guardian *ad litem*. Thus they may be responsive to the attorney's admonitions about the need to protect the child from excessive pressure. In general the guardian *ad litem* may function positively to remind participants of the central objective of the process—protecting the child's welfare (Ramsey, 1983).

The Child's Preference

The debate about the appropriate role of the child's attorney in custody disputes is related to another trend in the law that may mitigate the effects of the adversary process—the growing emphasis on the child's preference as an important factor in the decision (Jones, 1984). This development is a recognition of the child's interest in the outcome of a decision that is crucial to his or her welfare; it is also an acknowledgment of the capacity for self-determination of older children. There is growing social science evidence that the law's traditional presumption that minors are incapable of participating in decisions regarding their welfare is erroneous (Weithorn, 1983; Weithorn & Campbell, 1982). The emphasis on the child's preference in custody decisions reflects a more general trend in the law away from a wholly paternalistic approach to children, a trend reflected, for example, in laws allowing mature minors to make medical decisions independently (Wadlington, 1983). This trend also is reflected in the conception of the role of guardian *ad litem* as advocate for the child's wishes.

At least 20 states require the judge to consult with the mature child regarding his or her preference for custody (Franklin & Hibbs, 1980; Siegel & Hurley, 1977). In Georgia and a few other states, a child over the age of 14 has an absolute right to choose between fit parents, and the choice is binding on the court (Siegel & Hurley, 1977). Most laws allow for more judicial discretion and merely direct that the judge consider the child's preference along with other factors. In general, the older the child, the more weight given his or her preference regarding custodian. As one court stated, "from a practical viewpoint we think it would be rather a vain and useless act to order children who are approaching the age of maturity to . . . live with one of their parents with whom they do not wish to live" (*Patrick v. Patrick,* 1968). Other factors that seem to be important in the weight given the child's preference include the intensity of the preference and the reasons the child gives for choosing one parent over the other. The latter factor seems to be directed at assessing the competency and maturity of the decision, although no law designates what would constitute competency in this context.

Weithorn has offered a developmental analysis that may be useful in determining whether a child's expressed custodial preference is "competent" (Weithorn, 1984). Most critical to the determination of competence is the child's ability to conceptualize the custodial alternatives and to consider the possible consequences of choosing one versus the other. Based on cognitive-developmental research, Weithorn (1984) suggests that a child of 12 or 14 years is likely to be capable. However, she points out, even a younger child who is not capable of the highest level of reasonable decision making may have a meaningful emotional or intellectual preference that should not be disregarded (Weithorn, 1984). Greenberg (1983) conducted an empirical comparison of the capacity to express a custodial preference of children ages 9 through 14 and age 18. She concluded that the study "provided empirical support for the common judicial practice of granting considerable weight to the custodial preference of children 14 years of age or older" (p. 159). However, she concluded further that during the critical transition years of 9 to 14, assessments of cognitive decision making capacity on a case-by-case basis may be more useful than will be determinations based on age.

The increasing emphasis in the law on the child's preference is generally based on a benevolent desire to take into account the wishes of the individual most profoundly affected by the custody decision. If a child has strong preferences regarding the custodial arrangement, the failure of the process to provide a means for his or her wishes to be heard may negatively affect the child's postdivorce adjustment. While there may be cases in which it is necessary, a decision about custody contrary to a child's strong wishes may be detrimental. Particularly for an older child, it seems likely that the decision may result in feelings of resentment and helplessness.

Although its purpose is benign, the trend toward emphasizing the child's preference raises a number of questions. Little is known about children's response to being given a central role in deciding the custody dispute. In some cases the law's focus on the child's wishes may mean substantial pressure is put on the child by the parents and their attorneys, since the child's support may be a significant advantage. Many children, already feeling that their loyalties are divided, may not wish to be put in the position of choosing one parent over the other and may want to stay as removed from the conflict as possible (Westman, 1979). Some may experience even the unbiased solicitation of their desires as coercion. While no law requires children to express a preference, they are far more likely to become directly involved in the legal dispute if the law invites their participation.

Another important issue is the way the child's preference is solicited. This is generally a matter of judicial discretion, with little guidance from the law (Lombard, 1984). Some commentators have recommended that the child speak to the judge alone in chambers (Jones, 1984). This may be less traumatic to the child in most situations than testifying as a witness in a hearing and being examined and cross-examined. However, some adherents of the adversary process question the fairness of a judge's resting the custody decision on evidence that is not subject to examination and cross-examination by the parties' attorneys. This view seems to weight the rights of parents more heavily than the best interests of the child. Very little empirical research has been conducted on the process by which children's opinions are elicited or on the effect different approaches have on children.

Older children who wish to live with one parent should have a significant if not dispositive role in determining their custodians. If younger children have strong feelings about the matter, considering their preference may lessen their feelings of helplessness and frustration. However, efforts should be made to avoid coercion and pressure on the child to prefer one parent. In some sense the great enthusiasm for considering a child's preference may be an acknowledgment of the failure by other decision makers and an abdication of this difficult role to the child.

The Role of the Mental Health Professional

Mental health professionals may be called upon to consult in custody disputes in two ways that may have very different implications for their role. Clinicians may be employed as experts by either parent to support a petition for custody. Alternatively, they may be brought into the process by the judge or the guardian *ad litem* and requested to perform an evaluation of the whole family for the court (Reppucci, 1984; Wood, 1984).

The clinician who is employed by one parent is at a disadvantage that may hamper effectiveness. The judge may understandably believe that the expert's opinion is biased; the clinician will be strongly identified with one side in the dispute. Thus the clinical observations and opinion favoring one parent's custody may be discounted, since the parent is the expert's employer.

Aside from the appearance of bias, the expert employed by a parent may in fact not have a complete basis for forming an opinion. Often he or she will not have access to the other parent and may be unable to observe that parent with the child. Even if an interview is permitted, cooperation is unlikely and observations may be distorted. In general, the psychologist or other mental health professional who performs a custody evaluation for one party will be identified with that party and may have difficulty maintaining a neutral clinical perspective. Even if the clinician is able to render an opinion objectively, all other participants in the process will view him or her as an ally of the parent seeking the consultation. Where each party brings in a mental health professional to support the custody suit, the "battle of the experts" may reduce the credibility of both professional opinions.

The mental health professional who serves as a consultant to the judge or the guardian *ad litem* is in a different position. The consultant may avoid the appearance of bias; further, objectivity and neutrality of clinical observations and opinions may actually be more feasible (Derdeyn, 1975). That the expert's evidence is brought into the process not by one of the parties but by the judge or the guardian *ad litem* makes it inherently less adversarial in nature.

The mental health professional who performs an evaluation for the court has a substantial advantage in that all participants are motivated to cooperate with the assessment. A fuller and more comprehensive picture of the family is likely to result from this kind of evaluation. Thus a mental health professional may have greater access to information about the family and more opportunity to observe interaction among family members than the consultant employed by a parent. Many commentators have recommended that, if at all feasible, the consultant performing a custody evaluation do so as a friend of the court (Derdeyn, 1975). This may be possible even if the original referral is from one party.

The limited value of the contribution of mental health expertise in resolving custody disputes is examined elsewhere in this volume. Further, clinicians may be understandably reluctant to become involved in a consultation in which their opinion is challenged and scrutinized by attorneys (Benedek & Benedek, 1972). Nonetheless, a clinician who participates in a custody proceeding as a "friend of the court" may serve the useful function of focusing the inquiry on the child's well-being and thereby defusing its destructive potential. Further, the clinician may be able to help the court separate abilities and behavior of the parents that are relevant to the child's welfare from those that may contribute to a negative or positive impression but have little effect on the child. Many "life-style" issues may fall into this category.

The input of neutral clinical expertise and the other reforms that have thus far been discussed offer promise of mitigating the negative effects of the adversary process. They do not fundamentally alter the system or offer an alternative mechanism for resolving custody disputes. Such an alternative mechanism is offered by divorce mediation. Many view this development as the most positive trend in custody law in recent years and as the one with the greatest potential to reduce the acrimony of divorce.

Divorce Mediation

Because of the dissatisfaction with the adversary system, there has been an increased interest in developing alternative methods of resolving child custody disputes. In the past several years, divorce mediation has grown dramatically as the major alternative to either litigation or out-of-court negotiation between attorneys. On January 1, 1981, the state of California enacted legislation mandating that all parties requesting a custody or visitation hearing must first attempt to settle the dispute in mediation (*California Civil Code,* 1983). At this time, the states of Delaware and Maine have also enacted mandatory mediation legislation (Freed & Foster, 1984; *Maine Revised Statutes Annotated,* 1984). In Alaska, Colorado, Connecticut, Florida, Iowa, Massachusetts, Michigan, New Jersey, and Pennsylvania, statewide mediation services are available to couples who wish to use them voluntarily and to parents who are ordered into mediation based on individual judicial discretion (Comeaux, 1983; Freed & Foster, 1984). In addition to these statewide programs, over 400 local divorce mediation programs exist in various jurisdictions throughout the country (Comeaux, 1983).

In divorce mediation the divorcing parties meet with an impartial third party (or parties) to identify, discuss, and, one hopes, settle the disputes that result from marital dissolution. While it shares features with some types of marital and family therapy, mediation can be distinguished from many forms of psychotherapy in that it is short term and problem focused. The process also requires that the mediator be knowledgeable in the legal and economic as well as the social and psychological consequences of divorce. Furthermore, mediation differs from therapy in its objectives, and the exploration of emotional issues is circumscribed by the goal of negotiating a fair and acceptable agreement. Finally, unlike marital therapy, the goal of mediation is *not* reconciliation.

Divorce mediation embraces a model of dispute resolution considerably different from that characterizing the adversary process. Whereas in mediation the parties give up some procedural control in that the mediator directs much of the process, decisional control is not handed over to a third party as it is in adjudication. That the parents retain decisional control also distinguishes mediation from arbitration. Arbitration, like mediation, may encompass less formal procedures than does litigation, but unlike the mediator, the arbitrator is expected to make a decision for the parties if they do not do so themselves. As with an agreement negotiated out of court by their attorneys, the parties themselves retain the authority to accept or reject a mediated agreement. The judiciary technically retains the right to reject any negotiated settlement that does not promote the best interests of the child. As with agreements reached through attorney negotiations, however, most judges will "rubber stamp" a mediated agreement (Mnookin, 1975).

While mediation therefore is similar to attorneys' out-of-court negotiations in that decisional control is maintained by the parties involved, it differs from that process in a number of important ways. Since the mediator, unlike the attorney or arbitrator, can resolve disputes only through negotiation, the process emphasizes cooperation rather than competition between the parties. As a result, the mediator is likely to discourage rather than support strategic bargaining wherein the parties take extreme stances at first to gain advantage in later "trading down" toward the middle. Strategic bargaining also is discouraged in mediation in that communication takes place with a single professional. By caucusing with parents individually and shuttling back and forth between them, the mediator can explore the range of options that each is willing to consider as a potential compromise. Such alternatives also can be, and commonly are, explored in face-to-face meetings.

Although the model of dispute resolution is designed to emphasize cooperative settlement and to avoid strategic bargaining, it would be naive to assume that all adversarial elements are removed from the mediation process. Based on their own plans or their attorneys' advice, parents may continue strategic bargaining in mediation; they may not disclose the full range of acceptable compromises; or they may withhold valuable information. Moreover, the process may be used not as a means of negotiation but instead as an opportunity to discover the opposing party's position. Finally, just as attorneys "shop" for judges in attempting to have a case heard by a judge who holds biases favorable to their clients, they may also "shop" for mediators as their biases become known to the legal community. Attorneys may be more or less supportive of a given client's participation in mediation based, for example, on the mediator's record of negotiating a high percentage of joint custody agreements.

Given that there is considerable potential to use mediation in a manipulative manner and that the mediator also lacks the authority of decisional control, the method of negotiation in mediation highlights process control. The parents' motivation to reach an agreement in mediation is based primarily on their own preexisting desire to negotiate a cooperative settlement or on the mediator's ability to persuade them that such a method of settlement is in their own and their children's best interests. The mediator has an advantage in this regard in that it is likely that most parties wish to settle disputes on their own and to avoid relinquishing decisional control to a third party (Rubin, 1980). However, given the emotional intensity of most custody disputes, negotiated settlements are not easily made. A mediator therefore must possess considerable interpersonal skill. We turn now to a brief discussion of some of the assumptions divorce mediators make about the mediation process and some of the techniques they use to promote settlement.

The Process of Custody Mediation

Some divorce mediators attempt to settle all four of the major issues that must be decided in divorce: property division, spousal support, custody and visitation, and child support. Almost all mediators, however, work in public court settings and limit their practice to the issues of custody and visitation (Comeaux, 1983). Mediation may be a particularly appropriate method of dealing with these child-related issues because of the indeterminacy of child custody law and research on the effects of parental conflict on children (Emery & Wyer, 1985). Moreover, a greater number of attorneys appear to accept the notion that custody mediation can be appropriately conducted by mental health professionals, who make up the vast majority of court mediators (Pearson, Ring, & Milne, 1983). Finally, it appears that the process by which the dispute is settled—the transaction costs—is particularly important in child custody dispute resolution. The process by which decisions are reached and the impact it has on the parents' relationship is critical to the integrative decisions regarding child rearing, since both parents are likely to maintain at least some contact with their children after a divorce.

Given that mediation has only recently been offered as an alternative to the adversarial settlement of custody and visitation disputes, it should not be surprising that diverse approaches are advocated in conducting mediation sessions (Bienenfeld, 1983; Coogler, 1978; Haynes, 1981; Saposnek, 1983). There are, however, several common assumptions about divorce and divorcing families that many mediators seem to share, and some common procedural details can be used to characterize the process.

Assumptions Made by Mediators
Perhaps the single most important assumption divorce mediators make is that the settlement of custody disputes is not a zero-sum game. That is, what is often viewed as a win/lose situation is seen as having win/win possibilities. Each party is seen as potentially able to gain from a negotiated settlement, rather than one parent's "losing" by the same amount that the other party "wins." Part of the reason mediation is seen as having win/win possibilities has to do with transaction costs. Dispute settlement through mediation may be less costly in terms of time, emotional energy, and economics. Moreover, it may be that more innovative and mutually acceptable child care arrangements can be negotiated in mediation. For example, parenting time may be scheduled to capitalize on opportunities for each parent to spend "quality time" with their children, while simultaneously offering the other parent respites from child care. Judges' caseloads typically allow little time to consider factors such as the fit between two parents' schedules when deciding the details of a custody and visitation arrangement. Similarly, out-of-court negotiations may be conducted with an adver-

sarial tone where neither parent shows much concern for the convenience of the other.

One of the major reasons divorce settlement is seen as a non-zero-sum game is that dispute resolution itself is an important part of the cost of the settlement. This concept is far from new to attorneys, who use various delaying tactics in procedural justice to encourage out-of-court settlement or discourage litigation. What is new is the divorce mediation procedure itself and the different transaction costs it entails. As noted earlier, most divorcing partners with children must maintain their relationship in some form, and evidence indicates that continued conflict takes a psychological toll both on parents and on children (Bloom, Asher, & White, 1978; Emery, 1982). Advocates argue that the cooperative process of mediation is likely to help set a pattern of interaction that will promote more healthy relationships between parents than the pattern established by the adversary process. They hope that mediation not only will help resolve current disputes, but also will teach divorcing parents a way of approaching future problems.

Another assumption that most mediators seem to make is that many of the problems inherent in a custody or visitation dispute are as much interpersonal issues as legal ones. Terms such as *custody* and *visitation* hold tremendous symbolic value for divorcing parents. Whereas parents may be outraged at the idea of "visiting" their child only on weekends while the other parent has "sole custody," they may view a "joint custody" arrangement where the child resides with the other parent on weekdays as eminently fair. In fact, many of the joint legal custody agreements negotiated by mediators resemble traditional sole custody settlements in terms of actual physical care (Koopman, Hunt, & Stafford, 1984). In other situations, mediators note that sometimes a legal dispute about custody or visitation is in fact motivated by a desire for retribution. Although judges and attorneys also recognize this motivation, the adversary process is not designed to uncover such underlying issues. Though not always successful, mediation constitutes a forum in which such manipulative behavior can be identified and challenged.

Mediation Procedures

In attempting to establish or maintain a cooperative parenting relationship between divorcing spouses, mediators typically use many of the skills of marriage and family therapists in uncovering underlying issues, managing conflict, and allowing for emotional expression. This is most commonly done with a short-term, problem-solving focus. Although individual styles vary greatly, in mediation significant attention can legitimately be paid to the psychological aspects of divorce and child rearing.

Fisher and Ury's (1981) general negotiation model provides a useful framework for organizing a brief overview of the process of mediation (cf. Emery, Shaw, & Jackson, in press). These authors delineate four critical aspects of principled negotiation: (1) separating the people from the problem, (2) focusing on common interests rather than on strategic bargaining positions, (3) inventing options for mutual gain, and (4) using objective criteria to evaluate the options being considered. The use of these four strategies in mediation is briefly described below.

In regard to separating people from their problems, perhaps the most important goal of divorce mediation is to help the parties distinguish their roles as parents from their roles as spouses (Emery, Shaw, & Jackson, in press). Although the latter role ends with a divorce, the former continues and needs to be redefined. In a marriage, the spousal and parental roles are intertwined; in a divorce they must be separated to prevent anger at the former spouse from disrupting mutual interests regarding parenting.

Focusing on the parents' mutual interests—the welfare of the children involved—is a second important aspect of the mediation process. The attorney's ethical obligation in a custody or visitation dispute is to promote the interests of the client—one or the other parent. The mediator's ethical obligation, however, is the same as the judge's—to protect the best interests of the children involved (Standards of Practice for Family Mediators, 1984). Mediators work to help parents recognize that what is in their children's best interests ultimately is in their own mutual interests as well. In trying to help parents reach custody and visitation decisions that are in concert with this common goal, mediators attempt to disengage them from their original bargaining positions and help them develop creative compromises.

The third aspect of mediation—inventing options for mutual gain— is akin to the "brainstorming" component of the psychotherapeutic problem-solving model (D'Zurilla & Goldfried, 1971). Parents are asked to suspend judgment in regard to various solutions to their disagreements and to brainstorm regarding new, creative, and mutually acceptable options. This brainstorming set can be used as an opportunity for parents to "float trial balloons" regarding options they have previously considered but not yet discussed and also to invent new options that had not occurred to either party (Emery et al., in press). For some problems, such as one parent's wishing to move across the country, there may be a very limited number of potential solutions; for others, inventive options can be discussed face to face in mediation that might be arrived at only through lengthy attorney negotiations.

Fisher and Ury (1981) argue for using objective criteria in evaluating the options raised as potential solutions to a dispute. This can be of great value in settling property disputes, since objective estimates of monetary worth can be obtained relatively easily (Haynes, 1981). There are, however, no satisfactory objective criteria for determining the best interests of the child. If there were, judges would have few problems in deciding custody or visitation disputes. In mediation, it is the *parents'* criteria regarding what is best for their children that guide the selection among the various parenting alternatives. The decision is a matter of private ordering based on the parents' rather than the state's values, provided the child is not endangered (Mnookin, 1975). Parents are encouraged to apply their own standards of fairness to the options they create. They are given the authority to make decisions about their children, and, difficult as that may be, mediators hold that they should do their best to do so.

The Four C's

To this point, we have reviewed problems inherent in using the adversary process for settling custody disputes and have made suggestions regarding the potential of mediation as a less disruptive method of dispute resolution. We now turn to a review of some research in which the two processes have been compared.

Proponents have argued that mediation will have benefits in areas that have been termed the "four C's" (Emery, 1983). That is, mediation is said to reduce *conflict,* increase *cooperation,* give people more *control* over important decisions in their lives (Burger, 1982; Irving, Benjamin, Bohm, & MacDonald, 1981; Pearson & Thoennes, 1982a), and achieve these goals at a reduced public or private *cost* (Bahr, 1981a). In reply to such arguments, it has been asserted that the adversary process may enhance parents' and children's sense of fairness and control (Melton & Lind, 1982), that mediation will ultimately fail and further undermine parental cooperation ("Mediation Can," 1983), that the individual parties' rights will not be protected in mediation, since the dominant party will control the process (Schulman & Woods, 1983), and that costs will actually rise as a new step is added to the already intricate process of obtaining a divorce (Cohen, 1984). We turn now to some of the research that has compared the two methods of dispute resolution along these four dimensions (see Emery & Wyer, 1985, for further critical evaluation of this literature).

Control: Are Agreements Made in Mediation?

A logical question to address in evaluating the alternative is whether agreements can be negotiated in mediation that would not be reached elsewhere. The best data on this question come from court-based programs in states where mediation is commonly used. In Los Angeles County, where couples who request a custody or visitation hearing are automatically referred to mediation first, 55% of these parents reach an agreement in mediation (McIsaac, 1982). In Connecticut's court-based mediation programs, where referrals to the program are based on local practices and judicial discretion, of the 3,272 cases that had been seen as of November 1982, 64% reached an agreement in mediation (Salius & Maruzo, 1982). Other smaller public mediation services similarly have reported reaching mediated agreements with between one-half and three-quarters of all couples (Irving et al., 1981; Pearson & Thoennes, 1982b).

Court-based mediators are succeeding in negotiating agreements between parents who had planned to litigate their dispute, and since only about 10% of all divorces result in a court hearing (Bodenheimer, 1977), these partners are likely to have more acrimonious relationships than most divorcing couples. Unfortunately, no useful data are available on how successful mediators are in negotiating agreements with the full spectrum of the divorcing population. It is safe to speculate, however, that agreement rates would be considerably higher if the entire group was included.

Even those divorcing spouses who fail to negotiate an agreement in mediation nonetheless may benefit from the process. Data indicate that people who do not reach an agreement in mediation are more likely subsequently to settle out of court than are divorcing partners who never attempt mediation (Pearson, Thoennes, & Vanderkooi, 1982). Informal observations also support the idea that mediation can be of benefit even when it does not result in an agreement. Mediation gives divorcing parents an opportunity to discuss their parenting concerns at a time when few such opportunities exist (Emery et al., 1985). Thus mediation may promote a more cooperative approach toward resolving disputes even when the disputes are not directly settled in mediation.

Cooperation and Conflict: Do Mediated Agreements Work?

If statistics indicate that most divorcing parents can maintain decisional control by negotiating their own custody and visitation agreements in mediation, what is the quality of mediated agreements? Certainly social psychological research suggests that people are more likely to value and abide by decisions they participate in (Brehm & Brehm, 1981); however, one cannot readily generalize from laboratory evidence.

Initial data do indicate that divorcing parties are more satisfied with the mediation process than with proceedings associated with litigation. In three studies where families were randomly assigned to either mediation or the adversary process, it was found that: (1) three times as many people who went through mediation reported that "things had gotten much better" six weeks after the settlement than those who went through litigation (Irving, 1981); (2) at six- to twelve-month follow-up, parties who mediated divorce settlements, as opposed to members of a litigation contrast group, reported more satisfaction, were more likely to view their settlement as fair, and indicated a higher level of understanding and cooperation with their former spouses (Pearson & Thoennes, 1982a); and (3) when interviewed a short time after reaching a settlement, parents undergoing mediation found mediation to be less biased and more suited to the family than parents undergoing traditional court adjudication found adjudication to be (Watson & Morton, 1983).

Whether parents return to court with postdissolution litigation, which occurs in as many as one-third of all divorces that involve children (Foster & Freed, 1973–1974), is another, objective measure of the quality of mediated agreements. It has been found that parents randomly assigned to mediate their visitation disputes were only one-sixth as likely to return to court two years subsequently as were parents who proceeded through the adversary system (Margolin, 1973). In another study using random assignment, parents in mediation were less than half as likely to become involved in a subsequent court proceeding as parents who reached a settlement by other means (Pearson & Thoennes, 1982a). Similarly, in two studies that did not employ random assignment but obtained matched contrast groups, the post-dissolution litigation rate following mediation was approximately one-third of what it was following an adversarial settlement (Doyle & Caron cited in Bahr, 1981a; Milne, 1978). Thus both self-report and behavioral data suggest that mediation promotes cooperation and reduces conflict between divorcing partners.

Costs: Is Mediation Cost Effective?

In evaluating the cost effectiveness of mediation, it is important to distinguish the private costs for the divorcing spouses from public costs as calculated in terms of court time. The limited research available on the private cost of mediation indicates that the overall expense is not much different from the cost of litigation (Bahr, 1981b; Pearson & Thoennes, 1982b). This finding likely reflects the fact that many mediators encourage their clients to have an independent attorney review the agreement negotiated in mediation. Thus at the time of resolution of the initial dispute mediation may not result in much of a private cost reduction, though the reduced relitigation rate should lead to lower long-term private costs.

As for whether mediation is effective in terms of reducing public costs, evidence does suggest that a large percentage of cases can be successfully diverted from the more expensive custody hearing to the less expensive mediation session, that agreements are reached more quickly in mediation, and that mediated agreements last longer (Bahr, 1981a; McIsaac, 1982). As a result, fiscal analyses of a variety of court-based programs project that mediation reduces costs computed as a function of court time by 10% to 50% compared with a settlement obtained through a court hearing (Bahr, 1981a). However, to begin mediation programs additional social service staffing usually is necessary, so there typically are increased start-up costs in implementing a mediation service. Exactly what effect of court-based mediation programs will have on public costs can be expected to depend greatly on how the programs are implemented and administered.

Children: Do They Benefit from Mediation?

If mediation appears to lessen family conflict and increase cooperation, does this translate into an easier transition for those children
whose parents mediate divorce disputes? Based on research on the
effects of divorce on children, one would expect so (Emery, 1982).
To date there has been no systematic study of this important question, however; thus any suggestions about the consequences of mediation for children are purely speculative. Recently one of us (Robert
Emory) has begun a research project designed to provide data relevant to precisely this issue. The prediction of this line of research is
that mediation will protect children from some of the stresses of the
divorce process.

Some Questions About Mediation

Although initial data are optimistic about the positive effect
of mediation on families compared with the adversary process, a number of questions remain about the mediation alternative. Since many of
these issues have been discussed in detail elsewhere (cf. Emery &
Wyer, 1985) yet remain unresolved, here it will suffice simply to raise
some of these questions and the controversies surrounding them.

One set of questions about divorce mediation concerns who should
conduct the process, what issues should be mediated, and where mediation should take place. These questions encompass debates on
whether attorneys or mental health professionals are better trained to
conduct mediation, whether mediation should be conducted by teams
including one member of each profession, or whether a new, distinct profession must be created. Also debated is whether all divorce
disputes should be negotiated in mediation or whether mediation
should be limited to custody and visitation issues. Finally, whether
mediation should be promoted as a public service or as a private practice has generated considerable controversy. Although each of these
debates continues, it appears that divorce mediation will be most
widely used in public court settings where mental health professionals
attempt to mediate only custody and visitation settlements (Emery &
Wyer, 1985).

Another set of questions about mediation concerns who should be included or excluded: whether referrals to court-based mediation programs should be mandatory; whether participation in mediation should be completely voluntary; and whether parents should be referred to mediation at individual judges' discretion. These three options now are variously used in jurisdictions throughout the United States (Comeaux, 1983). It has also been asked whether certain cases should automatically be excluded from mediation: for example, cases where there are apparently great discrepancies in the parties' relative bargaining power, as where spouse abuse has occurred (Irving et al., 1981; Schulman & Woods, 1983), or where independent legal findings on matters such as child abuse or neglect must be made (Haynes, 1981; Salius & Maruzo, 1982; Schulman & Woods, 1983).

A third set of questions pertains to the process of mediation itself. Should children be included in mediation sessions? Should grandparents, stepparents, or other interested relatives have a role? What part should mediators play in deciding the content of the negotiated agreement? Should mediators, for example, work toward negotiating joint custody settlements? Moreover, should mediators refuse to be party to agreements they object to on ethical or psychological grounds? Important as such issues are, they remain largely unresolved, and policies vary among practitioners. Efforts have been made, however, to develop uniform standards of practice for mediators (Standards of Practice for Family Mediators, 1984).

Finally, a set of questions has been raised about what is to happen once mediation ends. What role should attorneys play in regard to a mediated agreement? Can a single attorney review the agreement, should it be reviewed by two attorneys who hold an adversarial perspective, or need it be reviewed by an attorney at all? Perhaps the most controversial debate about the termination of mediation, however, concerns the mediator's role in any subsequent court hearing. Some have argued that when a court hearing is held after mediation fails to produce an agreement, the mediator *should* make a recommendation to the court. Proponents of this perspective point to the fact that the mediator is already familiar with the family and that such a recommendation will avoid the duplication of efforts inherent in beginning a new custody investigation. Others argue that strict confidentiality is essential to the mediation process, though in many states a judge may ignore a guarantee of confidentiality (Emery & Wyer,

1985). Practice and judicial policy remain unresolved in regard to the important issue of confidentiality in most jurisdictions. It seems, however, that when the mediator makes a recommendation to the court, the process moves closer to becoming arbitration rather than mediation. This then raises the questions of what impact the knowledge that a recommendation will be made to the court will have on the parties in mediation and of who is properly invested with the authority to arbitrate custody disputes.

While these series of questions about mediation may seem overwhelming, many issues are in the process of being answered (Emery & Wyer, 1985). Until these questions are resolved, however, it is incumbent upon individual mediators to disclose their policies. Divorce mediation seems to hold the potential to be a useful alternative to the adversary process, especially as a means of resolving custody and visitation disputes. Nevertheless, this new practice is not a panacea, and it must be pursued with care and caution.

References

American Bar Association. (1969a). *Code of professional responsibility.* Canon 7. Washington, DC: Author.

American Bar Association. (1969b). Ethical consideration 7-10. In *Code of professional responsibility.* Washington, DC: Author.

Bahr, S. J. (1981a). An evaluation of court mediation: A comparison in divorce cases with children. *Journal of Family Issues, 2,* 39–60.

Bahr, S. J. (1981b). Mediation is the answer. *Family Advocate, 3,* 32–35.

Benedek, E., & Benedek, R. (1972). New child custody laws: Making them to do what they say. *American Journal of Orthopsychiatry, 42,* 825–834.

Bersoff, D. N. (1976–1977). Representation for children in custody decisions: All that glitters is not Gault. *Journal of Family Law, 15,* 27–49.

Bienenfeld, F. (1983). *Child custody mediation.* Palo Alto, CA: Science and Behavior Books.

Bloom, B. L., Asher, S. J., & White, S. W. (1978). Marital disruption as a stressor: A review and analysis. *Psychological Bulletin, 85,* 867–894.

Bodenheimer, B. M. (1977). Progress under the Uniform Child Jurisdiction Act and remaining problems: Punitive decrees, joint custody, and excessive modification. *California Law Review, 65,* 978–1014.

Brehm, S. S., & Brehm, J. W. (1981). *Psychological reactance: A theory of freedom and control.* London: Academic Press.

Brown, I. S. (1984). Good lawyers needn't be gladiators. *Family Advocate*, *6(4)*, 4-6, 42.

Burger, W. B. (1982). Isn't there a better way? *American Bar Association Journal*, *68*, 274-277.

California Civil Code. Section 4607 (West 1983).

Child Custody Commission. (1984). Report of the commission to study the matter of child custody in domestic relations cases, 111th Maine Legislature, Augusta, Maine.

Clingempeel, W. G., & Reppucci, N. D. (1982). Joint custody after divorce: Major issues and goals for research. *Psychological Bulletin*, *91*, 102-127.

Cohen, H. N. (1984). Mediation in divorce: Boon or bane? *Women's Advocate*, *5*, 1-2.

Comeaux, E. A. (1983). A guide to implementing divorce mediation in the public sector. *Conciliation Courts Review*, *21*, 1-25.

Coogler, O. J. (1977). Changing the lawyer's role in matrimonial practice. *Conciliation Courts Review*, *15*, 1-12.

Coogler, O. J. (1978). *Structured mediation in divorce settlement*. Lexington, MA: D.C. Heath.

Derdeyn, A. P. (1975). Child custody consultation. *American Journal of Orthopsychiatry*, *45*, 791-801.

Derdeyn, A. P. (1976). Child custody contests in historical perspective. *American Journal of Psychiatry*, *133*, 1369-1376.

D'Zurilla, T., & Goldfried, M. (1971). Problem solving and behavior modification. *Journal of Abnormal Psychology*, *78*, 107-126.

Ellison, E. S. (1983). Issues concerning parental harmony and children's psychosocial adjustment. *American Journal of Orthopsychiatry*, *53*, 73-80.

Ellsworth, P. C., & Levy, R. J. (1969). Legislative reform of child custody adjudication. *Law and Society Review*, *4*, 167-215.

Emery, R. E. (1982). Interparental conflict and the children of discord and divorce. *Psychological Bulletin*, *92*, 310-330.

Emery, R. E. (August 1983). *Divorce mediation and child custody dispute resolution*. Paper presented at the meeting of the 91st Annual Convention of the American Psychological Association, Anaheim, CA.

Emery, R. E., Hetherington, E. M., & DiLalla, L. F. (1985). Divorce, children, and social policy. In H. Stevenson & A. Siegel (Eds.), *Child development research and social policy*. Chicago: University of Chicago Press.

Emery, R. E., Shaw, D., & Jackson, J. A. (1984). *A comediational model for negotiating child custody and visitation disputes*. Unpublished manuscript, University of Virginia.

Emery, R. E., Shaw, D. S., & Jackson, J. A. (in press). A clinical description of a model of child custody mediation. In J. P. Vincent (Ed.), *Advances in family intervention, assessment, and theory* (Vol. 4). Greenwich, CN: JAI.

Emery, R. E., & Wyer, M. M. (1985). *Mediating disputes related to divorce.* Unpublished manuscript, University of Virginia.

Fain, H. M. (1967). The role and responsibility of the lawyer in custody cases. *Family Law Quarterly, 1,* 36–47.

Fisher, R., & Ury, W. (1981). *Getting to yes.* New York: Penguin.

Foster, H. H., & Freed, D. J. (1972). A bill of rights for children. *Family Law Quarterly, 6,* 343–375.

Foster, H. H., & Freed, D. J. (1973). Divorce reform: Breaks on breakdown. *Journal of Family Law, 74,* 443–494.

Franklin, R., & Hibbs, B. (1980). Child custody in transition. *Journal of Marital and Family Therapy, 6,* 285–291.

Freed, D. J., & Foster, H. H. (1984). Divorce in the fifty states: An overview. *Family Law Quarterly, 17,* 365–447.

Goldstein, J., Freud, A., & Solnit, A. (1979). *Beyond the best interests of the child.* New York: Free Press.

Greenberg, E. F. (1983). *An empirical determination of the competence of children to participate in child custody decision-making.* Unpublished doctoral dissertation, University of Illinois at Urbana-Champaign.

Haynes, J. M. (1981). *Divorce mediation: A practical guide for therapists and counselors.* New York: Springer.

Hetherington, E. M., Cox, M., & Cox, R. (1978). The aftermath of divorce. In J. H. Stevens and M. Mathews (Eds.), *Mother-child-father-child relations.* Washington, DC: National Association for the Education of Young Children.

Inker, M. L., & Perretta, C. A. (1971). A child's right to counsel in custody cases. *Family Law Quarterly, 5,* 108–120.

Institute of Judicial Administration–American Bar Association (IJA-ABA). (1980). *Juvenile justice standards: Standards relating to counsel for private parties.* Cambridge, Mass.: Ballinger.

Irving, H. H. (1981). *Divorce mediation.* New York: Universe Books.

Irving, H. H., Benjamin, M., Bohm, P., & MacDonald, G. (1981). *Final research report.* Toronto.

Jones, C. J. (1984). Judicial questioning of children in custody and visitation proceedings. *Family Law Quarterly, 18,* 43–91.

Kay, R., & Segal, D. (1974). The role of the attorney in juvenile court proceedings: A non-polar approach. *Georgetown Law Journal, 61,* 1401–1424.

Klaff, R. L. (1982). The tender years doctrine: A defense. *California Law Review, 70,* 335–372.

Koopman, E. J., Hunt, E. J., & Stafford, V. (1984). Child-related agreements in mediated and non-mediated divorce settlements: A preliminary examination and discussion of implications. *Conciliation Courts Review, 22,* 19–25.

Lambe, J. A. (1983). Handling contested custody cases. *Case and Comment, 88,* 3–7.

Landsman, K. J., & Minow, M. L. (1978). Lawyering for the child: Principles of representation in custody and visitation disputes arising from divorce. *Yale Law Journal, 87,* 1126–1190.

Lombard, F. K. (1984). Judicial interviewing of children in custody cases: An empirical and analytical study. *University of California at Davis Law Review, 17,* 807–808.

Long, L. (1983). When the client is a child: Dilemmas in the lawyer's role. *Journal of Family Law, 31,* 607–640.

Maine Revised Statutes Annotated, title 19, 752 (1984).

Margolin, F. M. (1973). *An approach to resolution of visitation disputes post-divorce: Short term counseling.* Unpublished doctoral dissertation, United States International University.

McCreery v. McCreery, 218 Va. 352, 237 S.E.2d, 167 (1977).

McFarland, A. S. (1984). A legal voice for children. *Family Advocate, 6,* 18–19.

McIsaac, H. (1982). Court-connected mediation. *Conciliation Courts Review, 21,* 49–56.

Mediation can do harm in child custody cases. (April 1983). *Marriage and Divorce Today* (p. 4).

Melton, G. B., & Lind, E. A. (1982). Procedural justice in family court: Does the adversary model make sense? *Child and Youth Services, 5,* 63–81.

Michigan Statutes Annotated. Section 25.312(3) (Callaghan 1984).

Milne, A. L. (1978). Custody of children in a divorce process: A family self-determination model. *Conciliation Courts Review, 16,* 1–6.

Mlyniec, W. J. (1977–1978). The child advocate in private custody disputes: A role in search of a standard. *Journal of Family Law, 16,* 1–17.

Mnookin, R. H. (1975). Child-custody adjudication: Judicial functions in the face of indeterminacy. *Law and Contemporary Problems, 39,* 226–292.

Mnookin, R. H., & Kornhauser, L. (1979). Bargaining in the shadow of the law: The case of divorce. *Yale Law Journal, 88,* 950–997.

Painter v. Bannister, 258 Iowa 1390, 140 N.W.2d, 152 *cert. denied* 385 U.S. 949 (1966).

Palmore v. Sidoti, 466 U.S. 429 (1984).

Patrick v. Patrick, 212 So. 2d 145 (La. 1968).

Pearson, J., Ring, M., & Milne, A. (1983). A portrait of divorce mediation services in the public and private sector. *Conciliation Courts Review, 21,* 1–24.

Pearson, J., & Thoennes, N. (June 1982a). *Mediating and litigating custody disputes: A longitudinal evaluation.* Paper presented at the American Bar Association's Conference on Alternative Means of Family Dispute Resolution, Washington, DC. Reprinted in *Family Law Quarterly, 17,* 497–524 (1984).

Pearson, J., & Thoennes, N. (1982b). The mediation and adjudication of divorce disputes: Some costs and benefits. *Family Advocate, 4,* 26–32.

Pearson, J., Thoennes, N., & Vanderkooi, L. (1982). The decision to mediate: Profiles of individuals who accept and reject the opportunity to mediate contested custody and visitation issues. *Journal of Divorce, 6,* 17–35.

Ramsey, S. H. (1983). Representation of the child in protection proceedings: The determination of decision-making capacity. *Family Law Quarterly, 17,* 287–326.

Reppucci, N. D. (1984). The wisdom of Solomon: Issues in child custody determination. In N. D. Reppucci, L. A. Weithorn, E. P. Mulvey, & J. Monahan (Eds.), *Mental health, law, and children* (pp. 59–78). Beverly Hills: Sage.

Roth, A. (1977). The tender years presumption in child custody disputes. *Journal of Family Law, 15,* 423–462.

Rubin, J. Z. (1980). Experimental research on third-party intervention in conflict: Toward some generalizations. *Psychological Bulletin, 87,* 379–391.

Rutter, M. (1971). Parent-child separation: Psychological effects on the children. *Journal of Child Psychology and Psychiatry, 12,* 233–260.

Rutter, M. (1981). Epidemiological/longitudinal strategies and causal research in child psychiatry. *Journal of the American Academy of Child Psychiatry, 20,* 513–544.

Salius, A. J., & Maruzo, S. D. (1982). *The use of mediation in contested child custody and visitation disputes.* Unpublished manuscript.

Saposnek, D. T. (1983). *Mediating child custody disputes.* San Francisco: Jossey-Bass.

Schneider v. Richardson, 411 A.2d 656 (Me. 1979).

Schulman, J. & Woods, L. (1983). Legal advocacy v. mediation in family law. *Women's Advocate, 4,* 3–4.

Scott, E. S., & Derdeyn, A. P. (1984). Rethinking joint custody. *Ohio State Law Journal, 45,* 455–498.

Siegel, D. M., & Hurley, S. (1977). The role of the child's preference in custody proceedings. *Family Law Quarterly, 13,* 1–58.

Spanier, G. B., & Anderson, E. A. (1979). The impact of the legal system on adjustment to marital separation. *Journal of Marriage and the Family, 41,* 605–613.

Standards of Practice for Family Mediators. (1984). *Family Law Quarterly, 18,* 455–460.

Thibault, J., & Walker, L. A. (1975). *Procedural justice: A psychological analysis.* New York: Erlbaum/Halstead.

Thibault, J., & Walker, L. A. (1978). A theory of procedure. *California Law Review, 66,* 541–566.

Wadlington, W. J. (1983). Consent to medical care for minors: The legal framework. In G. B. Melton, G. P. Koocher, & M. J. Saks, *Children's competence to consent.* New York: Plenum Press.

Walker, L. A., LaTour, S., Lind, E. A., & Thibault, J. (1974). Reactions of participants and observers to modes of adjudication. *Journal of Applied Social Psychology, 4,* 295–310.

Wallace, D. L. (1982). When the child becomes a prize—that child needs a lawyer. *Barrister, 9*(2), 16–20.

Watson, A. S. (1969). The children of Armageddon: Problems of custody following divorce. *Syracuse Law Review, 21,* 55–86.

Watson, M. M., & Morton, T. L. (1983). *Mediation as an alternative to social study in child custody disputes.* Unpublished evaluation report of the family court of the First Circuit Court, Honolulu, Hawaii.

Weithorn, L. A. (1983). Involving children in decisions affecting their own welfare: Guidelines for professionals. In G. B. Melton, G. P. Koocher, and M. J. Saks (Eds.), *Children's competence to consent.* New York: Plenum Press.

Weithorn, L. A. (1984). Children's capacities in legal contexts. In N. D. Reppucci, L. A. Weithorn, E. P. Mulvey, & J. Monahan (Eds.), *Mental health, law and children* (pp. 25–55). Beverly Hills: Sage.

Weithorn, L. A., & Campbell, S. B. (1982). The competency of children and adolescents to make informed treatment decisions. *Child Development, 53,* 1589–1598.

Weitzman, L. J., & Dixon, R. B. (1979). Child custody awards: Legal standards and empirical patterns for child custody, support, and visitation after divorce. *University of California, Davis Law Review, 12,* 471–521.

Westman, J. C. (1979). *Child advocacy.* New York: Free Press.

Westman, J. C., Cline, D. W., Swift, W. J., Kramer, D. A. (1970). The role of child psychiatry in divorce. *Archives of General Psychiatry, 23,* 416–420.

Whatley v. Whatley, 31 So. 2d 149 (1975).

Wood, G. H. (1984). The child as witness: How to make the adversarial process less destructive. *Family Advocate, 6,* 14–19.

PART II.

The State of Knowledge

3.

The Best Interests of the Child
in Custody Disputes

Linda Whobrey Rohman, Bruce D. Sales, and Mimi Lou

In 1969 Ellsworth and Levy, having reviewed the empirical
social science data for the National Conference of Commissioners on
Uniform State Laws, at that time attempting to promulgate a uniform
marriage and divorce law, concluded:

> psychological research that can be considered both relevant and
> useful to the problems of custody adjudication is minimal. . . .
> Similarly, judgments based upon psychological tests of either
> the parents or the child are not likely to be well founded, since
> there is little evidence that such test results have any implica-
> tions in terms of the person's actual behavior. The same is true
> of individual personality assessments made by psychologists
> and psychiatrists. (p. 198)

(See also Bradbrook, 1971; Mnookin, 1975.)
Seven years later Okpaku (1976) conducted a less exhaustive review of the empirical literature but reached similar conclusions regarding its relevance within the custody context. However, unlike earlier
reviewers Okpaku asserted,

[t]he discussion . . . cannot end here. To the extent that custody litigants are allowed to adduce psychological evidence, a number of threats to the integrity of custody decision making become apparent. Judges may rely on psychological testimony to justify decisions at variance with custom or to circumvent established judicial guidelines. Since psychological hypotheses are sufficiently elastic to be pressed into the service of virtually any opinion or prediction, psychological testimony could easily be used to justify questionable custody awards, functioning as the cover under which unacceptable decisional factors gain expression. Further, judges may give credence to psychological testimony as a means of escaping the frustrations of attempting to reach the "correct" result in a difficult case. (pp. 1144–1145)

Okpaku would, at least by implication, foreclose the use of psychological data and expertise within the custody context. At least three major considerations support the more moderate view that the proper role of psychological and other social science data and expertise should be something other than an all or nothing proposition.

First, the social sciences are finally in a position to begin making significant contributions to child custody law. For the first time, direct studies of different types of custody arrangements have been undertaken (see e.g., Abarbanel, 1979; Benedek & Benedek, 1979; Clingempeel & Reppucci, 1982; Grief, 1979; Hetherington, Cox, & Cox, 1976, 1979a, 1979b, 1981; Kelly & Wallerstein, 1976; Orthner & Lewis, 1979; Roman & Haddad, 1978; Steinman, 1981; Wallerstein & Kelly, 1974, 1975, 1976, 1980). Clinical methodologies designed to assess the functioning and relationships of the parties to a custody conflict have been and continue to be developed (Levy, 1978; McDermott, Tseng, Char, & Fukunaga, 1978; Musetto, 1981; Swerdlow, 1978). Finally, we have also learned more in recent years about how to improve the quality of intervention services for members of a divorcing family unit (Crossman & Adams, 1980; Kelly & Wallerstein, 1977; Swerdlow, 1978; Wallerstein & Kelly, 1977).

Second, the use of social science data and expertise does not necessarily contradict the policy of treating a custody determination as one to be based on an exercise of judicial discretion. As a legal principle, the best interests standard "provides a purpose or objective [while] it leaves a decisionmaker the task of figuring out how to achieve that objective and the weight to be accorded to that objective when there are other principles pointing in other directions" (Mnookin, 1975, p. 231). Previously, a decisionmaker faced with this task could safely rely upon a variety of legal presumptions (e.g., the maternal preference rule, the tender years doctrine, the parental preference rule, and the fault concept) that functioned as intermediate rules under the best interests standard. As these presumptions become outmoded, child custody decisionmakers are left with an increasing amount of uninformed and unbridled discretion. While there is no doubt that judges are burdened by the weight of their discretionary powers under the best interests standard (see, e.g., Botein, 1952), practical and precedural legal rules prevent a judge from engaging in the blatantly unethical practices Okpaku (1976) considered threats to the integrity of custody decisionmaking (see, e.g., *People ex rel. Kessler v. Cotter,* 1955; *Gumphrey v. Gumphrey,* 1962). "As long as supposed experts in psychology are required to articulate the basis for their judgments, we are confident that judges . . . can be relied upon to distinguish between those psychological opinions that are well buttressed by the underlying facts of the case and the force of logic, and those psychological opinions which have no more weight behind them than the expert's titles" (Litwack, Gerber, & Fenster 1979–1980).

Finally, one can advocate the use of social science data and expertise in formulating legislative and judicial policies in the custody context and simultaneously acknowledge the inherently speculative nature of any specific application of those policies. While social science cannot guarantee that a particular judge has made the "right" decision in a particular case, social science data and expertise can provide an additional source of information and an additional perspective on what, in all the circumstances and in light of judicial discretion, appears to be in a child's best interests. Furthermore, social science experts can arguably provide a particularly valuable perspective within the custody context because, unlike judges, they are accustomed to making person-oriented determinations that are typically prospective in character and involve interdependent personal relationships (Duquette, 1978; Mnookin, 1975; Weiss, 1979a).

The purpose of this chapter, then, is to review the state of our knowledge relevant to the current custody criteria, to comment upon the strengths and limitations of that data base, and to identify fruitful areas for further research. The first section will consider the individual factors that currently constitute and define the best interests standard. For the purpose of this analysis, these factors have been grouped into two categories depending upon their referent. The first group of factors focuses upon the child or children whose custody is in dispute. Specifically, these factors involve considerations that purport to enable the court to ascertain and weigh each particular child's needs in reaching a custody determination. The second group of factors focuses upon the custody claimants in terms of their potential for fulfilling custodial responsibilities should the custody dispute be resolved in their favor. Within these two broad categories, as each factor is discussed, we will review psychological theory and research data relevant to the particular factor, the underlying assumptions that support consideration of the particular factor, or both. The final section summarizes this discussion and makes tentative conclusions and recommendations.

Current Custody Criteria

Currently, the best interests of the child is the governing standard in virtually all child custody disputes between natural parents arising within the fifty states.[1] Some states have also specified factors focusing on the needs of the child whose custody is subject to dispute or on the parental factors that will affect the child's best interests that a judge can use when applying that standard.[2] The criteria vary in form

1. The standard may or may not be applied in custody disputes between a biological parent and a nonparental third party, depending upon the status of the parental rights doctrine within the jurisdiction where the particular case arises. A great deal of literature exists concerning the special problems encountered by a nonparental third-party claimant to the custody of a child against the biological parent(s) of that child (see, e.g., Curtis, 1980; Goldstein, Freud, & Solnit, 1979; McGough & Shindell, 1978; Muench & Levy, 1979). An in-depth discussion of those problems is beyond the scope of this chapter. We will attempt, however, to point out these problems where appropriate within our more general discussion of the best interests standard.

2. Statutes in sixteen of these jurisdictions are essentially identical to Section 402 of the Uniform Marriage and Divorce Act in the factors they specify. Factors listed in Section 402 include:

and application from state to state and often from court to court within the same jurisdiction.

The Child's Needs

Although the best interests of the child standard has remained largely undefined, the focus of the court under the standard is supposed to be child centered rather than adult or parent centered. Ideally, the task of the court is to discover the child's physical, emotional, and developmental needs and attempt to satisfy them rather than to referee an adversarial contest for custody between two or more parties.[3]

Children's needs considered relevant to custody decisions under the standard can be classified in terms of four categories: physical/material needs, mental/emotional needs, religious/moral needs, and cultural/racial needs.

Physical/Material Needs

Acting as *parens patriae*,[4] the state has the power to intervene in the parent-child relationship when it is necessary to protect the health and well-being of a child. Therefore the physical needs of the child are considered relevant to a judge's determination of which placement is in the child's best interests. Among the factors considered are the child's present physical health and integrity and each party's ability to provide material benefits, food, clothing, and medical and other remedial care.

---

1) the wishes of the child's parent or parents as to his custody;
2) the wishes of the child as to his custodian;
3) the interaction and interrelationship of the child with his parent or parents, his siblings, and any other person who may significantly affect the child's best interest;
4) the child's adjustment to his home, school, and community; and
5) the mental and physical health of all individuals involved.

3. In spite of this goal, resolutions of child custody cases often turn upon objective considerations concerning the relative ability of each litigant to provide for what the court presumes to be the needs of children generally rather than upon subjective consideration of the proven needs of each particular child who comes before the court.

4. *Parens patriae* refers to the sovereign power of the state to act as a guardian in place of the parent to protect the person and property of persons under disability. Disability includes incompetence, insanity, and infancy. For a review of the doctrine and its origins see Custer (1978).

Social scientists would not dispute the assumption, implicit in the law, that the physical environment determined by a parent's socioeconomic status has an effect upon child development and adjustment to parental divorce. Although research data are sparse, one study has indicated that many children of divorcing parents expressed some concern, at least initially, about their own physical care and security (Kelly & Wallerstein, 1976; Wallerstein & Kelly, 1974, 1980). Younger children usually expressed concern about physical necessities like food and clothing, while adolescents were more likely to express concern about their chances to attend college.

Demographic data present an economic profile of the postdivorce family that indicates such insecurities may have some rational basis (see, e.g., Jenkins, 1978). However, Watson (1969) has pointed out that the more immediately apparent and perhaps "the main impact that the material need question may have on the children (beyond subsistence) relates to what it reveals of 'fairness' as mother, father, and the court demonstrate it" (p. 68). Wallerstein and Kelly (1980), citing information from their longitudinal study of 131 children of divorced parents, indicate that such children's loyalties were often swayed from one parent to the other depending upon their perceptions of "fairness" in terms of how the divorce affected both parents and each parent's ability to cope emotionally and financially with the postdivorce situation. Perceived inequity in the judicial resolution of financial disputes may also affect a child's postdivorce adjustment because it can create conflict between the parents that continues beyond the divorce (Ahrons, 1981; Cline & Westman, 1971). Continued hostility between divorced parents has been implicated as a major factor in children's postdivorce adjustment and development (Berg & Kelly, 1979; Hess & Camara, 1979; Hetherington et al., 1976, 1981; Jacobson, 1978b; Longfellow, 1979; Rosen, 1977; Wallerstein & Kelly, 1975, 1980; Westman, Cline, Swift, & Kramer, 1970).

Finally, courts should not assume that because a potential custodian has access to greater financial and economic resources a custodial award in his or her favor will usually further the best interests of a child. From a social science perspective, child-specific variables like the child's age, prior standard of living, and the presence of unique physical needs, handicaps, or disabilities that necessitate financial expenditures would be more valid indicators of such interests. In a custody trial, evidence of economic and financial resources *beyond* what is needed to sustain life should be of less import unless tied to the special needs of the child involved.

Mental/Emotional Needs

Few states' laws explicitly specify the relevance of the children's emotional needs in applying the best interests standard. However, the majority of states indirectly invoke this consideration by including five general types of criteria under the standard: the age and sex of the child; the affectional ties between the child and significant others; the child's wishes; the desirability of maintaining stability and continuity; and the child's mental and emotional health.

Age and sex of the child. Law in most states provides that the age and sex of a child are permissible considerations under the best interests standard. Age and sex have traditionally been closely associated within child custody law owing to widespread acceptance of the tender years doctrine. That doctrine established a legal presumption that the best interests of all young children, regardless of their sex, and the best interests of minor girls, regardless of their age, are best served by maternal custody (Roth, 1977). The doctrine was dispositive of a custody case unless evidence could be produced to refute the presumption (e.g., by proving the mother unfit for custody of her child) (Roth, 1977).

Recent reviews of state child custody statutes have revealed a trend toward abolishing the tender years doctrine and equalizing maternal and paternal rights to custody regardless of the age and sex of the children (Freed & Foster, 1979, 1981, 1983, 1984; Roth, 1977). However, the judiciary in some states has been slow to give practical effect to this legislative trend. For example, Lowery (1981) noted that 88% of the judges and commissioners hearing divorce cases in Kentucky who responded to her survey indicated a preference for maternal custody if a child was younger than $8\frac{1}{2}$, even though such a preference had been outlawed by a 1978 state statute.

The tender years doctrine is only one of a number of ways to conceptualize how the age and sex of a child relate to the best interests standard. The age of a child at the time of parental separation and divorce has been implicated as a major factor determining the child's postdivorce behavior and adjustment. Generally, the earlier parental divorce occurs in the life of a child beyond infancy, the more profound is its effect. Although Kalter and Rembar (1981) failed to verify an inverse relation between a child's age and degree of emotional disturbance in a clinical sample of children of divorced parents, such a relation has been supported by three other lines of social science evidence. First, developmental literature concerning attachment and parental deprivation has indicated that the early years of child's life constitute a critical period during which permanent or frequent disruption of parent-child attachment bonds may interfere with the child's later social and emotional development (Rutter, 1979). Second, research concerning the effects of fathers' absence upon their offspring has established that such effects are more pronounced the earlier in a child's life the father's absence occurs (Biller & Bahm, 1971; Herzog & Sudia, 1973; Hetherington, 1972; Hetherington et al., 1979a; Lamb, 1977; Santrock, 1975, 1977; Shinn, 1978). Several of these studies specifically investigated the effects of fathers' absence owing to divorce. Finally, direct studies of children of divorced parents have reported an inverse relation between a child's age at the time of the divorce and child adjustment after the divorce (Kelly & Wallerstein, 1976; Kurdek, Blisk, & Siesky, 1981; Kurdek & Siesky, 1980a; Wallerstein & Kelly, 1974, 1975, 1976, 1980). For example, in their five-year longitudinal study of the children of 60 pairs of divorced parents, Kelly and Wallerstein (1976; Wallerstein & Kelly, 1974, 1975, 1976, 1980) found that after the divorce and parental separation the psychological status of 44% of the preschoolers (2–6-year-olds) had deteriorated. In contrast, they reported finding evidence of deterioration in the psychological/emotional condition of only 23% of the children in early latency (7–8-year-olds), 24% of the children in later latency (9–12-year-olds), and a few of the children in adolescence (13 years old and above).

The negative correlation between age at the time of parental divorce and the incidence of emotional/psychological disturbance has been attributed to the notion that though the trauma produced by divorce may be equally intense at any age, the experience of divorce differs qualitatively for children as a function of their cognitive/emotional developmental status (Hetherington, 1979). For example, Kurdek et al. (1981; Kurdek & Siesky, 1980a, 1980b) have reported that age-related differences in children's experiences of and responses to parental divorce are mediated by their acquisition of an internal locus of control and cognitive sophistication regarding interpersonal behavior (i.e., the ability to infer motives, feelings, and thoughts of other persons and to generate reasons for their behavior). On the basis of this and other research (Crossman & Adams, 1980; Hetherington et al., 1979a, 1979b; Jacobson, 1978a, 1978b, 1978c; Kelly & Wallerstein, 1976; Kurdek et al., 1981; Kurdek & Siesky, 1980a, 1980b; Longfellow, 1979; Magrab, 1978; McDermott, 1968; Reinhard, 1977; Sorosky, 1977; Tooley, 1976; Wallerstein & Kelly, 1974, 1975, 1976, 1980; Weiss, 1979b), distinct emotional and behavioral response patterns of four age groups of children to the experience of parental divorce have been identified.

The data hold at least two implications for the resolution of custody disputes. First, they support the practice, discussed below, of awarding custody of young children to the parent who has functioned as their primary caretaker. Second, they indicate that a preference as to custody elicited from a preadolescent child must not be taken at face value (see below, The Child's Wishes). Rather, it must be interpreted in light of that child's developmentally determined emotional and behavioral response to the divorce, which may include a tendency to "take sides" with one parent against another (Wallerstein & Kelly, 1976, 1980). Children in this age group have been found to feel particularly angry toward their parents and to perceive them as either exclusively "good" or exclusively "bad" (Wallerstein & Kelly, 1976, 1980).

The sex of a child may be equally determinative of his or her reaction to parental divorce. Research suggests that boys have a tendency to be more seriously affected by parental divorce than girls (Hess & Camara, 1979; Hetherington, 1979; Hetherington et al., 1979a, 1979b, 1981; Kelly & Wallerstein, 1976; McDermott, 1968; Wallerstein & Kelly, 1974, 1975, 1976, 1980). However, these data must be interpreted with caution. A number of variables related to a child's sex may intervene in the relation between a child's sex and severity of response to parental divorce. First, there is substantial evidence that boys and girls often receive qualitatively different care from adults both before and after divorce. For example, studies have shown that, within the predivorce family, boys are both more likely to be exposed to parental conflicts and more likely to receive inconsistent parenting than are girls (Hetherington, 1979; Hetherington et al., 1979b). In the postdivorce period, boys are less likely than girls to receive positive support and nurture from parents, teachers, and other adults even though behaviorally they may experience equal or greater subjective distress and consequent desire for adult attention (Hetherington et al., 1979b). Additionally, custodial mothers have reported greater subjective stress in dealing with their sons than with their daughters (Hetherington, 1979; Hetherington et al., 1979a, 1979b). Such reports have been substantiated by the observations of objective researchers (Hetherington et al., 1979a, 1979b; Kelly & Wallerstein, 1976, 1977; Santrock & Warshak, 1979; Santrock, Warshak, & Elliott, 1981; Tooley, 1976) and have given rise to the proposal that fathers be preferred for custody of sons and mothers for custody of daughters (Bradbrook, 1971; Mnookin, 1975; Thompson, 1983).

Yet the data do not provide a sufficient basis for adopting a legal preference for same-sex custody. For example, the finding that parent-child opposite-sex pairs experienced a more stressful relationship after divorce than parent-child pairs of the same sex has usually been based upon observation of custodial parent-child relations in the first year after divorce. Hetherington (1979; Hetherington et al., 1979a) described a number of sociocultural variables operative within the initial postdivorce period that could account for turbulence within the mother-son relationship during that period. In general, children have been shown to be more likely to obey a man and complain to a woman. This tendency has been found to be particularly prevalent among boys. Given this and the additional fact that within our society boys more than girls are encouraged to express their aggressive feelings, the finding that boys have often presented more serious behavior problems to their custodial mothers than have girls is not surprising.

But should this fact be dispositive of custody decisions? We would argue that it should not. Although some mothers may be unequal to the task of controlling their sons' aggressive behavior in the initial postdivorce period because they are less familiar with the disciplinarian role—a role typically occupied by fathers within the intact family structure—they can learn to manage their sons' aggression through discipline. Tooley (1976) reported that stressful mother-son relationships after divorce were improved by appropriate psychological interventions. Additionally, Hetherington et al. (1976, 1979a, 1979b, 1981) reported that stress within the mother-son relationship after divorce usually peaked at one year and subsided over time thereafter as the mother acquired parenting skills.

Second, several recent studies of the extended postdivorce relationship between opposite-sex parent-child pairs have failed to find any indication that such relationships are more stressful than custodial relationships between parent-child pairs of the same sex or that such relationships are detrimental to the long-term adjustment and development of the children involved (Kurdek et al., 1981; Lowenstein & Koopman, 1978).

Finally, establishing a preference for custody of a child by the parent of the same sex would amount to substitution of one sex-biased rule for another (Santrock et al., 1981). Clearly, the traditional practice of awarding the custody of children to their mothers regardless of sex has lacked the requisite flexibility to be responsive to children's needs. Formal legal recognition of the "same sex" proposal could create an equally inflexible preference.

Affectional ties. Section 402 of the Uniform Marriage and Divorce Act (1979) provides that in deciding the custody of a child according to the best interests of that child, a court "shall consider . . . the interaction and interrelationship of the child with his parent or parents, his siblings, and any other person who may significantly affect the child's best interests." Generally, emphasis is placed upon the child's relationships with siblings, with potential custodians, and with other relevant members of each potential custodian's household.

The affectional ties between a child and each of the parties competing for custody is an important consideration under the best interests standard. There is a central presumption that the best interests of a child, emotional and otherwise, are served by placing the care of that child in the hands of an adult who loves the child and whom the child loves in return. Although this is a simple notion, judicial implementation of it has been fraught with great practical difficulty, particularly in cases where strong affectional ties exist between both parties and the child (e.g., when the parties are the child's parents and in parent–third-party disputes where the child's affections lie with the third-party litigant rather than with the biological parent).

Commentators have argued that the court should concentrate upon discovering the psychological parent of a child and award custody to that "parent" (Goldstein, Freud, & Solnit, 1979). A psychological parent has been defined as "one who, on a continuing, day-to-day basis, through interplay, and mutuality, fulfills the child's psychological needs for a parent, as well as the child's physical needs" (Goldstein et al., 1979, p. 98). However, members of the legal community have proved to be among the most vocal critics of the psychological parenthood doctrine. (See, e.g., Crouch, 1979, and Katkin, Bullington, & Levine, 1978, for excellent reviews of the critical and judicial reception of *Beyond the Best Interests of the Child* and its recommendations concerning psychological parenthood.) Criticism has centered upon three major points.

First, critics of the doctrine have charged that psychological parenthood is essentially a theoretical construct that may or may not reflect the realities of parent-child relationship dynamics. Unfortunately, within *Beyond the Best Interests of the Child,* Goldstein et al. neglected to cite any social science data to establish the empirical validity of the doctrine. However, the relationship between an adult and a child that Goldstein et al. referred to as "psychological parenthood" is essentially equivalent to parent-child attachment, a relationship that has received a great deal of attention within the developmental psychology research literature. Attachment has been defined as

> an affectional tie that one person forms to another specific person, binding them together in space and enduring over time. . . . Attachment implies affect. Although the affects may be complex and may vary from time to time, positive affects predominate, and we usually think of attachment as implying affection or love. (Ainsworth, 1973, p. 2)

An observer can reliably conclude that an attachment relationship exists between a child and a particular adult if the child exhibits behaviors that "promote proximity, contact, and communication with" that adult (Ainsworth, 1973, p. 2). Such behaviors are thought to indicate attachment

> only when they are differentially directed to one or a few persons rather than to others. Through such behaviors a [child] initiates and maintains interaction with and seeks to avoid sepa-

ration from an attachment figure; through them also [a child] keeps within range of this figure while occupied with other activities and seeks protection and reassurance from it when faced with a frightening situation. (Ainsworth, 1973, p. 2)

The second line of criticism that has been directed toward the psychological parenthood doctrine is the contention that the doctrine is of little value in the context of "difficult" child custody cases (Mnookin, 1975; Okpaku, 1976). While these critics may concede "that psychologists and psychiatrists can rather consistently differentiate between a situation where an adult and a child have a substantial relationship of the sort we characterize as parent-child and that where there is no such relationship at all," they contend "that existing psychological theories [do not] provide the basis to choose generally between two adults where the child has some relationship and psychological attachment to each" (Mnookin, 1975, pp. 286–287). If it were valid, this argument would, at least by implication, logically preclude the use of psychological expertise within all child custody cases: within "easy" cases, because such cases could by definition be confidently disposed of by way of traditional judicial guidelines, and within "difficult" cases, because in such cases both psychological and judicial guidelines would "fail to provide meaningful guidance in choosing between custody alternatives" (Okpaku, 1976, pp. 1120, 1129).

Although research concerning parent-child attachment has confirmed that a child forms strong attachment bonds with both parents and, consequently, both parents may be "psychological parents" of their child (Lamb, 1981; Lamb & Lamb, 1976; Rutter, 1979; Thompson, 1983), further studies have revealed

a basic difference in each parent's role vis-à-vis the baby. . . . In most instances, the mother is the infant's *primary caregiver*. . . . That is, she more typically provides for the baby's basic needs—feeding, bathing, diaper-changing, soothing of distress, preventative protection from harm, and similar ministrations—as well as being a salient social partner in low-key play. In contrast, the father's typical role as a *secondary caregiver* is less focused around specific caregiving activities and is more focused on vigorous, physically stimulating play with the baby. Play is thus a more basic interactive context for infants with their fathers than with their mothers; in addition, different kinds of play activities also distinguish each parent. (Thompson, 1983)

Because each parent performs a distinct role when interacting with the child, the child begins in infancy to "know and develop expectations for each parent in somewhat different social contexts" (Thompson, 1983). The infant's expectations, in turn, begin to shape the baby's behavior toward each parent. When a baby becomes distressed or frightened, studies have shown that he or she will usually prefer the parent who has been the primary caregiver to the parent who functions in the secondary role. However, when a child is otherwise secure and seeks to initiate play or social interaction, he or she will probably prefer the parent who has functioned in the secondary caregiving role (Thompson, 1983).

Thompson (1983) has interpreted these findings to indicate that, other considerations being equal, within the child custody context the primary caregiver should be the preferred custodian for a child whose custody is subject to dispute (but see Atkinson, 1984). This interpretation has received some support from research specifically designed to investigate the effects of parental divorce and subsequent custodial relationships upon children. The experience of parental divorce has been characterized and studied as a stressful event within the life of a child (Bloom, Asher, & White, 1978; Hetherington, 1979; Wallerstein & Kelly, 1980). Because children have been found to prefer contact with their primary caregiver during times of general emotional distress, perhaps they would fare better in the custody of their primary caregiver during the crisis of parental divorce. And since child adjustment has been found to be strongly associated with the quality of custodial parent-child relations during the postdivorce period (Santrock & Warshak, 1979; Wallerstein & Kelly, 1975, 1980), it should not be surprising that the quantity and quality of parental attention to children's individual problems and needs has been shown to foster their abilities to cope with the parental divorce experience (Jacobson, 1978c; Shinn, 1978).

Furthermore, it may be particularly important to place the very young child with the primary caretaker for three reasons. First, physical ministrations by the primary caretaker are perhaps the most salient social interactions a young child experiences (Thompson, 1983). Second, substitution of even the child's secondary caregiver in the primary parenting role would "require a more significant renegotiation of relational expectations" than would be required by placing the child with the primary caregiver (Thompson, 1983). Because very young children have shown a greater propensity to succumb to the psychological and emotional stress imposed by parental divorce than any other age group, a preference that minimizes the environmental and relational instability they experience during the postdivorce period is highly desirable. Finally, research has not adequately investigated the responses of older children to distinct parental roles within the child care context. Such research is necessary before extension of the proposed preference to older children could be advocated (Thompson, 1983).

The final type of critical response to the psychological parenthood doctrine has focused upon the recommendation by Goldstein et al. that the custodial "psychological" parent of a child be granted complete control over the noncustodial parent's future access to the child. In support of this proposal, Goldstein et al. (1979) and others (see, e.g., Jenkins, 1977) reason that a child's psychological parent can be trusted, unselfishly and objectively, to do what is best for the child regarding access to the noncustodial parent. If a child's psychological parent were to elect to prevent all contact between the child and the noncustodial parent, Goldstein et al. (1979) maintain that the benefit to the child of the continuity of care and the stability of the custodial environment gained thereby would far outweigh any harm inflicted by complete loss of access to a noncustodial parent.

Social science data have documented the incidence of a great deal of personal and legal strife between parents during the postdivorce period (Ahrons, 1981; Cline & Westman, 1971; Hetherington et al., 1976; Wallerstein & Kelly, 1975, 1980; Westman et al., 1970), and studies have confirmed that children of divorced parents suffer psychologically and emotionally as a result (Berg & Kelly, 1979; Hess & Camara, 1979; Hetherington et al., 1976; Jacobson, 1978c; Lowenstein & Koopman, 1978; Wallerstein & Kelly, 1975, 1980; Westman et al., 1970). Because visitation of the child by the noncustodial parent usually necessitates some contact between parents as well, interparental hostility is often vented within the visitation context (Benedek & Benedek, 1977; Wallerstein & Kelly, 1980). Therefore, to the extent that the proposal of Goldstein et al. would allow the custodial parent to control visits, with the option of totally denying the noncustodial parent access to the child should visitation prove detrimental (i.e., become an arena for the expression of interparental hostility), and to the extent that it would simultaneously eliminate a noncustodial parent's right to legal redress of visitation grievances, the proposal would eliminate a number of proven threats to children's postdivorce adjustment.

However, there is little evidence to support the assumption that the custodial parent of a child would responsibly wield the authority to permit or deny visitation by the noncustodial parent. Fulton (1979) reported that 40% of the custodial mothers he interviewed confessed they had denied their former spouse access to the children at least once out of spite. Similarly, Mnookin and Kornhauser (1979) have noted that often a custodial parent's most immediate weapon of retaliation against a noncustodial parent who defaults on child support obligations is denial of visitation rights. Clearly, given the generally poor quality of interparental relations after divorce, a custodial parent's denial of the other parent's access to their child might frequently be motivated by other than rational, objective consideration of the child's best interests.

Perhaps the most significant flaw in the visitation proposal of Goldstein et al. is that it underestimates the importance to a child of both parents. A number of studies have reported that maintaining positive relationships between a child and both parents following parental divorce aids the child's adjustment (Benedek & Benedek, 1977; Hess & Camara, 1979; Hetherington et al., 1976; Kurdek & Siesky, 1980b; Rutter, 1971; Wallerstein & Kelly, 1980; Westman et al., 1970). Children who succeeded in maintaining both parental ties were significantly better adjusted than children who maintained positive relations with only one parent or with neither parent. Furthermore, Hess and Camara (1979) reported that family process variables (i.e., interparental harmony, mother-child relations, and father-child relations) make a larger unique contribution to child outcomes than family type (i.e., divorced versus intact). Among family process variables, interparental harmony was less important in terms of child outcome than the quality of affective relations maintained between the child and each parent after divorce.

The policy implications of these findings are clear. Contrary to the proposal of Goldstein et al. concerning visitation, so far as possible child custody law should facilitate postdivorce relations between the child and each parent (Hess & Camara, 1979). Additionally, because hostile interparental relations of a personal and/or a legal nature after divorce have been shown to detrimentally affect child adjustment and child relations with one or both parents, child custody law should attempt to facilitate positive postdivorce interparental relations as well (Hess & Camara, 1979).

The child's wishes. Virtually every state allows a judge to consider the wishes of a child of any age concerning his or her own custody, depending upon the child's ability to express a reasoned and intelligent preference. The chronological age of a child usually determines whether a judge will elicit a preference and whether the preference, once elicited, will weigh heavily in the decision (Moskowitz, 1978).

Inclusion of the child's wishes as to his or her custodian as a factor under the best interests standard is related to the commonsense notion that to preserve the emotional welfare of a child, the child should be placed in the care of an adult who loves the child and whom the child loves. Ideally, when questioned, a child should voice a preference for the parent or party with whom he or she would rather live, probably the person who could be termed the child's psychological parent. However, even when a child involved in a custody dispute appears to express an intelligent, reasoned preference, that appearance may be deceptive (Levy, 1978). Especially at young ages, children may be prevented from giving a preference by their own developmental limitations. A child may lack the cognitive ability to understand what information the judge is attempting to elicit, the emotional maturity to formulate a preference, and/or the verbal ability to communicate a preference even if he or she can formulate one (Jones, 1984).

Further, we must consider whether a child is capable of making a choice based upon his or her best interests rather than one motivated by other factors. The child may choose the more lenient party, the party whose bribe seems most attractive, or one party in order to strike out at the other (Moskowitz, 1978; Weiss, 1979a; but see Jenkins, 1977).

Eliciting a preference may cause the child to experience guilt feelings later, particularly if the unchosen party interprets the choice as betrayal (Moskowitz, 1978; Weiss, 1979a). In such cases the child's emotional interests may best be served by not presenting the choice at all or by ensuring that the child's choice does not become a part of the record (Jones, 1984; Weiss, 1979a). Compounding all these obstacles is the simple fact that many lawyers and judges feel professionally inadequate to the task of eliciting a preference from a child in such an emotionally charged situation as a child custody case because they lack the psychological expertise that would give insight into the relevant emotional, mental, and physical developmental factors (Holz, 1978; Jones, 1984; Note, 1976; ; and Note, 1978).

Relevant social science data can assist in determining the legal age at which a reliable preference can be elicited from a child and can contribute appropriate assessment methods (see, e.g., Jones, 1984). Surveys of members of the judiciary have established that there is little consensus on the age when a child can express a reliable preference. The average age at which judges reported they would elicit a child's custodial preference was $8\frac{1}{2}$, but responses varied between 3 and 14 years of age (Kapner & Frumkes, 1978). Of the judges Lowery (1981) surveyed, 86% reported they would accord a child's preference more weight if the child was 12 years of age or older.

Wallerstein and Kelly (1974, 1976, 1980) reported in their longitudinal study of the children of divorcing parents that by later latency (9–12 years of age) most children were capable of a mature understanding of the reasons for and causes of parental divorce. However, not until adolescence did children involved in a parental divorce appear capable of sufficient cognitive/emotional distance from their parents to maintain positive relations with both while accurately perceiving each parent's individual deficiencies. Greenberg (1983) compared the reasoning skills and levels of understanding regarding divorce custody of children ages 9 through 14 and adults aged 18 in her study of children's competence to participate in custody decision making. Her findings suggest that, whereas adolescents 14 and older typically will be capable of expressing meaningful preferences regarding their custodial dispositions, level of cognitive development is a more reliable predictor of such capacity than is age. Her findings are consistent with Weithorn's (1984) analysis of the cognitive-developmental literature. Weithorn predicted that most children 12 or older would be capable of expressing independent preferences regarding their custody, but that many younger children also will be capable of meaningful participation in the process. Although more research is required, one can conclude that the current practice of eliciting custodial preferences from children 12 or older and according them more weight is consistent with the social science evidence.

Stability and continuity. Most states recognize the importance of stability and continuity in the environment to a child's emotional well-being. Commonly, a court's inquiry may focus upon one or more of three general factors: the need for stability, usually considered in terms of how long a child has lived in a particular stable, satisfactory environment and the desirability of maintaining continuity; the child's adjustment to home, school, and community; and the permanence, as a family unit, of the existing or proposed custodial home.

A review of decisional law reveals that concern for stability and continuity in a child's environment has usually arisen within the context of three types of cases: cases involving judicial review of or imposition of joint custody arrangements; interparental disputes over modification of preexisting custodial arrangements; and parent–third-party disputes over the custody of a child who has resided for a significant period in the custody of the third-party litigant. A child's need for environmental continuity and stability has often been cited as a major impediment to judicial recognition of joint custody, an option often requiring a child to alternate parental residences (Abarbanel, 1979; Benedek & Benedek, 1979; Clingempeel & Reppucci, 1982; Grief, 1979; Roman & Haddad, 1978; Steinman, 1981). Rules in most jurisdictions permit modifications in existing custodial arrangements to be ordered when there is a material change in the circumstances of the custodian or the child that affects the child's welfare (see, e.g., *Ponder v. Ponder,* 1973).

Finally, in the context of parent–third-party disputes, stability and continuity in the child's interpersonal, affectional relationships may be deemed so vital to the child's best interests as to outweigh parental right to custody.

Social science research indicates that in general within the custody context, a child's need for interpersonal stability and continuity may be more important to his or her well-being than a stable physical environment. First, the attachment literature, reviewed above, suggests that a child forms an attachment to both parents. However, during the temporary absence of either parent, the presence of the remaining attachment figure may compensate for the absence of the other and mitigate the effects of an unfamiliar physical environment (Rutter, 1971, 1972, 1979; Thompson, 1983). Second, a line of social science research has concerned the effect of visitation by the noncustodial parent upon child development and adjustment in the period following parental divorce (Hess & Camara, 1979; Kurdek & Siesky, 1978; Lowenstein & Koopman, 1978; Wallerstein & Kelly, 1980). This research has established that maintenance of positive relations between the child and both parents is more strongly indicative of child adjustment during the postdivorce period than either the degree of interparental harmony or the family structure.

In contrast to these findings, certain data indicate that in some instances maintenance of stability and continuity may actually be harmful to child adjustment. For example, a body of data has suggested that consistent interparental hostility in an intact nuclear family may be more detrimental to a child's adjustment than in divorce (Berg & Kelly, 1979; Despert, 1962; Nye, 1957). Further, Crossman and Adams (1980), Hetherington et al., (1979b), and Santrock (1975) have shown that where children had behavior problems at school subsequent to parental divorce, teachers or peers evaluated them negatively and that these negative evaluations persisted even when the problematic behaviors ceased. Conversely, Hetherington et al. (1979b) have found that such children were evaluated more positively if they changed schools between one and two years after the divorce. Clearly, more research is necessary to identify the specific situations and circumstances where consistency and stability promote or interfere with a child's best interests.

Mental/emotional health. Finally, the law focuses upon a child's mental and emotional health and integrity as relevant to the best interests standard. Concern for these factors is legitimate given the number of studies documenting that children of divorced parents as a group are overrepresented within clinical populations (Kalter, 1977; McDermott, 1970; Morrison, 1974; Sugar, 1970; Tuckman & Regan, 1966; Westman et al., 1970; but see Felner, Stolberg, & Cowen, 1975). Additionally, the nature of psychological/behavioral problems presented by children of divorced parents has been found to distinguish them as a group (Felner et al., 1975; Herzog & Sudia, 1973; Kalter, 1977; Levitin, 1979). Generally, this research finds a higher incidence of delinquency and depression and a lower incidence of anxiety, neurotic symptoms, and sleep disturbances in clinical samples of children whose parents divorced than in clinical samples of children whose parents' marriage remained intact and happy.

Within research specific to the issue of child adjustment after parental divorce, the mental/emotional integrity of a child at the time his or her parents divorce may affect how the experience affects the child (Hetherington, 1979; Wallerstein & Kelly, 1974, 1980). An otherwise stable child's experience of parental divorce has been compared to the grief or mourning response attendant upon the death of a loved one (Toomin, 1974). With time, grief subsides and life and growth continue. Accordingly, studies of the effects of parents' divorce upon their children have reported that many children recover from the experience within between two to three months and one to two years (McDermott, 1968; Hetherington et al., 1979b; Wallerstein & Kelly, 1980). However, it is generally agreed that if a child has experienced chronic or concurrent stress, parental divorce may enhance preexisting stressors to the extent that it becomes the proverbial straw that broke the camel's back (Hetherington, 1979; Wallerstein & Kelly, 1974). After the initial shock subsides, a few children actually have been found to experience a developmental spurt attributable to increased maturity demands imposed upon them by the separation of their parents (Wallerstein & Kelly, 1980).

Religious/Moral Needs

Although a few state statutes refer specifically to the religious needs or moral welfare of children as relevant to the best interests standard, the law in many jurisdictions countenances a specific inquiry into the religious beliefs and practices of potential custodians. However, because courts are required by constitutional provisions ensuring religious freedom to maintain an attitude of strict impartiality among religions and between religious and atheistic beliefs, the religious beliefs and practices of a potential custodian are weighed only in terms of their effects upon the child.

A few general policies concerning religion as a factor in accordance with the best interests of the child standard are evident in the law (Annotation, 1983). First, a child's welfare will not be sacrificed to permit or enhance the expression of religious beliefs held either by a potential custodian or by the child, should he or she be mature enough to embrace a particular faith. Thus, in making a custody determination a court will examine the religious beliefs of each potential custodian and of a mature child to determine if the practice of such beliefs could possibly threaten the child's physical or psychological welfare. Second, where the child has reached a sufficient age and level of intellectual maturity to embrace a particular faith as his or her own and has done so, courts have generally been reluctant to award custody to a party who appears unlikely or unwilling to provide the child with an opportunity to practice that faith. Third, if other considerations are equal and if the child has not yet been initiated into a particular faith, courts tend to award custody to the party who will raise the child in the faith professed by the natural parents. Finally, between natural parents of differing faiths whose child does not yet adhere to any particular faith, courts have tended to award custody of the child without regard to religious considerations.

More generally, the law has traditionally emphasized the moral character of the competing parties, presuming that the best religious/moral interests of any child are served by placement with the potential custodian who is of higher moral character (see below, Fitness and Conduct of Prospective Custodians).

To our knowledge, no social science research has systematically investigated the effect of a custodian's religious beliefs or moral behavior upon the well-being of a child. Of some relevance, however, are studies in the area of delinquency and criminology, including, specifically, investigations into the relation between parental behavior and criminal activities by children. Although neither the actual moral conduct nor the moral values of the parents have been examined in such studies, certain types of antisocial (i.e., criminal) parental behavior have been found to be significantly related to delinquency of the children (Glueck & Glueck, 1950; McCord, McCord, & Zola, 1959; West & Farrington, 1973). However, other studies (Gove & Crutchfield, 1982; West & Farrington, 1977) found that quality of the relationship between parents and their child are among the strongest predictors of juvenile delinquency. Thus it is possible that the quality of relationship shared with psychological parents, rather than the moral "character" of the parents, might be the more significant factor for consideration under the best interests standard.

Cultural/Racial Needs

Currently, child custody statutes in two states refer to the racial or cultural background of children and their potential custodians in conjunction with the best interests of the child standard. One statute permits consideration of the child's cultural background and the capacity and disposition of the parties to continue educating and raising the child within his or her culture (*Minnesota Statutes Annotated,* 1982). The other statutory provision prohibits reliance upon the race or color of a party as the sole basis of a custody determination although permitting racial/cultural considerations to be among a number of factors that provide the factual basis for such a decision (District of Columbia, 1981).

Generally, state courts have dealt differently with racial issues when they have arisen within one of two distinct fact situations (Annotation, 1981c). Consideration of race by the judge of a custody conflict has been held to be an abuse of discretion when race has been raised as an issue in a suit by a noncustodial parent to alter existing custodial arrangements because the custodial parent of the children has entered into a miscegenous relationship (*Palmore v. Sidoti,* 1984). Race has been held to be a legitimate consideration under the best interests standard where the child is the product of a miscegenous relationship and one potential custodian does not share the physical racial attributes of the child (Note, 1980d). Within the context of these cases, a few courts have presumed that the biracial child's interests are best served by placement with the potential custodian the child most closely resembles physically (Note, 1980d).

Some commentators feel that race has been used improperly by judges in the latter group of cases (Note, 1980d). They argue that courts should focus upon the children's identification with a particular cultural heritage and the willingness of the people who share that heritage to accept the children into their community rather than upon similarity of physical characteristics. As a result, courts confronted with this issue most recently have consistently held that while racial considerations remain relevant under the best interests standard, it is not permissible for such considerations to compose the sole basis of a custody determination (see, e.g., *Beazley v. Davis,* 1976; and *Tucker v. Tucker,* 1975).

Although social scientists are generally cognizant of the salience of race in determining behavior, no studies of father absence or parental divorce have adequately isolated the effects of race within the child custody context. However, several researchers have examined the racial identity and self-concept of nonwhite children adopted by white couples (Altstein & Simon, 1977; Howard, Royse, & Skerl, 1977; Ladner, 1977; Simon & Altstein, 1977). During the 1970s, when the incidence of transracial adoption was at its peak, minority groups objected to the practice as "a threat to the future of their communities" and an act of "cultural genocide" (Altstein & Simon, 1977, p. 64). However, a study of this issue (Altstein & Simon, 1977) found that "transracial adoption of nonwhite children by white families does not jeopardize the nonwhite child's racial awareness, identity, or attitude" (p. 70). On the basis of these results, Altstein and Simon advocate extension of the practice of transracial adoption as a viable alternative for many nonwhite children who are currently difficult to place in permanent adoptive homes.

Moreover, the data currently militate against using racial differences between a child and potential custodian as a reliable indicator of the custodial placement that will further the child's best interests. Further research in this area is necessary.

The Prospective Custodians

Child custody law has established the relevance of a number of factors that pertain to the characteristics or behavior of a prospective custodian with respect to ability to promote the best interests of a child. These factors include the sex of parental litigants; the physical and mental condition of the competing parties; the wishes and rights of the biological parents of the child whose custody is contested; and the fitness of each of the competing parties for parenthood, which is usually at least partially, if not wholly, based upon an inquiry into each party's conduct and general life-style.

Sex of Parental Litigants

During the nineteenth and early twentieth centuries a preference for maternal custody was established in the law governing divorce custody adjudications. Initially, the maternal preference rule reflected societal values concerning the sex-appropriate roles of men and women within the family vis-à-vis their children and, more generally, within society. As the governing legal standard changed from rules based on parental right or fault to the more amorphous best interests of the child principle, the maternal preference rule survived as an intermediate premise or corollary to the new standard. This rule functionally narrowed the wide judicial discretionary powers that had resulted from the change in the decision standard (Jaffe, 1967; Mnookin, 1975). Ellsworth and Levy (1969) recommended incorporating the maternal preference rule into the Uniform Marriage and Divorce Act for that reason. They proposed that the rule would resolve difficult value conflicts presented by custody cases and would discourage fathers from contesting maternal custody, thereby decreasing the number of such cases reaching the courts.

Contrary to Ellsworth's and Levy's contention, perpetuating the maternal preference rule has created many more value conflicts than it has resolved. Maternal custody has become and remains the prevalent custodial arrangement, regardless whether the custody disposition is the result of parental agreement or imposed upon the parents by a court of law (Goode, 1956, 1965; Marschall & Gatz, 1975; Weiss, 1975). Divorced fathers are actively discouraged from seeking custody by judges and by their own attorneys owing to rigid adherence to a preference for maternal custody within the legal community (Gersick, 1979; Marschall & Gatz, 1975; Roman & Haddad, 1978). As a practical matter, the ability of divorced fathers to gain custody of their children may often be completely dependent upon the clear unfitness of the mother for child custody or the mother's acquiescence in a custody arrangement permitting the father sole or partial custody of their children (Gersick, 1979; Marschall & Gatz, 1975; Orthner, Brown, & Ferguson, 1976).

Value conflicts have arisen to the extent that societal norms no longer uniformly support the notion that mothers are naturally superior caretakers of children (Weiss, 1979a). Given the increasing number of mothers employed outside the home and given changing sex roles within the family, the law can no longer assume with any confidence that a child's mother has been the child's primary caregiver or that custodial placement with the mother will automatically provide the child with a homebound parent (Weiss, 1979a). The courts also can no longer assume that the child's emotional relationship with the mother is unique, distinctly different from his or her relationship with others including the father (Ainsworth, 1973; Bowlby, 1969). Recent reviews of the attachment and parental deprivation literature have concluded that infants form attachments and bonds with both parents that may be very similar in quality and function from the child's perspective (Lamb & Lamb, 1976; Rutter, 1972, 1979) and that are dependent not upon the parent's sex but upon the character of the parent's interaction with the child (Thompson, 1983). Recent studies have indicated that fathers can be as competent and nurturant as mothers in caring for their infants and in responding to infant cues (Parke & Sawin, 1976; Parke & Tinsley, 1981) and that single divorced fathers can parent effectively (Friedman, 1980; Gasser & Taylor, 1976; Lamb, 1977, 1981; Mendes, 1976; Orthner et al., 1976; Orthner & Lewis, 1979).

In January 1978 the American Psychological Association adopted a resolution that stated: "It is scientifically and psychologically baseless . . . to discriminate against men because of their sex in the assignment of children's custody" (Salk, 1977, p. 49). Mnookin (1975) agrees: "There appears to be no substantial empirical evidence to justify, from the child's perspective, a rule that systematically "tilts" the process in favor of the mother where the parents disagree" (p. 284). He continued, "Sex-based rules have been tried historically and are now being discarded (correctly in my view) because they reflect value judgments and sexual stereotypes that our society is in the process of rejecting" (p. 284).

In short, a legal presumption that automatically equates maternal custody with a child's best interests is no longer an accurate reflection of sociofamilial realities. Within this social context, to discourage paternal suits for custody of children in the interest of clearing court dockets is inappropriate. In the extreme, it may qualify as sexual discrimination prohibited by the due process and equal protection clauses of state and federal constitutions (Derdeyn, 1976b, 1978; Weiss, 1979a).

Parental Wishes

Within contested custody cases, the relative strength and genuineness of parental wishes and desires constitute one of many factors a judge may consider in reaching a decision. Contrary to popular stereotype, however, the typical child custody case is not contested. Of the child custody cases resulting from parental divorce, 83% to 90% have been estimated to be uncontested as a result of parental agreement concerning custody arrangements before the custody hearing (Goode, 1956, 1965; Levy, 1984; Lowery, 1981). When the child's parents have agreed on custody arrangements, the law provides that their agreement will determine the child's custody if the court concludes that the best interests of their child will be promoted by fulfillment of its terms. In reality, judges seldom inquire into the terms of such agreements (Lowery, 1981; Mnookin & Kornhauser, 1979): "Typically, separation agreements are rubber stamped even in cases involving children" (Mnookin & Kornhauser, 1979, p. 955). As a result, parents' wishes may determine their child's custody if they can agree on the issue before a court hearing.

From a psychological standpoint, it may be in the best interests of the children involved for their parents to resolve custody disputes by mutual consent rather than to have a custodial arrangement imposed upon the family by judicial mandate. Arguably parents are in a better position than any stranger, including a judge, to know their child and their and their child's needs and desires concerning child custody (Coogler, 1978; Gardner, 1977; Mnookin, 1975; Mnookin & Kornhauser, 1979). Consequently, "a privately negotiated solution by those who will be responsible for care after the divorce seems much more likely to match the parents' capacities and desires with the child's needs" (Mnookin, 1975, p. 288).

Further, negotiated settlements of child custody disputes may facilitate postdivorce relations between parents and between each parent and the children (Mnookin, 1975; Pearson & Thoennes, 1984). For example, the adversary nature of legal proceedings has been cited as one source of personal animosity between divorcing parents (Coogler, 1978; Derdeyn, 1976a; Watson, 1969) that would be avoided if the parents agreed on custody before a hearing on the matter (see chap. 2). Unfortunately, owing to the dearth of social science research in the area, much of the literature on the role of parents' wishes in the promotion of the best interests of children within the custody context remains scholarly conjecture.

Fitness and Conduct of a Prospective Custodian

Historically, judicial determination of parents' fitness for child custody was analogous to traditional notions of fault within divorce law. Upon parental divorce within fault-based jurisdictions it was customary to award the custody of any children of a marriage to the parent who had been "faultless" within the divorce action (Annotation, 1969). Fault consisted of proof that during the marriage a spouse engaged in one or more behaviors defined by statute as necessary and sufficient legal grounds for termination of a marriage. Typically these behaviors included, but were not limited to, adultery; alcohol or drug abuse; spouse abuse, abandonment, or neglect; criminal activities; and mental illness.

Judicial inquiry into a party's fitness for child custody survived the advent of no-fault divorce and the best interests standard substantially unscathed. Although no-fault divorce laws no longer require a party to demonstrate the other party's responsibility for marital failure, the behaviors formerly considered probative of fault have continued to provide the basis for the legal definition of a party's unfitness within the custody context. Moreover, in the absence of evidence establishing one party or the other as absolutely unfit for a child's custody, state statutes and case law permit a judge to assess and compare the general moral character of each through evidence concerning particular acts, a course of conduct, or a life-style that can be characterized as moral or immoral according to prevailing societal standards. Generally the law presumes that the best interests of a child are served by placement with the custodian who appears relatively "more fit" for child custody as a result of this inquiry.

Because a court is concerned with the present relative fitness of the parties for child custody, proof of specific instances of a party's misconduct can reflect upon that party's current fitness for custody only if they occurred in the recent past or continue into the present. The current trend in the law favors a legal test that requires an assessment of whether the prospective custodian's behavior has a direct adverse impact on the child, while it prohibits consideration of conduct that does not have a direct adverse effect upon the child and the custodian's relationship with the child (Lauerman, 1977).

Three separate surveys have demonstrated the emphasis currently placed upon the fitness and conduct of a potential custodian under the best interests standard. Of the judges Kapner and Frumkes (1978) surveyed, 75% indicated they would place great weight upon the moral values of a party as evidenced by his or her personal conduct, even when the judges were told to assume the conduct in question would not have a direct adverse impact upon the child. More recently, Lowery (1981) reported that a party's moral character is a major factor in judges' assessment of his or her potential as a parent. Similarly, parents who had settled custody disputes by mutual agreement reported they considered freedom from past or present mental illness, alcoholism, and low morals minimally necessary criteria to establish fitness for child custody. Within each of these studies the sexual conduct of a potential custodian was regarded as particularly probative of that party's general moral character and consequent relative fitness for custody.

Three types of sexual conduct on the part of a custodian or prospective custodian have been discussed in a significant number of cases: extramarital affairs (adultery or promiscuity), cohabitation with a member of the opposite sex without the benefit of marriage (Note, 1980a), and sexual orientation considered socially deviant (homosexuality and lesbianism) (Annotation, 1981a; Atkinson, 1984; Comment, 1980; Hunter & Polikoff, 1975–1976; Note, 1980c). Formerly proof that a potential custodian engaged in any of these types of sexual behaviors was sufficient to prevent that party from receiving custody of a child because, as Mnookin (1975) has pointed out, "while there is [often little] consensus about what is best for a child, there is much consensus about what is very bad" (p. 261). Until recently, widely held societal values supported the judicial presumption that if a custodian's sexual conduct varied from the middle-class societal norm, the resultant custodial environment would necessarily be "very bad" for the child. According to this presumption, a custodian who personally engaged in socially unacceptable sexual practices would be unable to function as a child's role model for socially acceptable behaviors of either a sexual or a nonsexual nature.

Recently, however, a "nascent trend" toward a more neutral stance with respect to a party's sexual conduct has been reflected in the statutes and case law governing child custody adjudication in a number of states (Derdeyn, 1976b, p. 1375). (See also Atkinson, 1984; Bergman, 1968; Lauerman, 1977.) This trend is attributable to a variety of factors and supported by social science data. First, societal values defining socially acceptable and unacceptable sexual conduct have changed. There is no longer a clear consensus that sexual activity should be limited to the confines of marriage, as evidenced by the increasing number of open marriages and couples who live together without benefit of matrimony.

Second, just as there is no longer a consensus that nontraditional sexual conduct is in itself clearly bad, there is no longer a clear consensus that nontraditional sexual conduct on the part of a child's custodian will necessarily be detrimental to the child. The effect upon a child of his or her parent's resumption of postdivorce sexual relationships may vary depending upon the age of the child and the discretion with which the parent conducts such relationships (Wallerstein & Kelly, 1974, 1976). For example, Sorosky (1977) and Wallerstein and Kelly (1974) have noted the necessity for parents with adolescent children to maintain generational boundaries in their sexual conduct. The postdivorce adjustment of the adolescents in those studies was disturbed when they perceived their parents as sexual competitors in the same dating market. These findings support the adoption of the direct adverse impact test in gauging the probative value of a potential custodian's unfit acts within the child custody context.

Finally, there are few social science data to support either of the conservative judicial predictions that a sexually nontraditional custodian will be unable to parent effectively or that a child reared in a nontraditional environment will necessarily adopt nontraditional societal values as an adult. Several preliminary investigations of the most extreme nontraditional family units (homosexual, lesbian, and transsexual parents and their children) have concluded that parents' sexual orientation appears to have no significant effect upon children's adjustment in general or upon children's sexual orientation in particular (Green, 1978; Hoeffer, 1981; Kirkpatrick, Smith, & Roy, 1981). Unfortunately, the courts have not necessarily considered the direction of the psychological data when rendering decisions on the fitness of homosexual parents. For example, the Supreme Court of Virginia reversed a joint custody order in a case where a homosexual father was living with a male lover (*Roe v. Roe,* 1985). Although there was no independent evidence that this relationship was harmful to his 9-year-old daughter, who was reported to be "well adjusted," the court decided that his exposing his daughter to "his immoral and illicit homosexual relationship rendered him an unfit and improper custodian as a matter of law" (*Roe v. Roe,* 1985, p. 694).

As mentioned previously in the section on Religious/Moral Needs, there has been in fact no research evidence showing exactly what are the effects of a parent's (positive) moral values or behaviors on a child. It certainly has not been demonstrated that there is in any sense a one-to-one relation between parents' values and children's values. In fact the literature from the separate social science fields of attachment and of delinquency suggests that the quality of the relationship between parent and child may be the most significant factor influencing the social development of the child, more important than the professed values of the parent.

Physical and Mental Condition of Litigants

The physical and mental condition of each party may be considered under the best interests of the child standard (Annotation, 1960; Annotation, 1981b; Note, 1980b). As to physical condition, recent court decisions have uniformly held that the physical disability of a party is not prima facie evidence[5] that the party is not capable of caring for children (Annotation, 1981b; Note, 1980b). Rather, the central consideration under the best interests standard is whether the party's disability will have a substantial and lasting adverse effect on the child (see, e.g., *In re marriage of Carney,* 1979).

The mental health of the parties competing for the custody of a child may also be considered under the best interests standard. In cases where the mental or emotional health of one or both prospective custodians is at issue, courts are forced to rely heavily upon expert

---

5. Prima facie evidence is a legal expression to describe evidence that is "good and sufficient on its face; . . . sufficient to establish a given fact, or the group or chains of facts constituting [a] party's claim or defense, and which if not rebutted or contradicted, will remain sufficient" and therefore decisive of the case. *Black's Law Dictionary* (4th ed., 1951), pp. 1353–1354.

psychological or psychiatric testimony (Annotation, 1960). A number of states authorize the courts to require that the parties undergo mental health examinations to aid in the adjudicatory process (Annotation, 1980). A few courts have required parties to submit to periodic examinations as a condition to the award or retention of a child's custody (see, e.g., *Barnes v. Barnes*, 1970). However, it has been held an abuse of discretion for a court to delay a determination until a party submits to some type of mental therapy (see, e.g., *Snell v. Snell*, 1978). Generally, courts have tended to weigh the questionable mental status of a parent suing for custody more heavily against that parent if the opposing party is the other parent of the child rather than a third-party litigant (Annotation, 1960).

Survey studies have revealed a high incidence of mental health problems within the general population of divorced persons (Briscoe, Smith, Robins, Marten, & Gaskin, 1973; Morrison, 1974). Wallerstein and Kelly (1980), for example, estimated on the basis of clinical interviews, self-reports, and interviews with former spouses that approximately two-thirds of the divorced parents in their study had been moderately to severely disturbed during their marriages. In another study of divorced persons, 65% of the reasons cited for obtaining a divorce related to psychological problems of one spouse or another (Sorosky, 1977).

Owing to the nature of the divorce experience, even otherwise well-adjusted persons undergo mental and emotional crises during a divorce that continue into the postdivorce period. There has been some indication of sex differences in parents' responses to the divorce crisis, with divorced fathers typically appearing more deeply troubled during the initial postdivorce period but readjusting more quickly than their ex-wives (Hetherington et al., 1976; Wallerstein & Kelly, 1980).

Research suggests that recently divorced parents make fewer maturity demands upon their children (Hetherington et al., 1976, 1981), communicate less well with them (Hetherington et al., 1976, 1981; Jacobson, 1978c), express less affection (Hetherington et al., 1976, 1981), discipline their children less consistently (Hetherington et al., 1976, 1981; McDermott, 1970; Tooley, 1976), and are less likely to reason and more likely to issue commands than parents in intact families (Hetherington et al., 1976, 1981; Santrock, 1975; Santrock &

Warshak, 1979; Santrock et al., 1981). The quantity as well as the quality of parental attention has been related to a child's ability to adjust to the divorce (Jacobson, 1978c; Shinn, 1978). Jacobson (1978c) noted that, although parental attentiveness to children's problems and needs during the postdivorce period accounted for most of the variance in child adjustment at one year after parental divorce, the vast majority of parents she studied were either unable or unwilling to help their children because of their own inability to cope. One may speculate that these findings support the notion that the mental health problems experienced by some divorced parents may interfere with their parenting skills. It is essential, however, that neither legal nor mental health professionals presume parental ineffectiveness in the face of a parental psychological problem. Rather, case-by-case analyses are critical to ascertain the effect of any specific problem upon parenting abilities.

There has been some indication that the mental/emotional status of the respective custody claimants is weighted heavily in decisions regarding child custody regardless whether the decision is made by the child's parents or by a judge (Lowery, 1981; Marschall & Gatz, 1975). Yet in reaching these decisions, do the parents and judges utilize the appropriate mental health expertise? It appears not. For example, in spite of the broad powers conferred upon the judge under present child custody laws to consult mental health experts or to require that a child's custodian submit to treatment, the majority of judges have failed to take full advantage of mental health resources available in their jurisdictions (Swerdlow, 1978; Woody, 1977). Similarly, attorneys reported that they seldom referred a client to such services even when the client appeared mentally or emotionally disturbed (Swerdlow, 1978). The failure effectively to utilize mental health expertise and mental health services has been attributed to the fact that legal professionals are unaware of their existence (Herrman, McKenry, & Weber, 1979), unconvinced of their usefulness (Mnookin, 1975; Saxe, 1975), or not convinced that referring clients to such services is within the scope of their responsibilities (Kressel, Lopez-Morillas, Weinglass, & Deutsch, 1978). It is the responsibility of the mental health professions to educate legal professionals about the unique expertise they can bring to divorce and child custody issues and to work together with them in this context.

Summary and Conclusions

In child custody decisions, parents or parental figures ask society through the courts to step into and arbitrate what otherwise is considered a private arena. Once asked in, courts have had difficulty fulfilling their original desire for minimal state intervention. "The best interests of the child" standard has led courts into realms where they had not previously ventured. It therefore is not surprising that judges have had great difficulty implementing the best interests standard without bringing in their own values for child rearing and family life.

As noted above, if parents can reach a mutually satisfactory agreement concerning the custody of their children informally or through divorce mediation, the benefits to the child may be great. If a dispute goes to trial, however, we propose the following. First, if courts hold true to the best interests of the child principle, child custody adjudication should promote continuity and stability of the relationships that are most psychologically salient to the child. Accordingly, an adult who shares a psychological parent-child relationship with a child should receive custody of that child regardless of the biological relationships between the child and other parties. Similarly, custody disputes between two psychological parents (attachment figures) of a child should generally be resolved in favor of the child's primary caregiver, particularly if the child is very young (Thompson, 1983). Second, the appointment of a representative for the child within contested custody cases and the judicious use of social science expertise concerning child development would provide the procedural means to promote children's best interests in both these respects. Third, and finally, to further inform judicial decisionmaking in the disposition of child custody, more social science research concerning the viability of alternative custodial arrangements such as joint custody is vital.

On a more general level, concerning the proper role of social science and social science experts within child custody disputes, Goldstein et al. (1979) have commented: "It is beyond the competence of any judge, or for that matter of any discipline, to appraise the amalgam of human factors in any child placement dispute for purposes of making long term predictions or dictating special conditions for custody. Those judges who [question the usefulness of psychological expertise within the custody context] confuse their *authority* to [decide custody cases] with their *capacity* to [render such decisions]" (p. 114). Furthermore,

> [U]nless custody disputes are to be determined by fixed and unbending rules—i.e., as long as custody decisions require consideration of which custody alternative is likely to serve the "best interests" of the child—some prediction must be made in custody cases. That being the case, the issue is not whether psychologists or psychiatrists can predict the outcome of alternative custody arrangements with anything approaching absolute accuracy, but whether psychological testimony can provide the court with information, *not otherwise readily available to the court,* which will increase, however slightly, the accuracy of the prediction the court must make. (Litwack et al., 1979–1980, pp. 282–283)

In this context it is important to note the distinction between the nomothetic data reviewed here and their application to individual cases. The data must be considered by mental health professionals who consult in child custody cases, but they must supplement and complement, not substitute for, case-by-case evaluations. In other words, even if data suggest a particular general trend, individual cases must be evaluated clinically to determine the applicability of general findings.

With this admonition in mind, let us reconsider the social science data contained in this chapter. They are really of two types: general findings gathered in pursuit of general knowledge of family functioning, and research specifically examining functioning and relationships in the divorce or custody framework. The bulk of the former type of research can be grouped into two categories (single-parent family research and clinical research), each with conceptual and methodological problems that threaten the validity and generalizability of their findings (Levitin, 1979). Although it is beyond the scope of this chapter to critique each study reviewed here individually, readers should be aware of the methodological limitations of much of the early social science research relevant to child custody litigation.

Single-parent family research studies have traditionally been concerned with broken homes, father absence, and maternal deprivation.

Unfortunately, many of the individual studies within this category have defined these terms differently or have omitted any clear definition of such terms from research reports. For example, within such research "broken home" may refer to a single-parent household created as a result of parental separation, desertion, divorce, death, or illegitimacy (Ellsworth & Levy, 1969). The consequences of growing up in a "broken home" may differ with the nature of the event that precipitated the breakup of a particular household. Similarly, "many of the so-called 'maternal deprivation' studies . . . examine the effects of institutionalization and/or *parental* deprivation [and] are thus not, strictly speaking, 'maternal' deprivation studies" (Okpaku, 1976, p. 1141). "Unfortunately, in this type of research, the problem of accurate definition of the [antecedent] variables is tremendously increased and compounded in the case of the presumed consequences [that] are generally much more subjective and ill-defined" (Ellsworth & Levy, 1969, p. 177).

Additionally, as a consequence of practical/ethical constraints preventing random assignment of subjects to groups, research studies within this category lack equivalent control groups for comparison. At worst such studies contain no comparison group. At best, researchers have employed quasi-experimental designs including nonequivalent comparison groups "matched" with the experimental group in terms of background variables deemed relevant (but see Ellsworth & Levy, 1969, for a discussion of matching used in this context).

Clinical research studies are subject to similar types of criticism. Clinical studies typically compare a group of children from divorced homes with a group of children from intact homes. Ellsworth and Levy (1969) argue that this is not a relevant comparison because an intact family situation "is not an option for children involved in custody decisions, nor does it represent the family situation obtaining prior to the divorce. . . . Nor is this type of control group, if taken alone, a proper comparison group for research purposes, since it places too much emphasis on the divorce (or current living arrangement) itself and not enough on the factors that led up to the divorce" (pp. 174–175).

Additionally, clinical research in this area has typically drawn subjects exclusively from psychiatric populations. Subjects from such samples are often very few in number and very disturbed psychologically. Data

derived from such research are primarily descriptive and, consequently, difficult to verify through replication. (See Levitin, 1979, and
Ellsworth & Levy, 1969, for comprehensive discussions of methodological problems involved in early research relevant to child custody
generally.)

More recent research concerning the effect of divorce upon children
shares some of the weaknesses that characterized earlier efforts
(e.g., overrepresentation of middle-class families, small sample size,
use of nonstandardized assessment measures). Fortunately, however,
recent studies have not suffered from many of the other methodological problems that flawed previous research. Levitin (1979), in reviewing some of this new work, made reference to a number of strengths
common to these studies and to much of the subsequent research in
the area. Recent studies have:

1) concerned the impact of divorce on normal, rather than
   atypical or clinical, samples of children . . . ;
2) employed longitudinal designs so that changes in the effects
   of divorce, over time, could be measured . . . ;
3) gathered initial data near the time of parental separation or
   divorce, and therefore, are not subject to the distortions and
   uncertainties associated with retrospective data. . . .
4) used direct observation of children and their families . . . ;
5) attempted to look at the family as a unit or system and to
   understand how differences in family functioning before, during, and after separation and divorce could have different
   consequences for children . . . ; [and]
6) employed dynamic, process variables and used multiple measures and procedures in order to understand more fully both
   continuity and change in the children and their families. (Levitin, 1979, p. 5)

Of final note is that the results of and conclusions drawn from such
research tend to be corroborative rather than contradictory (Levitin,
1979). These facts, taken together, bolster our confidence in making
the case for the involvement of social science in the resolution of custody conflicts.

References

Abarbanel, A. (1979). Shared parenting after separation and divorce: A study of joint custody. *American Journal of Orthopsychiatry, 49,* 320–329.

Ahrons, C. R. (1981). The continuing coparental relationship between divorced spouses. *American Journal of Orthopsychiatry, 51,* 415–428.

Ainsworth, M. S. (1973). The development of infant-mother attachment. In B. M. Caldwell and H. N. Ricciuti (Eds.), *Review of child development research* (Vol. 3, pp. 1–94). Chicago: University of Chicago Press.

Altstein, H., & Simon, R. J. (1977). Transracial adoption: An examination of an American phenomenon. *Journal of Social Welfare,* 63–71.

Annotation. (1960). Mental health of contesting parent as factor in award of child custody. *American Law Reports,* 2nd Series, *74,* 1073–1088.

Annotation. (1969). Award of custody of child to parent against whom divorce is decreed. *American Law Reports,* 3rd Series, *23,* 6–121.

Annotation. (1980). Right to require psychiatric or mental examination for party seeking to obtain or retain custody of child. *American Law Reports,* 3rd Series, *99,* 268–276.

Annotation. (1981a). Initial award or denial of child custody of homosexual or lesbian parent. *American Law Reports,* 4th Series, *6,* 1297–1300.

Annotation. (1981b). Parent's physical disability or handicap as factor in custody award or proceedings. *American Law Reports,* 4th Series, *3,* 1044–1048.

Annotation. (1981c). Race as a factor in custody award or proceedings. *American Law Reports,* 4th Series, *10,* 796–811.

Annotation. (1983). Religion as a factor in awarding custody of child. *American Law Reports,* 4th Series, *22,* 971–1039.

Atkinson, J. (1984). Criteria for deciding child custody in the trial and appellate courts. *Family Law Quarterly, 17,* 1–42.

Barnes v. Barnes, 458 S.W.2d 772 (Ky. 1970).

Beazley v. Davis, 92 Nev. 81, 545 P.2d 206 (1976).

Benedek, E. P., & Benedek, R. S. (1979). Joint custody: Solution or illusion? *American Journal of Psychiatry, 136,* 1540–1544.

Benedek, R. S., & Benedek, E. P. (1977). Postdivorce visitation: A child's right. *Journal of the American Academy of Child Psychiatry, 16,* 256–271.

Berg, B., & Kelly, R. (1979). The measured self-esteem of children from broken, rejected, and accepted families. *Journal of Divorce, 2,* 363–369.

Bergman, R. (1968). Custody awards: Standards used where the mother has been guilty of adultery or alcoholism. *Family Law Quarterly, 2,* 384–412.

Biller, H. B., & Bahm, R. M. (1971). Father absence, perceived maternal behavior, and masculinity of self-concept among junior high school boys. *Developmental Psychology, 4,* 178–181.

Bloom, B., Asher, S., & White, S. (1978). Marital disruption as a stressor: A review and analysis. *Psychological Bulletin, 85,* 867–894.

Botein, B. (1952). *Trial judge.* New York: Simon and Schuster.

Bowlby, J. (1969). *Attachment and loss* (Vol. 1). London: Hogarth; New York: Basic Books.

Bradbrook, A. (1971). The relevance of psychological and psychiatric studies to the future development of the laws governing the settlement of interparental child custody disputes. *Journal of Family Law, 11,* 557–587.

Briscoe, C. W., Smith, J. B., Robins, E., Marten, S., & Gaskin, F. (1973). Divorce and psychiatric disease. *Archives of General Psychiatry, 29,* 119–125.

Cline, D. W., & Westman, J. C. (1971). The impact of divorce on the family. *Child Psychiatry and Human Development, 2,* 78–83.

Clingempeel, W. G., & Reppucci, N. D. (1982). Joint custody after divorce: Major issues and goals for research. *Psychological Bulletin, 91,* 102–127.

Comment. (1980). Custody: Lesbian mothers in the courts. *Gonzaga Law Review, 16,* 147–170.

Coogler, O. J. (1978). *Structured mediation in divorce settlement: A handbook for marital mediators.* Lexington, MA: Lexington Books.

Crossman, S. M., & Adams, G. R. (1980). Divorce, single parenting, and child development. *Journal of Psychology, 106,* 205–217.

Crouch, R. E. (1979). An essay on the critical and judicial reception of *Beyond the best interests of the child. Family Law Quarterly, 13,* 49–103.

Curtis, C. (1980). The psychological parent doctrine in custody disputes between foster parents and biological parents. *Columbia Journal of Law and Social Problems, 16,* 149–192.

Custer, L. (1978). The origins of the doctrine of parens patriae. *Emory Law Journal, 27,* 195–208.

Derdeyn, A. P. (1976a). A consideration of legal issues in child custody contests: Implications for change. *Archives of General Psychiatry, 33,* 165–171.

Derdeyn, A. P. (1976b). Child custody contests in historical perspective. *American Journal of Psychiatry, 133,* 1369–1376.

Derdeyn, A. P. (1978). Child custody: A reflection of cultural change. *Journal of Clinical Child Psychology, 7,* 169–173.

Despert, J. (1962). *Children of divorce.* Garden City, NY: Dolphin Books.

District of Columbia Code, Section 16-911(a)(5) (1981).

Duquette, D. N. (1978). Child custody decision-making: The lawyer–behavioral scientist interface. *Journal of Clinical Child Psychology, 7,* 192–195.

Ellsworth, P., & Levy, R. (1969). Legislative reform of child custody adjudication: An effort to rely on social science data in formulating legal policies. *Law and Society Review, 4,* 167–233.

Felner, R. D., Stolberg, A., & Cowen, E. L. (1975). Crisis events and school mental health referral patterns of young children. *Journal of Consulting and Clinical Psychology, 43,* 305–310.

Freed, D. J., & Foster, H. H. (1979). Divorce in the fifty states: An overview as of 1978. *Family Law Quarterly, 13,* 105–128.

Freed, D. J., & Foster, H. H. (1981). Divorce in the fifty states: An overview. *Family Law Quarterly, 14,* 229–284.

Freed, D. J., & Foster, H. H. (1983). Family law in the fifty states: An overview. *Family Law Quarterly, 16,* 289–383.

Freed, D. J., & Foster, H. H. (1984). Family law in the fifty states: An overview. *Family Law Quarterly, 17,* 365–447.

Friedman, H. J. (1980). The father's parenting experience in divorce. *American Journal of Psychiatry, 137,* 1177–1182.

Fulton, J. A. (1979). Parental reports of children's post-divorce adjustment. *Journal of Social Issues, 35,* 126–139.

Gardner, R. A. (1977). Children of divorce—Some legal and psychological considerations. *Journal of Clinical Child Psychology, 6,* 3–6.

Gasser, R. D., & Taylor, C. M. (1976). Role adjustment of single parent fathers with dependent children. *Family Coordinator, 25,* 397–401.

Gersick, K. E. (1979). Fathers by choice: Divorced men who receive custody of their children. In G. Levinger and O. Moles (Eds.), *Divorce and separation: Context, causes, and consequences* (pp. 307–323). New York: Basic Books.

Glueck, S., & Glueck, E. (1950). *Unraveling juvenile delinquency.* Cambridge: Harvard University Press.

Goldstein, J., Freud, A., & Solnit, A. (1979). *Beyond the best interests of the child.* New York: Free Press.

Goode, W. (1956). *After divorce.* Glencoe, IL: Free Press.

Goode, W. (1965). *Women in divorce and separation.* New York: Free Press.

Gove, W. R., & Crutchfield, R. D. (1982). The family and juvenile delinquency. *Sociological Quarterly, 23,* 301–319.

Green, R. (1978). Sexual identity of 37 children raised by homosexual or transsexual parents. *American Journal of Psychiatry, 135,* 692–697.

Greenberg, E. F. (1983). *An empirical determination of the competence of children to participate in child custody decision making.* Unpublished doctoral dissertation, University of Illinois at Urbana-Champaign.

Grief, J. B. (1979). Fathers, children, and joint custody. *American Journal of Orthopsychiatry, 49,* 311–319.

Gumphrey v. Gumphrey, 262 Minn. 515, 115 N.W.2d 353 (1962).

Herrman, M., McKenry, P., & Weber, R. (1979). Attorneys' perceptions of their role in divorce. *Journal of Divorce, 2,* 313–322.

Herzog, E., & Sudia, C. (1973). Children in fatherless families. In B. M. Caldwell and H. N. Ricciuti (Eds.), *Review of child development research* (Vol. 3, pp. 141–232). Chicago: University of Chicago Press.

Hess, R. D., & Camara, K. A. (1979). Post-divorce family relationships as mediating factors in the consequences of divorce for children. *Journal of Social Issues, 35,* 79–96.

Hetherington, E. M. (1972). Effects of father absence on personality development in adolescent daughters. *Developmental Psychology, 7,* 313–326.

Hetherington, E. M. (1979). Divorce, a child's perspective. *American Psychologist, 34,* 851–858.

Hetherington, E. M., Cox, M., & Cox, R. (1976). Divorced fathers. *Family Coordinator, 25,* 417–428.

Hetherington, E. M., Cox, M., & Cox, R. (1979a). The development of children in mother-headed families. In D. Reiss and H. Hoffman (Eds.), *The American family: Dying or developing?* (pp. 117–145). New York: Plenum Press.

Hetherington, E. M., Cox, M., & Cox, R. (1979b). Play and social interaction in children following divorce. *Journal of Social Issues, 35,* 26–49.

Hetherington, E. M., Cox, M., & Cox, R. (1981). Effects of divorce on parents and children. In M. E. Lamb (Ed.), *Nontraditional families* (pp. 233–288). Hillsdale, NJ: Erlbaum.

Hoeffer, B. (1981). Children's acquisition of sex-role behavior in lesbian-mother families. *American Journal of Orthopsychiatry, 51,* 536–544.

Holz, M. (1978). The child advocate in private custody disputes: The Wisconsin experience. *Journal of Family Law, 16,* 739–749.

Howard, A., Royse, D., & Skerl, J. (1977). Transracial adoptions: The black community perspective. *Social Work, 22,* 184–190.

Hunter, N., & Polikoff, N. (1975–1976). Custody rights of lesbian mothers: Legal theory and litigation strategy. *Buffalo Law Review, 25,* 691–733.

In re Marriage of Carney, 24 Cal. 3d 725, 598 P.2d 36 (1979).

Jacobson, D. S. (1978a). The impact of marital separation/divorce on children. I. Parent-child separation and child adjustment. *Journal of Divorce, 1,* 341–360.

Jacobson, D. S. (1978b). The impact of marital separation/divorce on children. II. Interparent hostility and child adjustment. *Journal of Divorce, 2,* 3–19.

Jacobson, D. S. (1978c). The impact of marital separation/divorce on children. III. Parent-child communication and child adjustment, and regression analysis of findings from overall study. *Journal of Divorce, 2,* 175–194.

Jaffe, L. (1967). Was Brandeis an activist? The search for intermediate premises. *Harvard Law Review, 80,* 986–1003.

Jenkins, R. L. (1977). Maxims in child custody cases. *Family Coordinator, 26,* 385–389.

Jenkins, S. (1978). Children of divorce. *Children Today,* March–April, pp. 16–20.

Jones, C. J. (1984). Judicial questioning of children in custody and visitation proceedings. *Family Law Quarterly, 17,* 43–91.

Kalter, N. (1977). Children of divorce in an outpatient psychiatric population. *American Journal of Orthopsychiatry, 47,* 40–51.

Kalter, N., & Rembar, J. (1981). The significance of a child's age at the time of parental divorce. *American Journal of Orthopsychiatry, 51,* 85–100.

Kapner, L., & Frumkes, M. (1978). The trial of a custody conflict. *Florida Bar Journal, 52,* 174–178.

Katkin, D., Bullington, B., & Levine, M. (1978). Above and beyond the best interests of the child: An inquiry into the relationship between social policy and social action. *Law and Society Review, 8,* 669–687.

Kelly, J. (1981). The visiting relationship after divorce: Research findings and clinical implications. In I. R. Stuart and L. E. Abt (Eds.), *Children of separation and divorce: Management and treatment* (pp. 338–361). New York: Van Nostrand Reinhold.

Kelly, J., & Wallerstein, J. (1976). The effects of parental divorce: Experiences of the child in early latency. *American Journal of Orthopsychiatry, 46,* 20–32.

Kelly, J., & Wallerstein, J. (1977). Brief interventions with children in divorcing families. *American Journal of Orthopsychiatry, 47,* 23–39.

Kirkpatrick, M., Smith, C., & Roy, R. (1981). Lesbian mothers and their children: A comparative survey. *American Journal of Orthopsychiatry, 51,* 545–551.

Kressel, K., Lopez-Morillas, M., Weinglass, J., & Deutsch, M. (1978). Professional intervention in divorce: A summary of the views of lawyers, psychotherapists, and clergy. *Journal of Divorce, 2,* 119–155.

Kurdek, L., Blisk, D., & Siesky, A. (1981). Correlates of children's long-term adjustment to their parents' divorce. *Developmental Psychology, 17,* 565–579.

Kurdek, L., & Siesky, A. (1978). Divorced single parents' perceptions of child-related problems. *Journal of Divorce, 1,* 361–370.

Kurdek, L., & Siesky, A. (1980a). Children's perceptions of their parents' divorce. *Journal of Divorce, 3,* 339–378.

Kurdek, L., & Siesky, A. (1980b). Effects of divorce on children: The relationship between parent and child perspectives. *Journal of Divorce, 4,* 85–99.

Ladner, J. (1977). *Mixed families: Adopting across racial boundaries.* New York: Anchor Press/Doubleday.

Lamb, M. E. (1977). The effects of divorce on children's personality development. *Journal of Divorce, 1,* 163–174.

Lamb, M. E. (1981). *The role of the father in child development* (2nd ed.). New York: Wiley-Interscience.

Lamb, M. E., & Lamb, J. (1976). The nature and importance of the father-infant relationship. *Family Coordinator, 25,* 379–385.

Lauerman, N. (1977). Nonmarital sexual conduct and child custody. *University of Cincinnati Law Review, 46,* 647–724.

Levitin, T. (1979). Children of divorce: An introduction. *Journal of Social Issues, 35,* 1–25.

Levy, A. (1978). Child custody determination—A proposed psychiatric methodology and its resultant case typology. *Journal of Psychiatry and Law, 6,* 189–214.

Levy, R. (1984). Comment on the Pearson-Thoennes study and on mediation. *Family Law Quarterly, 17,* 525–533.

Litwack, T., Gerber, G., & Fenster, A. (1979–1980). The proper role of psychology in child custody disputes. *Journal of Family Law, 18,* 269–300.

Longfellow, C. (1979). Divorce in context: Its impact on children. In G. Levinger and O. Moles (Eds.), *Divorce and separation: Context, causes, and consequences* (pp. 287–306). New York: Basic Books.

Lowenstein, J., & Koopman, E. (1978). A comparison of self-esteem between boys living with single parent mothers and single parent fathers. *Journal of Divorce, 2,* 195–208.

Lowery, C. (1981). Child custody decisions in divorce proceedings: A survey of judges. *Professional Psychology, 12,* 492–498.

Magrab, P. (1978). For the sake of the children: A review of the psychological effects of divorce. *Journal of Divorce, 1,* 233–245.

Marschall, P., & Gatz, M. (1975). The custody decision process: Toward new roles for parents and the state. *North Carolina Central Law Journal, 7,* 50–72.

McCord, W., McCord, J., & Zola, I. K. (1959). *Origins of crime.* New York: Columbia University Press.

McDermott, J. (1968). Parental divorce in early childhood. *American Journal of Psychiatry, 124,* 1424–1432.

McDermott, J. (1970). Divorce and its psychiatric sequelae in children. *Archives of General Psychiatry, 23,* 421–427.

McDermott, J., Tseng, W., Char, W., & Fukunaga, C. (1978). Child custody decision making: The search for improvement. *Journal of the American Academy of Child Psychiatry, 17,* 104–116.

McGough, L., & Shindell, L. (1978). Coming of age: The best interests of the child standard in parent–third party custody disputes. *Emory Law Journal, 27,* 209–245.

Mendes, H. (1976). Single fathers. *Family Coordinator, 25,* 439–444.

Minnesota Statutes Annotated, Section 257.025(b) (1982).

Mnookin, R. (1975). Child custody adjudication: Judicial function in the face of indeterminacy. *Law and Contemporary Problems, 39,* 226–293.

Mnookin, R., & Kornhauser, L. (1979). Bargaining in the shadow of the law: The case of divorce. *Yale Law Review, 88,* 950–997.

Morrison, J. (1974). Parental divorce as a factor in childhood psychiatric illness. *Comprehensive Psychiatry, 15,* 95–102.

Moskowitz, L. (1978). Divorce-custody dispositions: The child's wishes in perspective. *Santa Clara Law Review, 18,* 427–452.

Muench, J., & Levy, M. (1979). Psychological parentage: A natural right. *Family Law Quarterly, 13,* 129–181.

Musetto, A. (1981). Standards for deciding contested child custody. *Journal of Clinical Child Psychology, 10,* 51–55.

Note. (1976). Family law: Custody and visitation. The judge's viewpoint—The lawyer's viewpoint. *New York State Bar Journal, 48,* 450–460.

Note. (1978). Lawyering for the child: Principles of representation in custody and visitation disputes arising from divorce. *Yale Law Journal, 87,* 1126–1190.

Note. (1980a). Child custody: Parental cohabitational relationships and the best interest of the child standard. *DePaul Law Review, 29,* 1141–1157.

Note. (1980b). Child custody—Physical disability that affects parent's ability to participate in purely physical activities with child is not a substantially changed circumstance that justifies change in custody—In re Marriage of Carney, 24 Cal. 3d 725, 598 P.2d 36 (1979). *Santa Clara Law Review, 20,* 253–257.

Note. (1980c). Child custody—Spouse's homosexuality not grounds for change of custody. *Seton Hall Law Review, 10,* 751–752.

Note. (1980d). Custody disputes following the dissolution of interracial marriages: Best interest of the child or judicial racism? *Journal of Family Law, 19,* 97–136.

Nye, F. (1957). Child adjustment in broken and in unhappy unbroken homes. *Marriage and Family Living, 19,* 356–361.

Okpaku, S. (1976). Psychology: Impediment or aid in child custody cases? *Rutgers Law Review,, 29,* 1117–1153.

Orthner, D., Brown, T., & Ferguson, D. (1976). Single-parent fatherhood: An emerging family life style. *Family Coordinator, 25,* 429–437.

Orthner, D., & Lewis, K. (1979). Evidence of single-father competence in childrearing. *Family Law Quarterly, 13,* 27–47.

Palmore v. Sidoti, 466 U.S. 429 (1984).

Parke, R., & Sawin, D. (1976). The father's role in infancy: A reevaluation. *Family Coordinator, 25,* 365–371.

Parke, R., & Tinsley, B. (1981). The father's role in infancy: Determinants of involvement in caregiving and play. In M. E. Lamb (Ed.), *The role of the father in child development* (2nd ed., pp. 429–458). New York: Wiley-Inter-science.

Pearson, J., & Thoennes, N. (1984). Mediating and litigating custody disputes: A longitudinal evaluation. *Family Law Quarterly, 17,* 497–524.

People ex rel. Kessler v. Cotter, 285 App. Div. 206, 136 N.Y.S.2d 515 (1955).

Ponder v. Ponder, 50 Ala.App. 27, 276 So. 2d 613 (1973).

Reinhard, D. (1977). The reaction of adolescent boys and girls to the divorce of their parents. *Journal of Clinical Child Psychology, 6,* 21–23.

Roe v. Roe, 324 S.E.2d 691 (Va. 1985).

Roman, M., & Haddad, W. (1978). *The disposable parent: The case for joint custody.* New York: Holt, Rinehart, and Winston.

Rosen, R. (1977). Children of divorce: What they feel about access and other aspects of the divorce experience. *Journal of Clinical Child Psychology, 6,* 24–27.

Roth, A. (1977). The tender years presumption in child custody disputes. *Journal of Family Law, 15,* 423–462.

Rutter, M. (1971). Parent-child separation: Psychological effects on the children. *Journal of Child Psychology and Psychiatry, 12,* 233–260.

Rutter, M. (1972). Maternal deprivation reconsidered. *Journal of Psycho-somatic Research, 16,* 241–250.

Rutter, M. (1979). Maternal deprivation, 1972–1978: New findings, new concepts, new approaches. *Child Development, 50,* 283–305.

Salk, L. (1977). On the custody rights of fathers in divorce. *Journal of Clinical Child Psychology, 6,* 49–50.

Santrock, J. (1975). Father absence, perceived maternal behavior, and moral development in boys. *Child Development, 46,* 753–757.

Santrock, J. (1977). Effects of father absence on sex-typed behavior in male children: Reason for the absence and age of onset of the absence. *Journal of Genetic Psychology, 130,* 3–10.

Santrock, J., & Warshak, R. (1979). Father custody and social development in boys and girls. *Journal of Social Issues, 35,* 112–125.

Santrock, J., Warshak, R., & Elliott, G. (1981). Social development and parent-child interaction in father-custody and stepmother families. In M. E. Lamb (Ed.), *Nontraditional families* (pp. 289–314). Hillsdale, NJ: Erlbaum.

Saxe, D. (1975). Some reflections on the interface of law and psychiatry in child custody cases. *Journal of Psychiatry and Law, 3,* 501–514.

Shinn, M. (1978). Father absence and children's cognitive development. *Psychological Bulletin, 85,* 295–324.

Simon, R. J., & Altstein, H. (1977). *Transracial adoption.* New York: Wiley-Interscience.

Snell v. Snell, 361 So. 2d 936 (La. App.), *cert. denied,* 363 So. 2d 536 (La. 1978).

Sorosky, A. (1977). The psychological effects of divorce on adolescents. *Adolescence, 12,* 123–136.

Steinman, S. (1981). The experience of children in a joint-custody arrangement: A report of a study. *American Journal of Orthopsychiatry, 51,* 403–414.

Sugar, M. (1970). Children of divorce. *Pediatrics, 46,* 588–595.

Swerdlow, E. (1978). Mental health services available to the bench and bar to assist in resolving problems relating to custody and visitation in family law cases. *Journal of Clinical Child Psychology, 7,* 174–177.

Thompson, R. (1983). The father's case in child custody disputes: The contributions of psychological research. In M. E. Lamb and A. Sagi (Eds.), *Fatherhood and social policy* (pp. 53–100). Hillsdale, NJ: Erlbaum.

Tooley, K. (1976). Antisocial behavior and social alienation post divorce: The "man of the house" and his mother. *American Journal of Orthopsychiatry, 46,* 33–43.

Toomin, M. (1974). The child of divorce. In R. Hardy and J. Cull (Eds.), *Therapeutic needs of the family: Problems, descriptions and therapeutic approaches* (pp. 56–90). Springfield, IL: Charles C. Thomas.

Tucker v. Tucker, 14 Wash. App. 454, 542 P.2d 789 (1975).

Tuckman, J., & Regan, R. (1966). Intactness of the home and behavioral problems in children. *Journal of Child Psychology and Psychiatry, 7,* 225–233.

Uniform Marriage and Divorce Act. (1979). *Uniform Laws Annotated,* 9A.

Wallerstein, J., & Kelly, J. (1974). The effects of parental divorce: The adolescent experience. In E. Anthony and C. Koupernik (Eds.), *The child in his family: Children at psychiatric risk* (Vol. 3, pp. 479–505). New York: Wiley.

Wallerstein, J., & Kelly, J. (1975). The effects of parental divorce: Experience of the preschool child. *Journal of the American Academy of Child Psychiatry, 14,* 600–616.

Wallerstein, J., & Kelly, J. (1976). The effects of parental divorce: Experiences of the child in later latency. *American Journal of Orthopsychiatry, 46,* 256–269.

Wallerstein, J., & Kelly, J. (1977). Divorce counseling: A community service for families in the midst of divorce *American Journal of Orthopsychiatry, 47,* 4–22.

Wallerstein, J., & Kelly, J. (1980). *Surviving the breakup: How children and parents cope with divorce.* New York: Basic Books.

Watson, A. (1969). The children of Armageddon: Problems of custody following divorce. *Syracuse Law Review, 21,* 55–86.

Weiss, R. (1975). *Marital separation.* New York: Basic Books.

Weiss, R. (1979a). Issues in the adjudication of custody when parents separate. In G. Levinger and O. Moles (Eds.), *Divorce and separation: Context, causes and consequences* (pp. 324–336). New York: Basic Books.

Weiss, R. (1979b). Growing up a little faster: The experience of growing up in a single-parent household. *Journal of Social Issues, 35,* 97–111.

Weithorn, L. A. (1984). Children's capacities in legal contexts. In N. D. Reppucci, L. A. Weithorn, E. P. Mulvey, & J. Monahan (Eds.), *Children, mental health, and the law* (pp. 25–35). Beverly Hills, CA: Sage.

West, D. J., & Farrington, D. P. (1973). *Who becomes delinquent?* London: Heinemann Educational Books.

West, D. J., & Farrington, D. P. (1977). *The delinquent way of life.* London: Heinemann Educational Books.

Westman, J., Cline, D., Swift, W., & Kramer, D. (1970). Role of child psychiatry in divorce. *Archives of General Psychiatry, 23,* 416–420.

Woody, R. (1977). Psychologists in child custody. In B. Sales (Ed.), *Psychology in the legal process* (pp. 249–268). New York: Spectrum.

4.

Child Custody Dispositions and Children's Adaptation Following Divorce

Robert D. Felner and Lisa Terre

Single-parent and blended families are rapidly approaching normative status in the United States, a condition that has forced society to reconsider traditional family role definitions and customary approaches to divorce and custody issues. In the absence of clear legal standards on which to base custody decisions (Felner, Terre, Farber, Primavera, & Bishop, 1985) and in response to public and legal pressures on the courts to adjust to the changing roles of family members in contemporary society (e.g., Folberg, 1984a; Reppucci, 1984), a growing judicial trend has emerged toward considering the range of options open to divorcing families. In addition to the traditional judicial commitment to sole maternal custody, courts have shown their present willingness to award sole paternal custody (e.g., Derdeyn, 1976; Salk, 1977; Santrock & Warshak, 1979; Schlesinger & Todres, 1976) or joint custody. The latter option in particular has gained popularity as well as apparent acceptance by the legal system. Since 1975, when this option was explicitly recognized in the statutes of only one state, 30 additional states have passed statutes either allowing for joint custody as one option for the courts to consider or making it a presumption (Freed & Foster, 1984). Further, many of the remaining states are considering legislation on joint custody (Derdeyn & Scott, 1984; Folberg, 1984b). Even in cases where joint custody is not seen as a viable option, the courts are encouraged to grant sole custody to the parent who is most tolerant of the child's continuing relationship with the other parent (Clingempeel & Reppucci, 1982; Derdeyn & Scott, 1984; Folberg, 1984b).

The increased exploration by the legal system of alternatives to sole maternal custody has been fueled not only by shifts in societal family patterns but also by social scientists who have taken strong positions for and against these changes (e.g., Goldstein, Freud, & Solnit, 1973; Roman & Haddad, 1978), often without clear data to support their positions (Felner & Farber, 1980). Indeed, in one of the most comprehensive considerations to date of the actual data relating to the differential viewpoint of sole versus joint custody, Clingempeel and Reppucci (1982) conclude that "The available studies are egregiously inadequate and for the most part the debate has been nourished solely by opposing ideologies" (p. 124). In the nearly five years since that review was carried out, there has been continued growth both in the movement to change the assumptions that surround custody decision making by the courts and in empirical literature addressing these issues. Illustratively, Clingempeel and Reppucci (1982) noted at the time of their review that "at least five states . . . have either passed or have in progress legislation establishing joint custody as a viable alternative" (p. 105). By contrast, as noted above, 31 states now have such statutes, with the rest considering enabling legislation (Derdeyn & Scott, 1984; Folberg, 1984b; Freed & Foster, 1984).

In this chapter we will consider the current statutory guidelines and empirical data pertaining to custody arrangements. However, since other chapters in this volume are devoted to exploring the shifting legal context in great detail, our primary goal is to consider the nature of the data social scientists have accumulated and used to buttress their arguments. In the following sections, we will first present a brief discussion of custody alternatives. The largest part of the chapter will be devoted to the empirical evidence relating to the adjustment of children in maternal sole custody, paternal sole custody, and joint custody, as well as the factors that may bear on these outcomes. Since there continues to be a paucity of studies that directly compare in any meaningful way children under different types of custody arrangements following divorce, we will review and judiciously extrapolate from other related research where pertinent. Finally, we consider the implications of these findings both for the arguments in favor of and opposed to various positions regarding child custody and for policy-makers in this area.

Distinction Between Single-Parent and Joint Custody

Any discussion of joint custody is hindered both by the lack of statutory uniformity and by pervasive imprecision and overlap in definitions. Statutes on coparenting differ greatly from state to state, and neither of the national model statutes, the Uniform Marriage and Divorce Act and the Uniform Child Custody Jurisdiction Act, even refers to joint custody (Folberg, 1984b). Without the guidance of the uniform model codes, it is likely that there will remain substantial variability across states for some years to come.

Difficulties in considering joint versus sole custody stemming from statutory inconsistencies among states are compounded by the lack of well-articulated and shared definitions for terms used to refer to joint custody and its variations. It is common to see the terms shared parenting, cocustody, concurrent custody, shared custody, coparenting, and joint managing conservators used interchangeably (albeit vaguely) in reference to joint parental responsibility and decisionmaking regarding the child's health, education, and welfare (Folberg, 1984a). For example, in split custody each parent is awarded sole physical custody of one or more of the children (Folberg, 1984a; Hyde, 1984); this living situation is also called divided custody at times. Arrangements in which a child resides solely with each parent either for extended portions of each year (e.g., spending summers with one parent and the academic year with the other) or in alternating years are usually alluded to as alternating custody but have also been called both divided and joint custody (Folberg, 1984a; Hyde, 1984). However, at other times these terms have more precise meanings; for example, some states (e.g., California, Colorado, Idaho, Illinois) distinguish between joint legal (decisionmaking) custody and joint physical (residential) custody (Folberg, 1984b).

An important practical factor, which interacts with the lack of clarity in formal terminology, further hinders efforts to evaluate the viability and impact of different types of custody arrangements. The multitude of day-to-day details involved in implementing joint custody defy policymakers' efforts to legislate them, with statutory definitions generally being broad enough to allow for a range of specific implementation patterns. Thus actual patterns of child care may vary significantly even within those forms of legal custody awarded by the court (Brown, 1984). For example, Levy and Chambers (1981) found that although 90% to 95% of joint custody rulings mandate joint legal custody, in most of these cases residential and caregiving arrangements are left to be worked out between the parties. Further, Ahrons (1980, 1981, 1983) notes that both court-awarded mother-custody and joint-custody families may be characterized by a wide range of father-child relationships, since parents awarded any particular custody disposition may shape and evolve it into any number of informal arrangements after the award is made (Abarbanel, 1979; Benedek & Benedek, 1979; Folberg, 1984a; Steinman, 1981).

Nevertheless, legally mandated joint and sole custody can be contrasted philosophically on at least two broad dimensions. First, in cases of joint custody, both parents are vested with equal legal authority for making important decisions pertaining to the welfare of their child. By comparison, in sole custody arrangements, the custodial parent is granted ultimate legal control over and responsibility for the child (Hyde, 1984; Roman & Haddad, 1978). Second, joint custody generally stipulates near parity with regard to child care. Sole custody, on the other hand, restricts the noncustodial parent's legal right of child access to that visitation set out by the court (Hyde, 1984; Roman & Haddad, 1978).

Divorce and the Process of Coping and Adaptation

As a prelude to our discussion of the voluminous, yet often fragmented, literature pertaining to the impact of various custody arrangements on children's adaptation, we will pause briefly to present a framework that provides a useful template for integrating this work. Felner and his colleagues have suggested that a "transitional events" (Felner, Farber, & Primavera, 1980, 1983; Felner, Rowlison, & Terre, in press) perspective may have considerable merit for guiding our efforts to understand how major life changes affect those who experience them. Drawing

from related work on the "stressfulness" of life events (e.g., Dohrenwend, 1979; Dohrenwend & Dohrenwend, 1984), this perspective
emphasizes that a specific event or major life change may have a quite
different impact on different individuals. The coping styles and attributes of each person, as well as situational factors that define the
context in which the event or change is occurring, are seen to contribute to shaping the individual's experiences of and adaptation to such
events. In addition, "life events" such as divorce are seen not as circumscribed, time-limited occurrences, but rather as "marker events"
in a prolonged process of change and readjustment both leading up to
and following "the event" proper. Thus, in attempting to understand
the consequences of such transitions, as well as the coping processes
required, the focus is not only on the brief period surrounding "the
event," but also on the circumstances that preceded it and its reper-
cussions in the lives of individuals or the family system. In the case of
divorce, the adaptation process required of family members may extend over a prolonged period during which they are confronted by a
complex set of personal and environmental stressors, changes, and
"adaptive tasks" (Felner, 1984; Felner, Farber, & Primavera, 1980,
1983; Felner, Rowlison, & Terre, in press; Felner, Terre, & Rowlison,
in press). These factors may interact with the individual's existing
coping abilities and resources to determine how well the child and the
family system negotiate this life transition.

Employing this "transitional events" (Felner, Rowlison, & Terre,
1986) framework, we shall now consider the current state of our
knowledge concerning the adaptive consequences of maternal, paternal, or joint-custody arrangements and the factors that relate to differential outcomes associated with each. The overwhelming majority of
studies to date pertain to maternal-custody conditions. Because the
issues raised by such work have often served as points of departure
for efforts to examine paternal and joint custody, we shall begin with
this literature.

Maternal Custody

Given the hundreds of studies that have been conducted on
single-parent maternal-custody families, a detailed review of all this
work is well beyond the scope of this chapter. For a more complete

discussion, readers are referred to one of the many comprehensive review papers or volumes that exist (cf. Felner et al., 1980; Felner, Terre, & Rowlison, in press; Longfellow, 1979; Shinn, 1978; Wolchik & Karoly, 1985). Employing a transitional events perspective and drawing on prior reviews and representative studies, we will present the current status of our understanding of the effects of maternal custody arrangements on children and the personal and situational factors that may be associated with different levels of risk and coping efficacy for children living in such households. Further, since many of the arguments in favor of alternative custody arrangements and studies of these alternatives are extrapolated from the work on maternal custody, we shall pay particular attention to those issues that are the focus of these arguments. Finally, it should be noted that research on child adjustment in maternal-custody households that includes comparison groups of children from other custody situations has only recently emerged. The handful of recent studies that do employ such comparisons will be discussed in the sections centered on paternal and joint custody.

Children's Adjustment and Mediating Factors: General Patterns of Adjustment

A number of studies, focusing predominantly on maternal-custody families, have attempted to unearth general patterns of adjustment specific to children of divorce that distinguish them from children who have not experienced this stressor. Consistent with a transitional events framework, the results of these studies have generally yielded mixed findings and have provided little support for any particular overall association between divorce and the adjustment problems of children. For example, while some studies have found that adolescent girls in maternal-custody households have difficulty interacting with males (e.g., Hetherington, 1972), other work (e.g., Hainline & Feig, 1978) has failed to replicate these results. Likewise, efforts to detect consistent self-concept differences among children raised solely by mothers have yielded contradictory findings (e.g., Berg & Kelly, 1979; Hainline & Feig, 1978; Parish & Taylor, 1979; Young & Parish, 1977).

Perhaps the most consistent pattern of difficulties found to be associated with parental divorce is increased "acting out," aggressive, or antisocial behavior. Heightened levels of acting out have been found by a number of authors focusing on children of divorce (e.g., Hethering-ton, Cox, & Cox, 1978a, 1978b; McDermott, 1968, 1970; Wallerstein & Kelly, 1975). Perhaps of even greater significance for the present work are the findings of those studies that have sought to disentangle the effects of divorce from the more general cases of father absence or family disruption. These studies also suggest that children from di-vorced households tend to display more aggressive, conduct disorder behaviors (e.g., Felner, Ginter, Boike, & Cowen, 1981; Felner, Stol-berg, & Cowen, 1975; Glueck & Glueck, 1950; McDermott, 1968, 1970); lower frustration tolerance (e.g., Felner et al., 1981); more difficulty following rules (e.g., Felner et al., 1981); and increased sex-ual "acting out" (e.g., Hetherington, 1972) than their counterparts ei-ther from intact families or from homes disrupted by a parent's death. By contrast, among children with a history of father loss through death, shy/withdrawn behaviors are more commonly reported (e.g., Felner et al., 1981; Hetherington, 1972).

Despite the consistent relationship between parental divorce and symptoms of child conduct disorder demonstrated by these studies, an investigative approach that seeks to find a general constellation of "effects" is not the most productive one for informing child custody decisions. Indeed, the consistent differences found among children from intact families and those that have been disrupted by different events (e.g., divorce versus death) underscore the fact that the *condi-tions surrounding* family disruption may be more important than *dis-ruption per se* in determining the adaptive consequences of such occur-rences (Felner, Terre, & Rowlison, in press). A more fruitful approach for developing guidelines to inform custody decisionmaking is to focus on those factors associated with differences in the responses of chil-dren following divorce. It is to these factors that we now turn.

Mediating Factors in Maternal-Custody Families

Child's Age and Gender
Two characteristics that have been the focus of much attention in both the empirical literature and the debate surrounding child custody are the child's age and sex. A number of studies and much theoretical speculation have been offered to support the position that the timing of

parental separation in a child's life may have a strong influence on the outcomes associated with that separation (e.g., Hodges & Bloom, 1984; Kalter & Rembar, 1981; Kurdek, Blisk, & Siesky, 1981). Influenced by psychoanalytic theory, much of the early work in the area of divorce alluded to "critical periods" such as early childhood, during which children might be particularly vulnerable (e.g., Despert, 1953; Gardner, 1977; Landis, 1960; McDermott, 1968; Neubauer, 1960; Westman, Cline, Swift, & Kramer, 1970). Findings from recent studies, however, have failed to provide evidence that some ages may be "worse" times for a divorce than others and suggest that the age at which the separation occurs may have greater salience for the *pattern* of a child's postdivorce coping efforts than for the *severity* of problems manifested (e.g., Kalter & Rembar, 1981; Kelly & Wallerstein, 1976; Wallerstein & Kelly, 1974, 1975, 1976). Moreover, even when age-related differences have been found in the severity of problems shown, the critical ages have been found to vary from study to study. For example, though some studies report that the early experience of divorce is associated with greater problems in adolescence or young adulthood (e.g., Hetherington, 1972), others have found that children who were younger when the divorce occurred rated themselves as happier, less upset, and more secure (e.g., Farber, Felner, & Primavera, 1985; Landis, 1960). Thus there appears to be little evidence supporting the once common belief that children adjust more easily to parental divorce with increasing age.

Age at the time of parental divorce may be most important in how it relates to the coping efforts children can bring to bear on the situation. That is, it is not age per se that is central here; rather, age-related competencies are the key to understanding the differential patterns of postdivorce adjustment found at different ages. Illustratively, Longfellow (1979) argues that the key factor underlying differential child reactions to divorce at varying ages may be the social-cognitive abilities associated with different developmental levels. Similarly, Kurdek and Siesky (1980a, 1980b) agree that age per se is an umbrella variable subsuming a broad array of more specific age-related processes that may influence children's perceptions and understanding of the divorce as well as their ability to draw on the available coping resources in their environments.

The evidence pertaining to the role of gender in children's response to divorce is similar to that relating to age in that gender is far more consistently related to the *patterns* than to the *magnitude* of the problems found. It seems that gender differences are primarily attributable to the different social-cognitive styles and abilities that derive from the different socialization experiences of males and females. Yet the findings relevant to gender are even less consistent than are findings for age. Despite some reports suggesting that boys cope less effectively than girls with divorce and separation (e.g., Biller, 1974; Hetherington, Cox, & Cox, 1978a, 1978b; Hodges & Bloom, 1984; Hodges, Wechsler, & Ballantine, 1979), others indicate no relation between children's gender and adaptation (e.g., Kurdek et al., 1981; Pett, 1982). Finally, some investigators have noted that females show more sex-role stereotypical signs of distress than males (Farber, Primavera, & Felner, 1984). Since those studies germane to both age- and gender-related effects have relied on maternal-custody families to an unfortunate extent, the generalizability of their findings to other family constellations is severely limited.

The Divorce Context

Divorce per se may not have any consistent, significant effect on children's functioning. Rather, the set of contextual factors associated with divorce may more immediately influence the children's environment and, thereby, their adaptive efforts. For those concerned with optimizing postdivorce adjustment by reaching custody arrangements that are truly in the child's best interests, existing literature on maternal-custody children points very clearly to a number of contextual mediators of adjustment that may be *directly* affected by the conditions set out in the custody decision. Key among these are: (1) the levels of pre- and postdivorce interparental conflict; (2) the quality of the relationship between the child and each parent as well as the conditions that surround such contact; (3) the degree of instability and change in the child's daily life surrounding the divorce; (4) the emotional well-being of the parents, particularly the primary caretaker; and (5) the level of economic stress and deprivation of the household in which the child lives. In the remainder of this section, we shall attempt to summarize the status of current research on each of these issues as they relate to the adjustment of children in divorced mother-headed households.

Interparental Conflict

It is by now widely acknowledged that parental conflict surrounding divorce, and the degree to which it persists or is exacerbated following divorce, may adversely affect the adaptation of the children involved. In particular, parental discord both before and after separation appears to have a pronounced effect on the coping efforts of children and has been repeatedly identified as an important precursor of childhood disorders in both intact and divorcing families (Ellison, 1983; Emery, 1982; Emery & O'Leary, 1982; Felner et al., 1975, 1981; Luepnitz, 1979; Nelson, 1981; Porter & O'Leary, 1980; Rosen, 1979). More specifically, research conducted by Felner and his colleagues (Felner et al., 1975, 1981) indicates that the heightened conduct problems found among children of divorce are more a function of the circumstances that surround divorce, especially parental conflict, than of father absence or of living in a single-parent family. Similarly, Jacobson (1978) found a significant association between the degree of parental hostility both before and after the divorce and the postdivorce adjustment of children, while Farber et al. (1985) report a like pattern for adolescents and young adults. Further, Wallerstein (1977) notes that the degree to which children were drawn into parental conflicts was a major factor differentiating children who coped well from those who coped poorly. Finally, Rutter (1981) reports that children from homes characterized by high levels of discord continued to manifest postdivorce adaptive difficulties only if parental conflict continued. However, in cases where separation was accompanied by a concomitant reduction in conflict, divorce was associated with a reduction in child problems.

In addition to exploring the relation between family conflict and adjustment within disrupted families, efforts have also been made to disentangle the relative contributions of family conflict and family configuration to children's adjustment. Again, the data highlight the importance of the former over the latter. Hetherington, Cox, and Cox (1979), for example, report that among a sample of children from middle- and upper-middle-class households, those from high-conflict divorced families exhibited the most adjustment problems, but those from high-conflict intact households manifested more problems than those from low-conflict intact households. These findings are consistent with those of a number of other authors who report more difficulties among children from high-conflict intact households than from low-conflict divorced families (e.g., McCord, McCord, & Thurber, 1962; Nye, 1957; Rutter, 1979).

Parent-Child Relationships

There are two discrete, although at times interwoven, lines of research pertaining to parent-child relationships in maternal-custody families. One of these focuses on the relationship between custodial mother and child, while the other centers on the relationship between child and noncustodial father. In both instances the relationships of concern are those that follow and precede the divorce.

Perhaps one of the most consistent findings is that when the relationship between custodial mother and child is strong or does not suffer disruption from the events or stresses associated with the divorce process (e.g., from parental conflict), then the child is significantly more likely to show a positive postdivorce level of adaptation. Hetherington et al. (1978a), for example, report that following divorce, changes may occur in both the quality and the quantity of custodial parent-child interactions, which in turn affects the level of problems the child displays. Specifically, if in an effort to adapt to their changed family circumstances, custodial mothers become less available or engage in ineffective child-management strategies, then children's behavior problems may increase. By contrast, close and mutually satisfying relationships between the mother and child were found to buffer the child against the negative effects of the disorganization surrounding the divorce (Hetherington et al., 1979). These authors further point out that the efficacy of child management behaviors may take several years to reach a new stable equilibrium following divorce-related disruption. However, once stable caretaking and discipline patterns are reestablished, and providing these patterns are equivalent to or better than those present before divorce, child behavior problems may decline to a level at or below that existing in the intact family. Indeed, Rutter (1981) indicates that both the mother-child relationship and child behavior may improve after divorce. Other authors have reported similarly strong correlations between the custodial mother-child relationship and the psychological status of the child at follow-up (e.g., Hess & Camara, 1979; Hodges, Buchsbaum, & Tierney, 1984; Pett, 1982; Wallerstein & Kelly, 1980b), with at least one of these (Hodges et al., 1984) reporting that maternal warmth and permissiveness was a better predictor of child adjustment than divorced or intact family status.

The preceding clearly suggests that the quality and consistency of the relationship between child and custodial mother may contribute to or mitigate the appearance or continuation of children's adjustment problems. Moreover, this work also suggests that negative changes in the mother-child relationship are not an inherent part of the divorce process but may be attributable to the stresses being experienced by the mother and the adequacy of her coping efforts.

The relationship between noncustodial father and child has also been the focus of a number of studies. Although the majority of these tend to center on "father absence," some have examined either the quality or the quantity of father-child contact. Even though the former constitute the bulk of the considerable work conducted in this area to date, this literature is flawed in its inclusion of a number of diverse family constellations and circumstances (Shinn, 1978). Given this, and considering the emphasis of this section, we shall focus primarily on those studies that have explored the nature of interactions between the noncustodial father and child.

Consistent with the position that children may benefit from a continued postdivorce relationship with both parents, the amount of contact between noncustodial fathers and their children has regularly been associated with more positive adjustment (Hess & Camara, 1979; Hetherington et al., 1978a, 1978b; Jacobs, 1982; Rosen, 1979; Wallerstein & Kelly, 1980a, 1980b). While these data have been used to support arguments favoring highly liberal visitation arrangements and joint custody, a further examination of the findings shows they are more complex than they initially appear. That is, while frequent contact with the noncustodial parent may indeed be correlated with child adaptation subsequent to divorce, there are two major qualifiers to this. First, there are certain conditions under which more frequent contact with the noncustodial parent may actually be detrimental to a child. Second, there is serious question whether the extant positive results should be attributed to the *frequency* of contact per se or to the *broader pattern of family interactions* associated with more frequent contact.

As discussed previously, parental conflict may have a substantial effect on the adjustment of children in both intact and divorced families. It should be no surprise, then, that level of discord between the former spouses may bear heavily on the outcomes associated with visitation by the noncustodial parent. Where conflict between former spouses is high (Felner, 1984; Hess & Camara, 1979; Hetherington et al., 1978a, 1978b; Wallerstein & Kelly, 1980a, 1980b) or where the noncustodial parent displays serious psychopathology (Hetherington et al., 1978a, 1978b; Wallerstein & Kelly, 1980a, 1980b), no positive association between visitation frequency and good adjustment has been found. Indeed, where heightened levels of parental conflict persist, frequent visitation may exacerbate such conflict and thus hamper children's coping efforts (e.g., Cline & Westman, 1971; Clingempeel & Reppucci, 1982; Ellison, 1983; Fulton, 1979; Hetherington et al., 1978a, 1978b; Jacobson, 1978; Kurdek & Blisk, in press; Kurdek et al., 1981; Rosen, 1979; Wallerstein & Kelly, 1980a, 1980b; Westman et al., 1970). Further, prolonged and even chronic conflict between former spouses may be more the norm than the exception (Cline & Westman, 1971; Johnston, Campbell, & Tall, 1985). For example, Wallerstein and Kelly (1980b) reported that 80% of the noncustodial fathers and 66% of the custodial mothers in their sample continued to be stressed by visitation in the year following divorce, and "nearly five years after the separation 29% of children were party to intense bitterness between parents, and even larger groups continued to be aware of limited frustration or anger" (Wallerstein & Kelly, 1980b, p. 189).

The hypothesis that the positive correlation between good adaptation by children and frequency of visitation may have less to do with visitation per se than with a broader pattern linking the child's successful coping efforts with better overall postdivorce family functioning is borne out in several ways. First, as just noted, visitation does not enhance children's adjustment when parental conflict is high. Second, in addition to its direct effects on the level of distress the child experiences, persistent discord between former spouses may result in lower levels of visitation over time regardless of the formal visitation agreements (Ahrons, 1981, 1983; Dominic & Schlesinger, 1980; Grief, 1979; Hetherington et al., 1978a, 1978b; Wallerstein & Kelly, 1980a, 1980b). Moreover, other predictors of reduced noncustodial father-child involvement include inconvenience associated with visiting

(Dominic & Schlesinger, 1980; Grief, 1979; Tepp, 1983); discomfort surrounding the ambiguity inherent in the visitor role (Tepp, 1983; Wallerstein & Kelly, 1980a, 1980b); remarriage of either of the former spouses (Tropf, 1984); fathers' feelings of depression or guilt, which may be exacerbated by continued contact (Dominic & Schlesinger, 1980; Grief, 1979; Tepp, 1983; Wallerstein & Kelly, 1980a, 1980b); and parental perception of rejection by the child (Hetherington et al., 1978a, 1978b; Wallerstein & Kelly, 1980a, 1980b). Thus, high levels of postdivorce father-child involvement typically exist in the context of a broader set of stable, satisfying, and low-conflict interactions among the members of the previously intact family. Further, when frequent father-child interactions continue under less optimal conditions, the child's adaptive efforts do not seem to be enhanced.

We shall return to the issues of parent-child relationships later in this chapter. To summarize briefly, it seems that where parental conflict is low in both intact and divorced families, a high-quality, continuing relationship with both parents is best for the child's growth and development. High levels of parent-child contact in difficult or hostility-laden circumstances not only may hinder more than help the child's adaptive efforts, but also may reduce the parenting effectiveness of the primary caretaker. Taken together, these data are very much in line with the position of Goldstein, Freud, and Solnit (1973) and others (e.g., Ellison, 1983; Emery, 1982; Felner & Farber, 1980; Felner, Farber, & Primavera, 1980; Reppucci, 1984; Rutter, 1981) that a stable, single-parent household may be better for a child than either a conflict-filled intact family or a divorced family where there is a high degree of non-custodial parent-child involvement but where high levels of conflict, distress, or disorganization accompany such contact.

Instability and Change in the Environment
Divorce is often accompanied by considerable family disorganization and disruption of daily routines (Felner, 1984; Felner, Farber, & Primavera, 1980; Felner, Terre, & Rowlison, in press). Recent work examining children in the custody of their mothers has shown that the maintenance or reestablishment of stable family household routines may significantly enhance a child's postdivorce adjustment (Felner, Farber, Ginter, Boike, & Cowen, 1980; Hetherington et al., 1978a, 1978b; Wallerstein, 1977). To the extent that disruptions persist, the

child's sense of well-being may be compromised. For example, Felner, Farber, Ginter, Boike, and Cowen (1980) examined disruptions in family functioning, shifts in economic circumstances, and levels of general family stressors among children in homes disrupted by parental divorce versus those that were intact or where a parent had died. Divorced households were characterized by significantly greater disorganization, general problems, and economic stresses. Moreover, the specific types of family problems found to be characteristic of divorce households, as compared with the other two types, were those that have been shown to relate strongly to the types of school behavior problems reported for children of divorce (Boike, Ginter, Cowen, Felner, & Francis, 1978). Stolberg and Anker (1983), in a similar work, examined changes in parent-child relationships, increased demands on the custodial parent or general family problem levels, and changes in parental income among children living with their divorced mothers versus children living with their married natural parents. Children of divorce, compared with children from intact families, tended to perceive their environments as more disorganized. Moreover, as the frequency of actual life changes increased, children perceived their environments as increasingly less predictable and felt less in control. Kurdek and Blisk (in press) also found that high levels of change in familiar routines and conditions (e.g., number of people in the home, hours of parent-child interaction, and signs of economic change such as shifts in the quality of the living quarters) were associated with increased difficulties in the psychological and social functioning of the child.

Disorganization in family routines and changes in living conditions may also exacerbate parenting stress levels or coping difficulties and thus lead cyclically to further instability in the child's life. Customary household patterns may be interrupted as a result of the increased demands on parents who are suddenly faced with all the responsibilities that go along with being a single head of household (see Parental Well-being below). Illustratively, Weinraub and Wolf (1983) found that, given the increased work load involved in being both primary caregiver and provider, single-parent mothers may have less time to manage the demands of child care and household responsibilities than mothers in intact households. This is a particularly salient issue when the custodial mother is required either to begin work for the first time or to increase her job responsibilities owing to the changes in economic circumstances that may result from the divorce settlement. However, in the absence of other interfering factors (e.g., continued conflict and accompanying instability), there is evidence that divorced mothers become more confident and efficient over time at managing competing child-care and employment demands (e.g., Johnson, 1983), and when other stressors are not present, custodial mothers seem able to establish effective care-giving routines within two years after a divorce (e.g., Hetherington et al., 1978a, 1978b).

Parental Well-being

One factor that clearly affects the child's adaptation directly and in turn is both influenced by and influences the three preceding contextual factors is the psychological status of the custodial parent. The direct effects of parental well-being have been illustrated in a number of studies suggesting that custodial mothers' coping efficacy and level of personal adjustment (e.g., feelings of confidence, self-esteem, state anxiety, and depression) are positively correlated either with the frequency of noxious and aggressive behaviors their children display (e.g., Hetherington et al., 1978a; Patterson, 1976) or with the degree to which the child feels rejected and unhappy (Zill, 1978).

A key factor bearing on the mother's coping efficacy is her appraisal of the desirability of the divorce. A positive maternal perception of the marital breakup has been found to help insulate the child against the development of problems (e.g., Biller, 1974; Santrock & Warshak, 1979). However, a negative maternal attitude toward the separation may represent yet another risk factor adding to the demands the child must cope with, thus leading to increased child vulnerability (Kopf, 1970).

The impact of divorce-related stresses and adaptive tasks on the psychological well-being of the custodial parent, and hence indirectly on the child, has received increasing attention (Felner, Farber, & Primavera, 1980; Felner, Terre, & Rowlison, in press). In a recent examination of the stresses faced by divorcing mothers and their children, Colletta (1983) found that maternal role performance is not the same for all divorced mothers but varies with specific stress factors such as income, the number of children in the family, and the sex of the particular target child. The presence of any combination of these factors as stressors has been found to be related to more restrictive and demanding child-rearing practices. Another frequently noted stressor that correlates inversely with the emotional health of the custodial parent is continued interaction between the former spouses, particularly when there is conflict pertaining to visitation or other child-related issues (Bloom, Asher, & White, 1978; Cline & Westman, 1971; Ellison, 1983; Fulton, 1979; Jacobson, 1978; Kurdek & Blisk, in press; Kurdek et al., 1981; Rosen, 1979; Westman et al., 1970). Finally, the overall level of change and demands for readjustment characterizing custodial parents' lives may hamper their efforts to cope effectively with the new challenges engendered by the divorce and may serve to exacerbate the perceived "stressfulness" of these changes (Felner, Farber, & Primavera, 1980, 1983; Hetherington et al., 1978a, 1978b; Longfellow, 1979).

Economic Stress
Several authors (e.g., Bane, 1979; Colletta, 1979, 1983; Felner, Farber, & Primavera, 1980; Felner, Terre, & Rowlison, in press; Herzog & Sudia, 1973) have argued that the increased economic stress and changed financial conditions experienced by divorced mothers constitute a key factor mediating many of the negative consequences of divorce and "father absence." The correlation between divorce and a sharp reduction in standard of living for female- (but not male-) headed single-parent families has been frequently demonstrated (Bahr, 1983; Bradbury, Danzinger, Smolensky, & Smolensky, 1979; Epenshade, 1979; Felner, Farber, Ginter, Boike, & Cowen, 1980; Hetherington, 1978a; LeMasters, 1971; Wolff, 1969). In investigating this phenomenon, Johnson (1983) surveyed 381 divorced custodial mothers and found that two factors help account for this economic downturn. First, many women are vocationally ill prepared to obtain employment that would allow them to maintain their prior living standards. Moreover, because low-level employment demands are often most compatible with parental responsibilities, divorced mothers may settle for lower-paying employment as a trade-off for increased availability to their children.

These sudden downward shifts in economic circumstances and the low levels of financial resources that characterize mother-headed single-parent families have consistently been found to be correlates of adjustment difficulties in children (Boike et al., 1978; Desimone-Luis, O'Mahoney, & Hunt, 1979; Felner, Farber, & Primavera, 1980; Fulton, 1979; Hodges, Wechsler, & Ballantine, 1979; Hetherington et al., 1978a; Nelson, 1981; Pett, 1982). Indeed, some studies have found that when family income is statistically controlled, differences in behavior problems between children from divorced and intact households disappear (Adams & Horovitz, 1980; Colletta, 1979, 1983; Desimone-Luis et al., 1979; MacKinnon, Brody, & Stoneman, 1982; Svanum, Bringle, & McLaughlin, 1982). For example, Desimone-Luis et al. (1979) found that, in their sample of children from divorced homes, subjects who showed behavioral problems were from families experiencing a severe drop in income (averaging 50%) immediately following parental separation. Work by Colletta (1979) also indicates that the negative consequences of divorce may be more strongly related to decreased income than to father absence. Based on similar data, MacKinnon et al. (1982) argue that "children within divorced households often spend several years in milieus that contain the stresses found in low income environments" (p. 1397). However, it should be noted that at least one study (Guidubaldi & Perry, 1984) suggests that single-parent status resulting from divorce predicts poor academic and school-entry competence for children in addition to and independent of socioeconomic status (SES). This work looked not at *changes* in income but rather at existing income levels, so it should not be taken to contradict other work in this area. Rather, the Guidubaldi and Perry data appear to reinforce the importance of changes associated with the divorce as being among the most significant factors influencing adjustment. That is, economic deprivation accompanying divorce may influence the child's adjustment not only directly by decreasing the level of material resources available to the child, but also less directly by leading to additional alterations (such as changes in mother-child interaction patterns, daily routines, and the quality or location of the child's home) or by contributing to the stress experienced by the custodial parent.

Taken together, the studies discussed above provide clear evidence that parental divorce and maternal custody may lead to a broad range of adaptive outcomes for a child, both positive and negative, and that the factors shaping the immediate context in which the child lives may be the most critical determinants of such outcomes. It is also clear that the custodial and financial arrangements surrounding the divorce may mold the child's environment and interactions with the custodial parent in ways that lead to predictable differential outcomes.

Paternal Custody

Although in approximately 10% of the families in the United States no mother is present in the household (Orthner, Brown, & Ferguson, 1976), there is a paucity of relevant research on such families. Perhaps the largest body of literature in this area consists of descriptive studies that rely on the perspectives of predominantly middle-class, white fathers who are primary caretakers. In general such work tends to report that these single fathers are basically satisfied with their lives and consider themselves adequate homemakers and effective, loving parents (Gasser & Taylor, 1976; Chang & Deinard, 1982; Keshet & Rosenthal, 1978; Mendes, 1976; Orthner et al., 1976).

Despite the general level of satisfaction found, these investigations have also highlighted some serious coping difficulties and problems custodial fathers may experience. Included among such stressors are the lack of community assistance programs designed to suit the needs of motherless families (Schlesinger & Todres, 1976; Orthner et al., 1976); role adjustment difficulties (Chang & Deinard, 1982; Gasser & Taylor, 1976; Keshet & Rosenthal, 1978; Schlesinger & Todres, 1967); feelings of task overload (Chang & Deinard, 1982; Gasser & Taylor, 1976) and lack of knowledge about normal childhood development (Mendes, 1976).

Generally speaking, these studies of fathers' experiences falter both in their assumption that single-parent fathers are a homogeneous group and in their failure to control adequately for the nature and amount of mother absence. Moreover, the results presented in most of these works rely exclusively on fathers' self-reports and fail to obtain direct data from spouses or children. Thus concerns must be raised about the lack of independent measures, the presence of rater bias, and the failure to include comparison groups representing other custody arrangements. Hence it is probably most useful to consider the findings from these studies regarding fathers' adjustment to single parenting as having suggestive value at best.

In contrast to the research above, Rosen (1979) focused on the effects of paternal versus maternal custody on the later adjustment of 92 white, middle-class children whose parents had divorced in the 10-year period before the investigation. She interviewed both custodial parents and children. Additionally, children were given projective tests to assess their current adjustment level. A control group of 25 subjects matched for age, sex, occupational/educational level, and religion was also interviewed and assessed clinically. In this study no significant differences were found between the maternal-custody and paternal-custody groups on any measure of child adjustment. Furthermore, when sex of the custodial parent was considered in relation to sex of the child and age at time of the divorce, no significant relationships emerged. Yet across groups, parental strife preceding or surrounding the divorce was found to be the single most significant predictor of children's dysfunction, with greater strife again related to poorer adaptive outcomes.

In what Santrock and Warshak (1979; Warshak & Santrock, 1983) describe as a systematic, well-controlled, multimethod investigation of paternal custody and its effect on children's social-skill development, they compared children between the ages of 6 and 11 living in paternal-custody, in maternal-custody, or in intact families. Their preliminary data suggest that children living with the same-sex parent uniformly show more competent social development than children living with the opposite-sex parent. Warshak and Santrock (1983) point out that, consistent with the results of prior work based on children in maternal custody (e.g., Gregory, 1965; Hetherington et al., 1978a, 1978b; Wallerstein & Kelly, 1980a, 1980b), the boys in their sample showed more demanding and less mature behavior with their mothers in a maternal-custody arrangement than with their fathers in a paternal-custody arrangement. However, it is worth noting that other adjustment measures were not administered. Moreover, neither the quality of parenting and support provided by the "absent father" to custodial mothers nor the level of parental conflict in these families was considered. Further, given the existing biases of the courts against awarding sole paternal custody at present, we have serious reservations about the representativeness of the family circumstances that characterize the participants in this and the other works in this area. For example, highly competent fathers with financial and material resources significantly better than those typical of custodial mothers may be over-represented in the paternal custody groups (Chang & Deinard, 1982).

A final issue that has received some attention in the paternal-custody literature concerns why some fathers seek custody of their children. For example, in a comparison of 20 fathers with and 20 fathers without child custody, Gersick (1976) found that fathers' decisions to seek custody were most strongly affected by relationships in their families of origin (men who were closer to their mothers, and later-borns with both male and female siblings tended to seek custody); feelings about the departing wife (with the more angry men being more likely to seek custody); wife's pretrial consent; and attorney's encouragement/attitude. In another such study, Turner (1984) found that fathers who seek custody fall into two categories: those who had been actively involved with their children during the marriage and sought custody to maintain their relationships with their children versus fathers who had not been actively involved, who waited at least two years to seek custody, and who did so either because of anger toward the former spouse or in the belief that she was a poor mother. Finally, a study by Felner et al. (1985) sounds a disturbing note with regard to paternal motivations for seeking custody. Legal professionals actively involved in family law were surveyed to obtain their perspectives on the custody process. While a majority of judges saw genuine concern and affection as among the primary motivations of fathers seeking custody, only a minority of attorneys expressed the same views. Moreover, revenge was seen as a primary motive of fathers seeking custody by a large minority of legal professionals. Finally, there was a high degree of agreement among attorneys and judges that fathers more often than mothers seek custody as a bargaining tool to obtain better financial arrangements.

Joint Custody

During the past decade there has been an acceleration of critiques and defenses regarding joint custody in social science, legal, and popular circles. Yet despite the increased attention focused on this custody option, estimates of the precise incidence of joint custody in the United States remain controversial (Abarbanel, 1979; Hyde, 1984), in part because of a lack of published prevalence figures (Abarbanel, 1979; Hyde, 1984). Nevertheless, the upsurge in publicity coupled with the growing legislative acceptance of this alternative is generally taken to indicate that the actual number of joint custody cases has increased since 1968 (Abarbanel, 1979; Hyde, 1984).

A variety of benefits and disadvantages have been offered to support the arguments for and against joint custody. Advocates of joint custody (e.g., Benedek & Benedek, 1979; Franklin & Hibbs, 1980; Grote & Weinstein, 1977; Ilfeld, Ilfeld, & Alexander, 1982; Morgenbesser & Nehls, 1981; Roman & Haddad, 1978) contend that, because this option attempts to closely replicate an intact family structure, it provides a remedy for both family and legal problems associated with sole-custody alternatives. Further, in terms of benefits to the divorcing family, enthusiasts argue that joint custody serves the best interests of both child and parents to a greater extent than other arrangements. Specifically, from this viewpoint, joint custody is thought to enhance the well-being of children by fostering their continued relationship with both parents and by eliminating the legal custody battles and adversarial climate that surround sole-custody contests, thereby minimizing their exposure to parental conflict. It is further argued that this arrangement may best meet parents' needs by alleviating the custodial parent's feelings of task overload as well as the noncustodial parent's sense of loss and role ambiguity (Clingempeel & Reppucci, 1982; Luepnitz, 1982; Roman & Haddad, 1978).

Finally, proponents claim that joint custody represents an attractive child-placement policy from the perspective of the court since it obviates the need for judges to decide which parent is likely to be the more competent custodian for the child (Derdeyn & Scott, 1984; Elkin, 1984; Roman & Haddad, 1978).

A number of opposing points have been marshaled by joint custody critics (e.g., Goldstein et al., 1973). First, because joint custody requires that former spouses not only continue to interact but also mutually decide matters relevant to their children's welfare, it is argued that this disposition may result in increased rather than decreased risk for strife. Therefore, they argue, the ability of former spouses to cooperate and interact without conflict is critical if joint custody is to be viable (e.g., Clingempeel & Reppucci, 1982; Felner & Farber, 1980; Felner, Farber, & Primavera, 1980; Felner, Terre, & Rowlison, in press; Reppucci, 1984; Wolchik, Fogas, & Sandler, 1984; Wolchik, Braver, & Sandler, 1985).

Another challenge to the benefits of joint custody centers on the effect on all family members of the more frequent disruptions in continuity of child care and shifting of children that coparenting may involve (Clingempeel & Reppucci, 1982; Felner, Terre, & Rowlison, in press). This concern is especially salient in light of the research collected with maternal-custody families suggesting that instability and change in the environment, particularly if persistent, may compromise the adaptationally focused efforts of children and parents alike. Moreover, children may experience alternation between homes and caregivers as particularly stressful if the parents either do not live in close geographic proximity or offer the children living conditions and life-styles that are markedly discrepant (Clingempeel & Reppucci, 1982; Goldstein et al., 1973). Finally, critics contend that joint custody and its accompanying discontinuity may impede the child's ability to maintain a close emotional bond based on daily interactions with at least one parent (Goldstein et al., 1973).

Children's Overall Adjustment and Joint Custody

Several recent studies have attempted to examine the differences in children's adjustment as a function of being in joint custody or some alternative family situation, although they do not attempt to investigate factors relating to differential outcomes within each family type. In general these works report no clear differences among family types as they relate to children's adjustment. For example, Nunan (1980) studied 40 children ages 7–11 who had experienced a parental divorce at least two years previously. Twenty children in joint custody and 20 in single-parent custody were matched on relevant demographic characteristics, and differences between the groups in anxiety, self-esteem, independence, and superego development were examined. Overall, no between-group differences were found on these measures. Moreover, both groups were found to compare favorably to norms for the general population on these indexes.

In a similar study, 40 children between ages 7–12 in maternal, paternal, and joint custody as well as from intact homes participated in a study by Welsh (1982). Using a multitrait, multimethod, multisource approach, seven areas of adjustment were examined including academic and social competence and self-concept. Data were collected from teachers, parents, children, and school records. Again no overall differences were found among groups. In addition, no differences were found in adjustment as a function of the child's sex. Finally, Trevisano (1982) investigated the behavioral adaptation, emotional functioning, and attitudes toward parental separation of three groups of children ages 7–11. Eight of the children were in joint custody, 14 in sole custody, and 10 in their intact families of origin. As in the Nunan and Welsh studies, no differences were found among the groups.

Interpretation of the findings above must be cautious. Potentially important information on how custody arrangements were determined (e.g., court-imposed versus mutually agreed-upon and desired by both parties) is lacking. However, based on an analysis of the statutes in effect at the time the studies were carried out, it is probably safe to surmise that the majority of joint-custody couples sought that arrangement voluntarily. Further, the samples are relatively homogeneous at least in terms of race and SES (white and middle class or above). Nonetheless, at least one of these studies appears fairly rigorous (Welsh, 1982), and if the biases noted do exist (e.g., parental agreement to seek joint custody) they should favor better outcomes for children in joint-custody households than those in others. Yet the more favorable outcomes that have been predicted by joint-custody proponents do not emerge on measures of children's functioning, and these findings raise questions about the validity of such claims.

These works also reaffirm the contention by Felner, Farber, and Primavera (1980) that simply comparing one type of family constellation or custody arrangement with another not only may be less than fruitful for illuminating the conditions that actually affect children's adjustment, but also may lead to erroneous conclusions. It could easily be concluded from the foregoing studies that specific custody arrangements have no effect on child outcome. Yet it is clear from much of the literature on maternal custody (as well as from that we are about to consider) that this simply is not so. Indeed, studies of factors that moderate differential adjustment underscore the extent to which complex interrelationships are masked by simple studies of "effects." As we shall see, the need to shift from a focus on "main effects" to "interactions" has significance far beyond the selection of research strategies, extending to the types of recommendations that are made concerning child-custody placement policy.

Factors Mediating Children's Adjustment in Joint Custody

A handful of studies have attempted to explore the factors that might influence differential adaptive outcomes for children in joint custody. Broadly conceived, these works employ a descriptive rather than methodologically rigorous approach, and the results thus yielded tend toward the impressionistic. Nonetheless, they do highlight a number of factors that may relate to the conditions under which joint custody may be a viable and appropriate alternative and the circumstances that may enhance children's development or increase the level of risk in joint-custody families.

In one of the earliest such reports, Abarbanel (1979) intensively studied four white, middle-class joint-custody families. Although no child spent more than two consecutive weeks with one parent, there was some variability in the scheduled alternations between households. In addition, parental division of child-care responsibility ranged from approximately equal to a roughly one-third to two-thirds ratio. Abarbanel interviewed children and parents separately, visited each of the eight parental homes, and interviewed the children's teachers. This information was supplemented by questionnaire data and informal observation. Parents reported that they were generally satisfied with their joint-custody arrangements and that, as time passed, they believed the advantages outweighed the disadvantages. The reactions of the children (who ranged in age from $4\frac{1}{2}$ to $12\frac{1}{2}$) were more variable. Although no severe behavioral problems were reported or observed and teachers rated the children as doing well after an initial period of some difficulty, the children's reports were somewhat different. In fact, for one adolescent moving back and forth became so disruptive that one primary home base was established with open access to the other parent. Abarbanel concludes that all the children had mixed experiences living alternately with both their parents and that joint custody was not necessarily good or bad but may work well under certain conditions. Specifically, she argues that in this sample factors that contributed to the success of joint custody included parental commitment to the arrangement, mutual parental support, flexible sharing of responsibility, and agreement on implicit rules of the system.

In an examination of children's psychological experiences living in joint custody, Steinman (1981) interviewed 32 children and their parents (24 families). Steinman acknowledges that her sample was an exceptional one. For example, she points out that the couples in her study "had a strong ideological commitment to joint custody . . . chose and implemented on their own . . . and opted for joint custody at a time when it was less fashionable and the law did not allow for it" (p. 406). Further, the participants actively valued each other as parents and had generally shared parenting during the marriage. All parents were white, with the exception of one black parent, highly educated, and financially comfortable. All but one of the mothers were working, and part of their motivation for joint custody was relief from full-time child-rearing obligations. Steinman reports, not surprisingly, that these parents were generally satisfied with the arrangements because they felt that the circumstances had "evolved from and suited their ideological, psychological and social needs" (p. 408). The reactions of the children, however, were less favorable. Approximately one-third felt burdened by shifting between the two households, some found negotiating the distance between their parents' homes frightening, and 25% experienced confusion, anxiety, and hostility about their schedules and switching homes. The last difficulty was a particular concern for younger children. In addition, teenagers found switching between parental homes antithetical to their needs. Significantly, even in these highly motivated families, Steinman notes that "the idea that loyalty conflicts are nonexistent for joint custody children was not borne out by this study. Rather, in the absence of overt conflict, the sense of responsibility for keeping things even and their parents happy was clearly burdensome to a number of these children" (p. 410). Steinman concludes that joint custody is not a beneficial solution for all families in that it requires considerable effort and commitment from both parents and that, even when the necessary parental cooperation and commitment are present, it may not suit the needs or abilities of the individual child. She cautions, "Certainly, much more research needs to be done before we can consider embracing joint custody as a broadly applicable policy" (p. 414).

Luepnitz's (1982) study of children's adjustment following divorce included 16 custodial mothers, 16 custodial fathers, and 18 parents with joint custody. All children under the age of 16 in each of the subjects' households were included, resulting in an overall sample of 91 children. Average time since the final separation for all custody groups was 3.5 years, with a minimum of 2 years having elapsed since the separation. Children completed a self-concept measure, and parents were asked to rate them on behavior problems, psychosomatic symptoms, self-concept, and changes in academic performance since the separation. Further, parents completed several measures of family functioning, personal adjustment, and sources of stress. Across all child-adjustment measures, no differences by custody type were found. The only variable found to predict poorer adjustment was parental conflict, with those children whose parents had higher levels of conflict attaining poorer self-concept scores.

It should be noted that several serious problems may exist in Luepnitz's (1982) data. First, it seems that all or at least most of the joint-custody couples in this study had sought these arrangements. Second, given that several years had elapsed since the separation, we might conclude that joint-custody couples who participated were those for whom this arrangement was at least minimally "working," because they had not yet relitigated. Despite these limitations and though no differences were found in the children's adjustment, the author concludes that "joint custody at its best is superior to single-parent custody at its best" (p. 150). When viewing this conclusion, it is also important to note that earlier in her volume she states: "From the outset I looked favorably on paternal and joint custody" (p. 17). We raise these points here not so much to criticize this particular work but because these quotations, which do not appear to be supported by the data the author obtained, nicely illustrate a problem that runs through much of the joint custody literature. That is, many of those who have carried out studies in this area have been strong proponents of such agreements, and often the conclusions presented may be somewhat stronger than is justified from the data.

In a more recent exploration of the experiences and adjustment of children in different types of custody situations Wolchik et al. (1985) focused on 133 children in joint or maternal custody. In all cases where joint custody was in effect, it had been voluntarily agreed to and sought by the parents rather than court imposed. Overall, 33% of the children were in joint custody and the remainder were in maternal custody. In three-fourths of the joint-custody families, a primary residential parent could be identified, and in 87% of the cases it was the mother. That is, only 25% of the children in the joint custody group regularly alternated households. In the joint-custody households where physical custody was shared, Wolchik et al. (1985) further note that there were several patterns of alternation. Children were interviewed and completed measures of self-concept, anxiety, depression, and self-worth as well as a divorce-experience scale. Parents completed a behavior checklist for each child and provided demographic information that included a description of their custody situation. Children in joint-custody arrangements reported more positive divorce-related experiences and exhibited better self-esteem than those in sole-custody households. However, only joint-custody boys reported fewer negative experiences than other children in the sample. There was no relation between psychological symptoms (as rated by either parents or children) and custody arrangement. A possible interpretation of these findings, consistent with other studies (e. g., Abarbanel, 1979), is that there may be lower levels of conflict and better-quality interactions between parents who voluntarily select joint custody than among those who do not mutually opt for this disposition. And the generally higher level of parental interaction and cooperation that characterizes individuals who select joint custody results in more positive divorce-related experiences for the child.

Generally similar results were found in another study of children in maternal custody versus joint custody conducted by Cowan (1982). Three areas of functioning (parent-parent relationships, parent-child relationships, and children's adjustment) were examined. The sample comprised 40 families, 20 in each custody group, each with at least one school-age child. While there were no clear differences in children's adjustment between the groups, wherever there was a high level of conflict or a low level of support between the parents, children showed more adjustment problems. Further, joint-custody families who shared residential custody of their children were found to differ from both sole- and joint-custody families who did not share residential custody. Parents with shared residential custody were more supportive of each other, and these fathers were more available to their children. Children in these households were rated as better adjusted by their mothers than those in the other two groups and were less likely to blame the father for the divorce. Finally, children's adjustment and perceptions of their parents as accepting were related to the opportunity to maintain positive relationships with both parents. It should be noted, however, that such opportunities were clearly associated with lower levels of parental strife and higher levels of support, and these factors influenced children's adjustment. What should be evident from this study is that those parents who choose joint custody may be very different from those who do not, both in their ability to relate to one another and in their emotional well-being. Where such circumstances exist, Cowan concludes that joint custody may be a viable option. However, where there is continuing discord or difficulties between parents, it may be less well advised.

Additional Research on Family Patterns in Joint Custody

Parental Involvement
In addition to the studies above, several others, although they fail to provide direct information on the differential adjustment of children in joint- or sole-custody arrangements, do provide data on associated coping factors that may bear on children's adaptive efforts. Joint-custody advocates have argued that among the primary benefits of joint custody are parents' increased involvement with their children, which enhances the well-being of both parents, particularly fathers. One of the earliest studies on this topic was carried out by Grief (1979), who interviewed 40 legally separated or divorced fathers of 63 children. These men were "largely white, Jewish, professional, and middle class." Although "a majority" of these fathers had originally wanted sole custody of their children, over 80% of the children were in the sole custody of their mothers. Hence a minority of this sample (8 fathers) was involved in joint custody. Fathers were asked to rate their degree of perceived parental influence in 10 areas (e.g., routine daily care and safety; intellectual, emotional, and moral development, etc.)

both before the separation and at the time of the study. Not surprisingly, Grief found that "the greater the father's involvement with his
child, the greater his sense of having an ongoing parental role in the
child's life after divorce" (p. 313). In this sample the fathers with joint
custody of their children reported the most satisfaction and did not believe the arrangement posed a difficulty for their children's social lives.
Children were not interviewed in this study. Grief further noted that
those men whose children were in the sole custody of their mothers
"accounted for all the low satisfaction scores" (p. 317). Although the
exact amount of father-child contact is not specified in any of the
cases, Grief concludes that "Fathers with joint custody are more likely
to involve themselves in all aspects of their child's growth and development" (p. 319). A critical point, not discussed by Grief, is the differences in parent-parent relationships and other circumstances that led
to the joint- versus sole-custody arrangements in the first place for
the couples in this sample. This seems particularly important given
the discrepancy noted between the numbers of men who wanted joint
custody and those who actually obtained it.

Parental involvement with children in joint-custody households was
also examined by Ahrons (1983). Forty-one divorced parents ("well
educated with considerably higher than average incomes") with joint
custody were interviewed for this study. Of the 41 respondents, 19%
were awarded alternating physical custody, 5% were awarded divided
custody (i.e., each parent had physical custody of at least one child),
and 76% (17 mothers and 14 fathers) were awarded sole physical custody. In all cases, the parents chose joint custody in advance of the
legal divorce and the court was used merely to bind the agreement.
Ahrons found that the frequency of contact and amount of time spent
with the child by the parent who did not have physical custody, as well
as the nature of that involvement, were quite variable. Frequency of
contact ranged from daily to a few hours monthly. Of those parents
without physical custody, 22% reported they were less involved with
their children at the time of sampling than they had been at the time of
separation, and 32% said they were less involved at present than during the marriage. Given the above, it is clear that at least in some
cases, as Ahrons points out, "joint did not necessarily mean equal"
(p. 201) and that joint custody did not necessarily lead to continued
high levels of involvement by the father.

Recent data from Bowman (1983) also bears on parental involvement under differing custodial conditions. Fifty-four maternal-custody couples and 28 joint-custody couples were interviewed approximately one year after divorce. Indicators of fathers' involvement in parenting showed that joint-custody fathers were significantly more involved with their children than were noncustodial fathers. It should be noted, however, that on two measures designed to examine the quality of the relationships between the divorced parents, joint-custody parents showed more positive relationships than did maternal-custody parents. Hence, as in sole-custody families, only better relationships between parents were related to greater involvement by fathers. On the issue of relitigation, joint-custody men indicated significantly less court use than did noncustodial men. There were no significant differences in women's responses about whether they had returned to court or planned to do so. This may indicate that whereas joint custody may be more satisfying for fathers, even when jointly agreed to, it may neither be preferred by mothers nor lead to reduced conflict.

Parents' Satisfaction

Several studies have focused on the factors that influence parents' satisfaction with coparenting arrangements, and overall, these studies find that those who voluntarily decide to share custody report general satisfaction but that, even for these couples, serious problems exist. However, where joint custody is entered into under duress, satisfaction levels may be even lower than for sole-custody families. For example, Rothberg (1983) explored parents' satisfaction and dissatisfaction among 30 white middle-class, joint-custody parents who opted for this arrangement extralegally. Although all parents shared parenting responsibilities, they were involved in a variety of time-sharing schedules (the most common being a split week with alternating weekends), and 37% of these parents felt that mothers were primarily responsible for caring for sick children and doing specific chores. Overall, 67% of this sample reported generally good feelings about the joint custody setup, 13% felt negative, and 20% were ambivalent. Interestingly, 20% of parents said they would not recommend joint custody to others, although they had elected it voluntarily. The benefits cited by satisfied mothers included relief from full-time child-care responsibilities and additional time to devote to careers and new relationships. By contrast, satisfied fathers were more likely to point to the continuity and structure added to their lives by shared parenting. Only 7% of the total sample expressed no problems with joint custody. Among the difficulties most frequently reported were problems with transitions, logistics, and the stress of children shifting between and adjusting to two environments (50% of parents); dealing with former spouses (23%); financial strain of maintaining two households (7%); and the necessity of parents' maintaining homes close to each other (10%). Two areas of particular parental conflict highlighted in this study included financial arrangements (men believed they paid too much, while women thought men's payments were insufficient), and jealousy and competition over the children (e.g., attempts to outbuy each other).

Factors bearing on parents' satisfaction with joint-custody agreements were also examined by Irving, Benjamin, and Trocme (1984). They present the preliminary results obtained from questionnaire responses of 201 parents involved voluntarily (i.e., not court imposed, and with a minority of respondents feeling pressured into joint custody) in shared parenting arrangements. Approximately two-thirds of respondents were in their 30s, earning between $21,000 and $60,000 per year, and had at least some university or postgraduate education. No information on race was provided. Irving and his colleagues report that in most cases (69%) the arrangement was in writing and "typically specified equal sharing of child care and control, with no primary residence" (p. 131). Approximately 50% shared residential custody equally, most frequently on a weekly rotation basis. The next largest group (30%) used a 75/25 split (typically spending the school week with one parent and weekends with the other). The remaining group (20%) "ran the gamut from splitting the week equally, to the school year with one parent and the summer vacation with the other" (p. 131). In this study parents living closer to each other had more equal timesharing arrangements. Parents' satisfaction with shared custody was related (a) negatively to court involvement (i.e., respondents who became involved in shared parenting as a result of court services were less satisfied than those whose arrangements arose informally); (b) inversely with guilt over the marital breakup; (c) inversely with level of preseparation conflict; and (d) positively with length of shared parenting arrangement. No relation was found between parents' satisfaction and the remarriage of one partner, physical arrangements of joint parenting schedules, or social class. These authors also point out the other limitations of this study (absence of data on children, lack of a comparative sole-custody sample, and reliance on descriptive statistics), beyond the fact that most of their sample sought joint custody.

Parental Conflict and Relitigation

The extent to which different custodial arrangements result in continued conflict and eventual relitigation has been central to the debate about joint custody. Yet relatively few empirical data are currently available on this issue. However, taken together with the research described above, the handful of existing studies fail to provide clear support for the contention that joint custody reduces parental strife or relitigation.

Ilfeld et al. (1982) examined data on 414 consecutive custody cases in a Los Angeles court over a two-year period, comparing relitigation rates of couples with exclusive and joint custody. They found that 91% of exclusive custody awards and 86% of joint custody awards were based on agreement between the parents. Ilfeld and his colleagues make the assumption that relitigation of custody "means that parents are in conflict with one another and that parental conflict strong enough to bring them to the courts has adverse effects on the children" (p. 63). Their finding that the proportion of relitigation for joint-custody families was one-half that for sole-custody families is interpreted as suggesting that "the custody arrangement most beneficial in terms of lack of subsequent parental conflict is joint custody" (p. 65). As these researchers note, they did not attempt to obtain information regarding the specifics of the custody arrangements (e.g., time sharing, decisionmaking styles, etc.). They also did not interview the families or investigate official court files to determine the basis of the court's decision. Further, the mean length of time between the divorce and data collection was not reported. Finally, and perhaps most telling, the frequency of relitigation among joint-custody families in which the arrangement was court imposed rather than mutually agreed upon was as high as for the sole-custody group. Thus the differences between these groups in overall levels of relitigation may have stemmed from the higher levels of parental agreement that characterized the joint-custody couples who sought the arrangement.

In a more recent study on relitigation, the public records of 500 divorces of parents with minor children were abstracted from the files of a county probate and family court in Massachusetts by Phear, Beck, Hauser, Clark, and Whitney (1984). Of 109 joint custody cases in this group only 17 represented original petitions for joint legal custody; the other 92 were originally petitions for sole custody. While joint legal custody was granted in over 30% of all cases, joint physical custody occurred in only 2% of the total cases. In contrast to the overall findings reported by Ilfeld et al. (1982), but consistent with the court-imposed subsample findings of that study, there was no significant difference in overall frequency of relitigation between joint- and sole-custody parents in the first 300 cases. Further, in an analysis of the last 200 cases, a greater percentage of the joint cases returned to court (20% of joint- versus 12% of sole-custody parents) and asked for "numerically and proportionally more changes in custody, visitation, and financial support" (p. 155). Moreover, these differences were particularly marked regarding relitigation about child-related matters, with joint-custody families returning to court significantly more often on these issues than sole-custody families.

The results of a study by Irving et al. (1984) are worthy of note here, since they raise questions about the use of relitigation as a direct indicator of higher levels of parental conflict, as is argued for by Ilfeld et al. (1982). Irving and his colleagues found that, although relatively few of those joint-custody parents in their sample had taken any legal action regarding their joint-custody agreement, there was no relation between dissatisfaction with the contract and the decision to relitigate. Other barriers or constraints may act to make relitigation rates a conservative estimate of conflict for joint-custody families. Indeed, many states require that certain conditions be met (e. g., a substantial change in circumstances) before relitigation may be brought, and litigation is always costly and contains some risks.

Together these studies provide little support for the contention that joint custody reduces the rate of relitigation, particularly when this custody disposition is not actively sought by both parties. Indeed, in the latter instance the opposite may be true. These initial studies involving court-imposed joint-custody conditions are at considerable disagreement with the findings from earlier studies where parents sought such arrangements, and they should give pause to joint custody proponents who base their views on the earlier works.

Conclusions

Over the past two decades, a number of authors (e.g., Clingempeel & Reppucci, 1982; Ellsworth & Levy, 1969; Felner & Farber, 1980; Felner, Farber, & Primavera, 1980; Reppucci, 1984; Weiss, 1979) have bemoaned the lack of a scientific basis for guiding public policy and decision making regarding child custody following divorce. Based on the preceding discussion of the relevant literature on children's adaptation under sole- or joint-custody conditions, it appears that we have made at least some progress toward addressing this deficit and toward making more informed decisions than may result from mere rhetoric. Indeed, there are several clear recommendations and statements we now appear able to make, as well as a number of points of caution that emerge from the available literature.

Perhaps the clearest statement that can be made is that no particular custody arrangement is "best." Arguments in favor of a presumption of one form over another are ill suited to the realities of family life and child development. The contention of Goldstein et al. (1973) that the child's relationship with the custodial or "psychological parent" may be damaged by the continued coequal involvement of the noncustodial parent does not appear to be necessarily true in all cases. However, neither is the contention by joint custody advocates that joint custody is the best alternative for all children. Let us now return to a brief consideration of the arguments for and against these positions in light of the empirical evidence available.

The central argument in favor of joint custody has been that children will show the most favorable adjustment following divorce with such an arrangement. However, not one of the studies considered here supports such a conclusion. In support of joint custody, we did see that children in joint-custody households may do as well as those in sole-custody families. Yet the adaptation of joint-custody children was not found to be superior to that of children in other groups. Indeed, these findings may be less positive for a joint custody position than they initially appear, given that most coparenting couples represented in the studies reviewed here voluntarily sought and agreed to this option or were highly motivated to ensure its success. That is, joint custody, under the most favorable of conditions, does not emerge as clearly superior to sole custody.

One factor that does appear critical, both in itself and as it interacts with other variables, is parental conflict. In both sole- and joint-custody families, such discord is consistently associated with more negative adaptive outcomes for the children as well as with higher levels of stress and lower levels of well-being for the parents, particularly mothers. Thus, by reducing the quality of the child's environment in a number of ways, conflict has the potential to hinder the child's efforts to cope with this life transition.

In considering factors that may contribute to the continuation of conflict following divorce, the existing literature also fails to support the contention that joint custody will reduce postdivorce conflict. Indeed, it may do just the opposite. Those studies that have in the past been cited as supporting the idea that joint custody may minimize conflict are, upon careful examination, seen to contain a critical methodological flaw that may account for this erroneous conclusion. Namely, until recently, the parents who have obtained joint custody were for the most part already atypical in their low degree of conflict and high level of cooperation compared with other divorced couples. Further, they generally sought or voluntarily entered into joint-custody arrangements. Thus the more accurate conclusion appears to be that low levels of parental discord and high levels of cooperation resulted in these joint-custody arrangements rather than vice versa.

Several related findings further support the argument that, where conflict exists, joint custody may exacerbate rather than reduce discord, stress, and disorganization. First, a number of studies discussed in this chapter found that high levels of parental contact in the presence of conflict only exacerbates that conflict. Next, and again contradicting the assertions of joint custody advocates, we do not find a reduction in litigation associated with joint custody. Where litigation or its threat has resulted in the joint-custody award, we have evidence that parents are less happy with these arrangements and are more likely to return to court (e.g., Ilfeld et al., 1982; Irving et al., 1984). The notion that parents should be able to put aside their differences to the extent necessary for both to remain fully involved in child rearing is a laudable ideal. Unfortunately it may be unrealistic for many families. In keeping with the findings of Wallerstein and Kelly and others, Johnston, Campbell, and Tall (1985, p. 112) note, "A significant proportion of divorced couples, however, do not settle their disputes within two years following the divorce; they battle continuously or sporadically for many years after the final divorce decree."

What then of the arguments for a legal presumption in favor of joint custody? We can only conclude that at this point such a move is not justified by the available data on children's adaptation to different forms of custody. Indeed, what evidence there is argues against such a presumption. That is not to say that joint custody should not be made an available option; but the manner in which the courts make it available must be careful and cautious. Indeed, recent empirical work (Felner et al., 1985) indicates that legal professionals may be aware of the need for caution in imposing a joint custody presumption. Surveyed judges and attorneys reported that they felt joint custody was neither the most desirable nor the most appropriate option in most cases. Further, consistent with the social science findings discussed above, these legal professionals questioned the ability and motivation of divorcing couples to cooperate to the extent necessary for joint custody to be viable. They felt that parental cooperation, mutual motivation for joint custody, more general positive relationships between the parents, and emotional stability of both parents all were needed for joint custody to be in the child's best interests.

A legal shift to joint custody as either an option or a presumption may also have unintended negative consequences for the process of negotiation between the parents. Reppucci (1984) notes that such a shift to joint custody may substantially increase the relative bargaining power of the father over the mother. While in some instances this redistribution of power may have a positive effect, in other instances it may have quite the opposite result. For example, mothers may agree to custody or visitation arrangements that keep the child locked in conflict out of fear that they may lose the child completely or obtain an even less desirable custody arrangement if they go to court. As Reppucci notes, "This may be unfortunate since the better parent may be the one who is more unwilling to risk a substantial reduction in contact with the child" (p. 73).

The presence of a joint custody option or presumption may also have profound implications for those parts of divorce settlements that have an indirect effect upon the child's adjustment but are not, strictly speaking, matters of custody. For example, considering that this equalization of power increases the risks associated with litigation, the threat of court action could be used as a bargaining weapon in persuading mothers to settle for lower levels of financial support or other material resources (e.g., a house). That this may occur much more frequently than we would like to believe is borne out by the findings of Felner et al. (1985), discussed above, in which legal professionals reported that fathers sought custody far more often as a means to obtain a better financial settlement rather than owing to an actual wish for custody. While this is certainly not true of all men seeking custody, it should remind us that the fathers in the joint- or paternal-custody families discussed in this chapter may not be representative of the more general population. Indeed, at least their demographic characteristics argue that they are rather atypical.

The findings concerning conflict and the issues raised by the equalization of legal power may also have implications for advocates of mediation. Although the search for a nonadversarial approach to the resolution of custody disputes, as well as other divorce-related issues, is one that the senior author of this chapter has long supported (Felner & Farber, 1980), we should not develop such solutions naively. Divorce mediation efforts, which are mandatory in some states, currently are based on rational, economic models of decisionmaking (Johnston et al., 1985). Yet the fact that such models are not always appropriate for understanding human behavior has been well demonstrated outside the custody literature (e.g., Kahneman & Tversky, 1982a, 1982b, 1982c). That we should expect rational models to apply in emotionally laden situations such as divorce is even more disconcerting. Couples come to mediation with long individual histories and long-standing patterns of interaction. To require by law that individuals engage in negotiations in a setting where power is equalized and where the involvement of legal counsel is not permitted without taking the couple's history into account may have devastating consequences. To illustrate, consider the difficulties inherent in mediation efforts between partners in a physically or psychologically abusive relationship. The battered spouse (often the wife) has learned to fear the abusive spouse. It is unlikely that the fearful partner in such a relationship will emerge from mediation conducted in the presence of an impartial stranger with a settlement that is actually in his or her best interests. Rather, owing to a combination of person and situation factors (e.g., a long history of being dominated, a perception of powerlessness, a lack of knowledge about his or her legal rights, the high level of affect aroused in the situation), the abused or frightened spouse may be apt to yield to the conditions proposed by the abusive spouse in order to get out of the highly noxious situation more quickly or out of fear of retaliation.

There are similar problems with statutes that favor the parent who is more open to allowing the child continued contact with the other parent. Such a policy may force a "good" parent to allow a visitation arrangement with a parent who may have been psychologically or physically abusive to the child, and who thus is detrimental to the child's well-being, for fear of losing custody if such contact is opposed (see chap. 2 for further discussion of the promise and problems of divorce mediation).

To summarize, no single custody arrangement seems to be clearly superior in promoting the child's well-being. Rather, the conditions that surround each custody agreement are most critical to the child's adaptation. Factors that have been shown to relate to consistently better adjustment by children following divorce include lower levels of parental conflict (or the opportunity for children to remove themselves from existing conflict), high environmental stability and low environmental flux following the divorce, and the psychological well-being of the child's primary caretaker(s). Arguments in favor of a presumption for joint custody do not seem to be supported by current data and certainly should be carefully reevaluated.

References

Abarbanel, A. (1979). Shared parenting after separation and divorce: A study of joint custody. *American Journal of Orthopsychiatry, 49*(2), 320–329.

Adams, D., & Horovitz, J. (1980). Psychopathology and fatherlessness in poor boys. *Child Psychiatry and Human Development, 10,* 135–143.

Ahrons, C. (1980). Joint custody arrangements in the postdivorce family. *Journal of Divorce, 3*(3), 189–205.

Ahrons, C. (1981). The continuing coparental relationship between divorced spouses. *American Journal of Orthopsychiatry, 51*(3), 415–428.

Ahrons, C. (1983). Predictors of paternal involvement postdivorce: Mothers' and fathers' perceptions. *Journal of Divorce, 6*(3), 55–69.

Bahr, S. (1983). Marital dissolution laws: Impact of recent changes for women. *Journal of Family Issues, 4*(3), 455–466.

Bane, M. (1979). Marital disruption and the lives of children. In G. Levinger & O. Moles (Eds.), *Divorce and separation: Context, causes and consequences* (pp. 276–286). New York: Basic Books.

Benedek, E., & Benedek, J. (1979). Joint custody: Solution or illusion? *American Journal of Psychiatry, 136*(12), 1540–1544.

Berg, B., & Kelly, R. (1979). Measured self-esteem of children from broken, rejected, and accepted families. *Journal of Divorce, 2,* 363–370.

Biller, H. B. (1974). *Paternal deprivation: Family, school, sexuality and society.* Lexington, MA: Heath.

Bloom, B., Asher, S., & White, S. (1978). Marital disruption as a stressor: A review and analysis. *Psychological Bulletin, 85,* 867–894.

Boike, M., Ginter, E., Cowen, E., Felner, R., & Francis, R. (1978). The relationship between family background problems and the competencies of young normal children. *Psychology in the Schools, 15,* 283–290.

Bowman, M. (1983). Parenting after divorce: A comparative study of mother custody and joint custody families. *Dissertation Abstracts International, 44,* 578A.

Bradbury, K., Danziger, S., Smolensky, E., & Smolensky, P. (1979). Public assistance, female headship, and economic well-being. *Journal of Marriage and the Family, 41,* 519–535.

Brown, S. (1984). Changes in laws governing divorce. *Journal of Family Issues, 5*(2), 200–223.

Chang, P., & Deinard, A. (1982). Single-father caretakers: Demographic characteristics and adjustment processes. *American Journal of Orthopsychiatry, 52*(2), 236–243.

Cline, D., & Westman, J. (1971). The impact of divorce on the family. *Child Psychiatry and Human Development, 2,* 78–83.

Clingempeel, W., & Reppucci, N. (1982). Joint custody after divorce: Major issues and goals for research. *Psychological Bulletin, 91*(1), 102–127.

Colletta, N. D. (1979). The impact of divorce: Father absence or poverty? *Journal of Divorce, 3*(1), 27–35.

Colletta, N. D. (1983). Stressful lives: The situation of divorced mothers and their children. *Journal of Divorce, 6*(3), 19–31.

Cowan, D. (1982). Mother custody versus joint custody: Children's parental relationships and adjustment. *Dissertation Abstracts International, 43,* 726A.

Derdeyn, A. (1976). Child custody contests in historical perspective. *American Journal of Psychiatry, 133,* 1369–1376.

Derdeyn, A., & Scott, E. (1984). Joint custody: A critical analysis and appraisal. *American Journal of Orthopsychiatry, 54*(2), 199–209.

Desimone-Luis, J., O'Mahoney, K., & Hunt, D. (1979). Children of separation and divorce: Factors influencing adjustment. *Journal of Divorce, 3*(1), 37–42.

Despert, J. (1953). *Children of divorce.* New York: Doubleday.

Dohrenwend, B. P. (1979). Stressful life events and psychopathology: Some issues of theory and method. In J. E. Barrett (Ed.), *Stress and mental disorder* (pp. 1–15). New York: Raven Press.

Dohrenwend, B. S., & Dohrenwend, B. P. (1984). Life stress and illness: Formulations of the issues. In B. S. Dohrenwend & B. P. Dohrenwend (Eds.), *Stressful life events and their contexts* (pp. 1–27). New Brunswick, NJ: Rutgers University Press.

Dominic, K., & Schlesinger, B. (1980). Weekend fathers: Family shadows. *Journal of Divorce, 3*(3), 241–247.

Elkin, M. (1984). Joint custody: In the best interest of the family. In J. Folberg (Ed.), *Joint custody and shared parenting* (pp. 11–15). Washington, DC: Bureau of National Affairs.

Ellison, E. (1983). Issues concerning parental harmony and children's psychosocial adjustment. *American Journal of Orthopsychiatry, 53*(1), 73–80.

Ellsworth, P., & Levy, R. (1969). Legislative reform of child custody adjudication. *Law and Society Review, 4,* 167–215.

Emery, R. (1982). Interparental conflict and the children of discord and divorce. *Psychological Bulletin, 92*(2), 310–330.

Emery, R., & O'Leary, K. D. (1982). Children's perceptions of marital discord and behavior problems of boys and girls. *Journal of Abnormal Child Psychology, 10*(1), 11–24.

Epenshade, T. (1979). The economic consequences of divorce. *Journal of Marriage and the Family, 41,* 615–625.

Farber, S., Felner, R., & Primavera, J. (1985). Parental separation/divorce and adolescents: An examination of factors mediating adaptation. *American Journal of Community Psychology, 13*(2), 171–185.

Farber, S., Primavera, J., & Felner, R. (1984). Older adolescents and parental divorce: Adjustment problems and mediators of coping. *Journal of Divorce, 7*(2), 59–75.

Felner, R. D. (1984). Vulnerability in childhood: A preventive framework for understanding children's efforts to cope with life stress and transitions. In M. C. Roberts and L. H. Peterson (Eds.), *Prevention of problems in childhood: Psychological research and applications.* New York: Wiley-Interscience.

Felner, R. D., & Farber, S. (1980). Social policy for child custody: A multidisciplinary framework. *American Journal of Orthopsychiatry, 50*(2), 341–347.

Felner, R. D., Farber, S., Ginter, M., Boike, M., & Cowen, E. (1980). Family stress and organization following parental divorce or death. *Journal of Divorce, 4,* 67–76.

Felner, R. D., Farber, S., & Primavera, J. (1980). Transitions and stressful life events: A model for primary prevention. In R. H. Price, R. F. Ketterer, B. C. Bader, & J. Monahan (Eds.), *Prevention in mental health: Research, policy, and practice* (pp. 81–108). Beverly Hills, CA: Sage.

Felner, R. D., Farber, S., & Primavera, J. (1983). Transitions and stressful life events: A model for primary prevention. In R. D. Felner, L. A. Jason, J. N. Moritsugu, & S. S. Farber (Eds.), *Preventive psychology: Theory, research, and practice* (pp. 199–215). New York: Pergamon Press.

Felner, R. D., Ginter, M., Boike, M., & Cowen, E. (1981). Parental death or divorce and the school adjustment of young children. *American Journal of Community Psychology, 9,* 181–191.

Felner, R. D., Rowlison, R., & Terre, L. (in press). Unraveling the Gordian knot in life change events: A critical examination of crisis, stress, and transitional frameworks for prevention. In S. M. Auerbach & A. L. Stolberg (Eds.), *Children's life crisis events: Preventive intervention strategies.* New York: Hemisphere/McGraw-Hill.

Felner, R. D., Stolberg, A., & Cowen, E. (1975). Crisis events and school mental health referral patterns of young children. *Journal of Consulting and Clinical Psychology, 43*(3), 305–310.

Felner, R. D., Terre, L., Farber, S., Primavera, J., & Bishop, T. (1985). Child custody: Practices and perspectives of legal professionals. *Journal of Clinical Child Psychology, 14*(1), 27–34.

Felner, R. D., Rowlison, R., & Terre, L. (1986). A life transition framework for understanding marital dissolution and family reorganization. In S. A. Wolchik & P. Karoly (Eds.), *Children of divorce: Perspectives on adjustment* (pp. 39–63). New York: Guilford Press.

Folberg, J. (1984a). Custody overview. In J. Folberg (Ed.), *Joint Custody and shared parenting* (pp. 3–10). Washington, DC: Bureau of National Affairs.

Folberg, J. (1984b). Issues and trends in the law of joint custody. In J. Folberg (Ed.), *Joint custody and shared parenting* (pp. 159–167). Washington, DC: Bureau of National Affairs.

Franklin, R., & Hibbs, B. (1980). Child custody in transition. *Journal of Marital and Family Therapy, 42,* 285–291.

Freed, D., & Foster, H. (1984). Family law in the fifty states: An overview. *Family Law Quarterly, 17*(4), 365–447.

Fulton, J. (1979). Parental reports of children's post-divorce adjustment. *Journal of Social Issues, 35,* 126–139.

Gardner, R. (1977). Children of divorce: Some legal and psychological considerations. *Journal of Clinical Child Psychology, 6,* 3–6.

Gasser, R., & Taylor, C. (1976). Role adjustment of single parent fathers with dependent children. *Family Coordinator,* October, 397–401.

Gersick, K. (1976). Fathers by choice: Divorced men who receive custody of their children. In G. Levinger & O. Moles (Eds.), *Divorce and separation* (pp. 307–323). New York: Basic Books.

Glueck, S., & Glueck, E. (1950). *Unraveling juvenile delinquency.* Cambridge: Harvard University Press.

Goldstein, J., Freud, A., & Solnit, A. (1973). *Beyond the best interests of the child.* New York: Free Press.

Gregory, I. (1965). Anterospective data following childhood loss of a parent. I. Delinquency and high school dropout. *Archives of General Psychiatry, 13,* 99–109.

Grief, J. B. (1979). Fathers, children, and joint custody. *American Journal of Orthopsychiatry, 49*(2), 311–319.

Grote, D., & Weinstein, J. (1977). Joint custody: A viable and ideal alternative. *Journal of Divorce, 1*(1), 43–53.

Guidubaldi, J., & Perry, J. (1984). Divorce, socioeconomic status, and children's cognitive-social competence at school entry. *American Journal of Orthopsychiatry, 54*(3), 459–468.

Hainline, L., & Feig, E. (1978). The correlates of childhood father absence in college-aged women. *Child Development, 49,* 37–42.

Herzog, E., & Sudia, C. (1973). Children in fatherless families. In B. M. Caldwell & H. N. Ricciuti (Eds.), *Child development and social policy.* Chicago: University of Chicago Press.

Hess, R., & Camara, K. (1979). Post-divorce relationships as mediating factors in the consequences of divorce for children. *Journal of Social Issues, 35,* 79–96.

Hetherington, M. (1972). Effects of father absence on personality development in adolescent daughters. *Developmental Psychology, 7,* 313–326.

Hetherington, M., Cox, M., & Cox, R. (1978a). The aftermath of divorce. In J. H. Stevens, Jr., & M. Mathews (Eds.), *Mother-child, father-child relationships* (pp. 149–176). Washington, DC: National Association for the Education of Young Children.

Hetherington, M., Cox, M., & Cox, R. (1978b). The development of children in mother-headed families. In H. Hoffman & O. Reiss (Eds.), *The American family: Dying or developing?* New York: Plenum Press.

Hetherington, M., Cox, M., & Cox, R. (1979). Play and social interaction in children following divorce. *Journal of Social Issues, 35,* 26–49.

Hodges, W., & Bloom, B. (1984). Parents' report of children's adjustment to marital separation: A longitudinal study. *Journal of Divorce, 8*(1), 33–50.

Hodges, W., Buchsbaum, H., & Tierney, C. (1984). Parent-child relationships and adjustment in preschool children in divorced and intact families. *Journal of Divorce, 7*(2), 43–58.

Hodges, W., Wechsler, R., & Ballantine, C. (1979). Divorce and the preschool child: Cumulative stress. *Journal of Divorce, 3,* 55–67.

Hyde, L. (1984). Child custody in divorce. *Juvenile and Family Court Journal, 35*(1).

Ilfeld, F., Ilfeld, H., & Alexander, J. (1982). Does joint custody work? A first look at outcome data of relitigation. *American Journal of Psychiatry, 139*(1), 62–66.

Irving, H., Benjamin, M., & Trocme, N. (1984). Shared parenting: An empirical analysis utilizing a large Canadian data base. In J. Folberg (Ed.), *Joint custody and shared parenting* (pp. 128–135). Washington, DC: Bureau of National Affairs.

Jacobs, J. (1982). The effect of divorce on fathers: An overview of the literature. *American Journal of Psychiatry, 139*(10), 1235–1241.

Jacobson, D. S. (1978). The impact of marital separation/divorce on children. II. Interparental hostility and child adjustment. *Journal of Divorce, 2,* 8–19.

Johnson, P. (1983). Divorced mothers' management of responsibilities. *Journal of Family Issues, 4*(1), 83–103.

Johnston, J., Campbell, L., & Tall, M. (1985). Impasses to the resolution of custody and visitation disputes. *American Journal of Orthopsychiatry, 55*(1), 112–129.

Kahneman, D., & Tversky, A. (1982a). The psychology of preferences. *Scientific American, 246*(1), 160–173.

Kahneman, D., & Tversky, A. (1982b). Variants of uncertainty. *Cognition, 11,* 143–157.

Kahneman, D., & Tversky, A. (1982c). On the study of statistical intuitions. *Cognition, 11,* 123–141.

Kalter, N., & Rembar, J. (1981). The significance of a child's age at the time of parental divorce. *American Journal of Orthopsychiatry, 51*(1), 85–100.

Kelly, J., & Wallerstein, J. (1976). The effects of parental divorce: Experiences of the child in early latency. *American Journal of Orthopsychiatry, 46,* 20–32.

Keshet, H., & Rosenthal, K. (1978). Single parent fathers: A new study. *Children Today,* May–June, 13–17.

Kopf, K. (1970). Family variables and school adjustment of eighth grade father-absent boys. *Family Coordinator, 19*(2), 145–150.

Kurdek, L., & Blisk, D. (in press). Dimensions and correlates of mothers' divorce experiences. *Journal of Divorce.*

Kurdek, L., Blisk, D., & Siesky, A. (1981). Correlates of children's long-term adjustment to their parents' divorce. *Developmental Psychology, 17*(5), 565–579.

150 The State of Knowledge

Kurdek, L, & Siesky, A. (1980a). Sex role self-concepts of single divorced parents and their children. *Journal of Divorce, 3*(1), 249–261.

Kurdek, L., & Siesky, A. (1980b). Children's perceptions of their parents' divorce. *Journal of Divorce, 3*(4), 339–378.

Landis, J. (1960). The trauma of children when parents divorce. *Marriage and Family Living, 22,* 7–13.

LeMasters, E. E. (1971). Parents without partners. In A. S. Skolnick & J. H. Skolnick (Eds.), *Family in transition* (pp. 403–410). Boston, MA: Little, Brown.

Levy, B., & Chambers, C. (1981). The folly of joint custody. *Family Advocate, 3*(4), 6–10.

Longfellow, C. (1979). Divorce in context: Its impact on children. In G. Levinger and O. C. Moles (Eds.), *Divorce and separation: Context, causes and consequences* (pp. 287–306). New York: Basic Books.

Luepnitz, D. (1979). Which aspects of divorce affect children? *Family Coordinator,* January, 79–85.

Luepnitz, D. (1982). *Child custody.* Lexington, MA: D. C. Heath.

MacKinnon, C., Brody, G., & Stoneman, Z. (1982). The effects of divorce and maternal employment on the home environments of preschool children. *Child Development, 53,* 1392–1399.

McCord, J., McCord, W., & Thurber, E. (1962). Some effects of paternal absence on small children. *Journal of Abnormal and Social Psychology, 64,* 361–369.

McDermott, J. F. (1968). Parental divorce in early childhood. *American Journal of Psychiatry, 124,* 118–126.

McDermott, J. F. (1970). Divorce and its psychiatric sequelae in children. *Archives of General Psychiatry, 23,* 421–427.

Mendes, H. (1976). Single fathers. *Family Coordinator,* October, 439–444.

Morgenbesser, M., & Nehls, N. (1981). *Joint custody: An alternative for divorcing families.* Chicago: Nelson-Hall.

Nelson, G. (1981). Moderators of women's and children's adjustment following parental divorce. *Journal of Divorce, 4*(3), 71–83.

Neubauer, P. (1960). The one-parent child and his oedipal development. *Psychoanalytic Study of the Child, 15,* 286–309.

Nunan, S. (1980). Joint custody versus single custody effects on child development. *Dissertation Abstracts International, 41,* 4680B–4681B.

Nye, F. I. (1957). Child adjustment in broken and in unhappy, unbroken homes. *Marriage and Family Living, 19,* 356–361.

Orthner, D., Brown, T., & Ferguson, D. (1976). Single-parent fatherhood: An emerging family life style. *Family Coordinator,* October, 429–437.

Parish, T., & Taylor, J. (1979). The impact of divorce and subsequent father absence on children's and adolescents' self-concepts. *Journal of Youth and Adolescence, 8*(4), 427–432.

Patterson, G. (April 1976). *Mothers: The unacknowledged victims.* Paper presented at the Society for Research in Child Development meeting, Oakland, CA.

Pett, M. (1982). Correlates of children's social adjustment following divorce. *Journal of Divorce, 5*(4), 25–39.

Phear, W., Beck, J., Hauser, B., Clark, S., & Whitney, R. (1984). An empirical study of custody agreements: Joint versus sole legal custody. In J. Folberg (Ed.), *Joint custody and shared parenting* (pp. 142–156). Washington, DC: Bureau of National Affairs.

Porter, B., & O'Leary, D. (1980). Marital discord and childhood behavior problems. *Journal of Abnormal Child Psychology, 8*(3), 287–295.

Reppucci, N. D. (1984). The wisdom of Solomon: Issues in child custody determination. In N. D. Reppucci, L. A. Weithorn, E. P. Mulvey, & J. Monahan (Eds.), *Children, mental health, and the law* (pp. 59–78). Beverly Hills, CA: Sage.

Roman, M., & Haddad, W. (1978). *The disposable parent.* New York: Holt, Rinehart and Winston.

Rosen, R. (1979). Some crucial issues concerning children of divorce. *Journal of Divorce, 3*(1), 19–25.

Rothberg, B. (1983). Joint custody: Parental problems and satisfactions. *Family Process, 22,* 43–52.

Rutter, M. (1979). Protective factors in children's responses to stress and disadvantage. In M. W. Kent & J. E. Rolf (Eds.), *Primary prevention of psychopathology: Social competence in children* (Vol. 3). Hanover: University Press of New England.

Rutter, M. (1981). Stress, coping and development: Some issues and some questions. *Journal of Child Psychology and Psychiatry, 22,* 323–356.

Salk, L. (1977). On the custody rights of fathers in divorce. *Journal of Clinical Psychology, 6*(2), 49–50.

Santrock, J., & Warshak, R. (1979). Father custody and social development in boys and girls. *Journal of Social Issues, 35,* 112–125.

Schlesinger, B., & Todres, R. (1976). Motherless families: An increasing societal pattern. *Child Welfare, 55*(8), 553–558.

Shinn, M. (1978). Father absence and children's cognitive development. *Psychological Bulletin, 85*(2), 295–324.

Steinman, S. (1981). The experience of children in a joint-custody arrangement: A report of a study. *American Journal of Orthopsychiatry, 51*(3), 403–414.

Stolberg, A., & Anker, J. (1983). Cognitive and behavioral changes in children resulting from parental divorce and consequent environmental changes. *Journal of Divorce, 7*(2), 23–41.

Svanum, S., Bringle, R., & McLaughlin, J. (1982). Father absence and cognitive performance in a large sample of 6–11 year old children. *Child Development, 53,* 136–143.

Tepp, A. (1983). Divorced fathers: Predictors of continued paternal involvement. *American Journal of Psychiatry, 140*(11), 1465–1469.

Trevisano, M. (1982). The effects of sole and joint custodial arrangements on the emotional functioning and behavioral adaptation of children of divorce. *Dissertation Abstracts International, 43,* 537B–538B.

Tropf, W. (1984). An exploratory examination of the effect of remarriage on child support and personal contacts. *Journal of Divorce, 7*(3), 57–73.

Turner, J. (1984). Divorced fathers who win contested custody of their children: An exploratory study. *American Journal of Orthopsychiatry, 54*(3), 498–501.

Wallerstein, J. (1977). Responses of the preschool child to divorce: Those who cope. In M. F. McMillan & S. Henao (Eds.), *Child psychiatry: Treatment and research* (pp. 269–292). New York: Brunner/Mazel.

Wallerstein, J., & Kelly, J. (1974). The effects of parental divorce: The adolescent experience. In E. J. Anthony & C. Koupernik (Eds.), *The child in his family: Children at psychiatric risk* (Vol. 3, pp. 479–506). New York: Wiley.

Wallerstein, J., & Kelly, J. (1975). The effects of parental divorce: Experiences of the preschool child. *Journal of the American Academy of Child Psychiatry, 14,* 600–616.

Wallerstein, J., & Kelly, J. (1976). The effects of parental divorce: Experiences of the child in later latency. *American Journal of Orthopsychiatry, 46,* 256–269.

Wallerstein, J., & Kelly, J. (1980a). Effects of divorce on the visiting father-child relationship. *American Journal of Psychiatry, 137*(12), 1534–1539.

Wallerstein, J., & Kelly, J. (1980b). *Surviving the breakup: How children and parents cope with divorce.* New York: Basic Books.

Warshak, R., & Santrock, J. (1983). Children of divorce: Impact of custody disposition on social development. In E. J. Callahan & K. A. McCluskey (Eds.), *Life-span developmental psychology: Nonnormative life events* (pp. 241–263). New York: Academic Press.

Weinraub, M., & Wolf, B. (1983). Effects of stress and social supports on mother-child interactions in single- and two-parent families. *Child Development, 54,* 1297–1311.

Weiss, R. (1979). The adjudication of custody when parents separate. In G. Levinger & O. Moles (Eds.), *Divorce and separation: Context, causes, and consequences* (pp. 324–336). New York: Basic Books.

Welsh, O. (1982). The effects of custody arrangements on children of divorce. *Dissertation Abstracts International, 42,* 4946B.

Westman, J., Cline, D., Swift, W., & Kramer, D. (1970). Role of child psychiatry in divorce. *Archives of General Psychiatry, 23,* 415–420.

Wolchik, S., Braver, S., & Sandler, I. (1985). Maternal versus joint custody: Children's post-separation experiences and adjustment. *Journal of Clinical Child Psychology, 14*(1), 5–10.

Wolchik, S., Fogas, B., & Sandler, I. (1984). Environmental change and children of divorce. In J. H. Humphrey (Ed.), *Stress in childhood.* (pp. 79–96). New York: AMS Press.

Wolchik, S., & Karoly, P. (Eds.). (1985). *Children of divorce: Perspectives on adjustment.* Lexington, MA: D. C. Heath.

Wolff, S. (1969). *Children under stress.* New York: Basic Books.

Young, E. R., & Parish, T. S. (1977). Impact of father absence during childhood on the psychological adjustment of college females. *Sex Roles, 3,* 217–227.

Zill, N. (1978). *Divorce, marital happiness and the mental health of children: Findings from the Foundation for Child Development National Survey of Children.* Prepared for the National Institute of Mental Health Workshop on Divorce and Children, Bethesda, MD.

PART III

Psychological Expertise, Professional Roles, and Ethics

5.

Psychological Evaluations in Divorce Custody: Problems, Principles, and Procedures

Many commentators have raised concerns about the value, relevance, and appropriateness of many forms of psychological and psychiatric testimony in divorce custody cases (e.g., Grisso, 1986; Hall & Hare-Mustin, 1983; Halleck, 1980; Melton, Petrila, Poythress, & Slobogin, 1987; Mnookin, 1975; Okpaku, 1976; Reppucci, 1984; Watson, 1969). Melton et al. (1987) have reflected the tone of these criticisms:

> There is probably no forensic question on which overreaching by mental health professionals has been so common and so egregious. Besides lacking scientific validity, such opinions have often been based on clinical data that are irrelevant, on their face, to the legal questions in dispute. (p. 330).

In this chapter we shall review some of the more common problems of divorce custody evaluations performed by psychologists. We will

Portions of material reported in this chapter were developed with the assistance of Research Grant #37231 from the Center for Studies of Antisocial and Violent Behavior, National Institute of Mental Health, to Thomas Grisso.

then identify certain principles and procedures that can guide clinical consultation in divorce custody cases so that it is competent, relevant to the proceedings, and appropriately cautious. The closely aligned ethical considerations will be reviewed in a companion chapter, chapter 6.

Legal Standards for Divorce Custody

State statutes differ somewhat in their elucidation of legal standards for adjudication in divorce custody cases. Each state, however, has adopted some form of the "best interests" standard (Rohman, Sales, & Lou, chap. 3 of this volume). Section 402 of the Uniform Marriage and Divorce Act (1979) is cited frequently for specification of those factors guiding judicial consideration of the child's best interests, in part because it has served as the model for the statutes of many states (Grisso, 1986; Rohman et al., chap. 3 above).

> The court shall determine custody in accordance with the best interests of the child. The court shall consider all relevant factors including:
> (1) the wishes of the child's parent or parents as to his custody;
> (2) the wishes of the child as to his custodian;
> (3) the interaction and interrelationship of the child with his parent or parents, his siblings, and any other person who may significantly affect the child's best interests;
> (4) the child's adjustment to his home, school, and community; and
> (5) the mental and physical health of all individuals involved.
> The court shall not consider conduct of a proposed custodian that does not affect his relationship to the child (Uniform Marriage and Divorce Act 1979, sec. 402)

A review of analyses of statutes and case law (e.g., Atkinson, 1984; Brownstone, 1980; Foster & Freed, 1964; Lawrence, 1981; Lowery, 1981; Oster, 1965; Watson, 1969; Rohman et al., chap. 3 above; Woody, 1977, 1978) suggests the following summary of variables as relevant to judicial determination of a child's best interests: (*a*) *child variables* (e.g., age, sex, physical or psychological functioning, individual needs, preference concerning custody); (*b*) *parent variables* (e.g., age, sex, physical or psychological functioning, history of meeting and capacity to meet the child's physical, educational, moral, emotional, and other needs); (*c*) *environmental variables* (characteristics of environments offered by each custodial option, e.g., degree to which each environment promotes continuity and stability in child's life); and (*d*) *interactive variables* (e.g., quality of relationships between child and prospective custodians and significant others).

State statutory and case law typically do not set priorities for these factors in relation to one another. Instead, judges adjudicating individual custody disputes retain significant individual discretion in applying these standards, a fact that has led Mnookin (1975) to comment on the problems attendant of the "indeterminacy" to the best interests standard. As will be discussed below, this factor probably also has contributed to the overreaching noted by Melton et al. (1987).

Common Problems Encountered in Divorce Custody Evaluations

Invading the Domain of the Court

In its report, the American Psychological Association Task Force on the Role of Psychology in the Criminal Justice System concluded that: "Since it is not within the professional competence of psychologists to offer conclusions on matter of law, psychologists should resist pressure to offer such conclusions" (Monahan, 1980, p. 9). Although the focus of the Task Force was psychology's role in the criminal justice system, its conclusions are clearly applicable to other forms of forensic expert testimony. Determining which of two adequate parents is the "better" custodian or whether a particular parent is "fit" is a matter of law. Psychologists unfamiliar with the legal system may react to this assertion by stating that the clinical techniques and scientific data base of psychology render psychologists uniquely qualified to address such questions. We do not dispute that psychologists may be able to make important contributions to courts' considerations of the legally enumerated factors. The later sections of this chapter are devoted to elaboration of principles and procedures for such contributions. However, in the courtroom, final determinations as to which placements are in children's "best interests" necessarily become value laden and nonscientific (Grisso, 1986; Melton et al., 1987; Mnookin,

1975), as do judgments about most "ultimate legal issues" (e.g., whether a defendant is insane, whether a defendant should receive the death penalty, whether a mentally retarded person should be sterilized). While psychological evidence is sometimes relevant, it is never dispositive because our courts are imbued with the power and responsibility to weigh the social and moral factors that inevitably must be considered in reaching an ultimate judgment.

Unfortunately, it is all too typical for lawyers and judges to encourage psychologists to reach dispositional conclusions in custody (and other forensic) cases. Attorneys are seeking firm conclusory testimony from experts who will advocate for their clients' interests. Judges, torn by the difficult choices raised by most divorce custody cases, often believe that psychologists have scientifically valid methods for determining what is "best" for a child. Courts may be only too willing to be relieved of the responsibility of playing guessing games about a child's future if they are persuaded that experts' crystal balls hold the answer. In reality, however, judgments on whether religious upbringing is more or less important or beneficial than opportunities for diverse peer relationships, for example, are based not on scientific or clinical data, but on cultural, moral, and other subjective values. Thus, while informing the courts of the roles such factors seem to play in children's lives may be extremely useful, drawing legally dispositive conclusions based upon them is invading the domain of the court. The same cautions are relevant to conclusory determinations of whether the parenting deficits observed by a psychologist actually render that parent unfit. "How much deficit is enough to render a parent unqualified?" also is a legal question, and psychologists should not pretend that their research suggests a threshold of parenting capacity below which a parent should be deprived of custodial rights. The research may suggest thresholds below which certain developmental effects are predicted, but the data do not address when those developmental effects outweigh constitutionally granted parental discretion.

Thus, in offering opinions on which of two or more adequate options is "best" for a child, psychologists are performing not as "experts" but as individuals with personal biases and life-style preferences. It is unavoidable that divorce custody decisions will be influenced by someone's personal biases and life-style preferences, because there is no other way to decide many such evenly balanced questions. However, the person whose decision should prevail is the judge, who is that individual empowered by society to make such legal, and inevitably moral, decisions.

The Scientific Basis of Divorce Custody Testimony

Rohman, Sales, and Lou (chap. 3 above) emphasize the paucity of behavioral science data relevant to the adjudication of divorce custody cases (see also Bradbrook, 1971; Ellsworth & Levy, 1969; Mnookin, 1975; Okpaku, 1976). Chapters 3 (Rohman et al.) and 4 (Felner & Terre) in this volume review the state of our knowledge in psychology about which factors and dispositions promote the "best interests" of children whose parents are divorcing. The conclusions of these authors are consistent with those of Melton et al. (1987) and others (Clingempeel & Reppucci, 1982; Mnookin, 1975; Ochroch, 1982; Reppucci, 1984) in firmly underscoring *the lack of any methodologically sound empirical evidence allowing psychological predictions as to the effects of various types of custodial placements on children, or whether joint custody, in general, is a better option than single-parent custody.*

Nevertheless, our general knowledge in psychology (e.g., child development, normal and pathological individual and family functioning, and recent studies of the effects of divorce on children) may provide a scientific basis for the testimony of a psychologist on more limited questions of considerable relevance to the court. For example, we have a relatively firm base for describing psychological functioning, characterizing interpersonal interactions and relationships, and making limited inferences about the current and possible future impact of certain conditions and situations upon the well-being of a child. We remain on shakiest ground when speculating about the consequences of custody arrangements, however, in that our predictive skills in psychology frequently lack demonstrated accuracy (Grisso, 1986; Ochroch, 1982; Mnookin, 1975; Reppucci, 1984). There is debate over whether clinical experts should offer *any* theoretical inferences or formulations in their testimony. Morse (1978a, 1978b, 1982, 1983) suggests that theoretical explanations typically represent mere speculation with no empirical support, although they may ostensibly be "scientific." As such they may influence the fact finder inappropriately, thus invading the domain of the court. By contrast, others (Bonnie & Slobogin, 1980;

Melton et al., 1987) make the case for "informed speculation" by clinicians. They emphasize, however, that clinicians then bear the responsibility to report to the fact finder the limitations of their testimony and the scientific and theoretical underpinnings of their speculations.

The Limitations and Misuse
of Psychological Assessment Techniques

In child custody assessments, as in any psychological evaluations, psychologists must be familiar with the psychometric properties (e.g., reliability and validity) of the measures they use (American Educational Research Association [AERA], American Psychological Association [APA], & National Council on Measurement in Education [NCME], 1985). Further, they must indicate any reservations regarding such properties in the reporting of their assessment findings (APA, 1981). A psychologist's inquiry into the suitability of certain measures must not stop at a perusal of the data on reliability and validity that exist *generally* for a method. Rather, one must consider whether the assessment technique is valid for the specific context, purpose, and examinees in the evaluation in question. Standard 6.3 of the Standards for Educational and Psychological Testing states the requirement clearly: "When a test is to be used for a purpose for which it has not been previously validated, or for which there is no supported claim for validity, the user is responsible for providing evidence of validity" (AERA, APA, & NCME, 1985).

Some writers have suggested that standardized psychological tests have little or no demonstrated utility and validity in divorce custody evaluations (Ellsworth & Levy, 1969; Okpaku, 1976). However, we believe that some psychological measures can be useful if employed in the assessment of specific, limited questions within the broader evaluation, and if psychometric and other properties of the measures are adequate and appropriate to the limited question. For example, in the course of a custody evaluation, in order to describe to the court the academic and psychosocial needs of a child who is performing poorly in school, a psychologist might administer certain educational or psychological tests. Or an evaluator may wish to examine the potential of two parents to cooperate in a coparenting relationship to aid the court in determining the suitability of joint custody. For the latter assessment one may consider administering one or more measures that permit direct measurement of couples' interactive functioning (see generally O'Leary, in press).

Grisso (1986) reviews the psychometric properties and possible utility of several measures developed to assess dimensions of psychological functioning or interaction particularly relevant to divorce custody cases. One of those measures reviewed is the Children's Reports of Parental Behavior, or CRPB (Schaefer, 1965). This instrument consists of item statements about parental behavior, feelings, and attitudes (e.g., "My mother often speaks of the good things I do"; "My father almost always punishes me in some way when I am bad"). Children are asked to indicate whether each statement is "like," "somewhat like," or "not like" the parent in question. There have been different versions of this measure, and scales representing various categories of child reports of parent behavior have been developed through factor analysis. Grisso (1986) considers the psychometric properties of the measure to be generally adequate, with some qualifications, and suggests that it may be useful to some evaluators in custody cases:

> If the CRPB results are interpreted merely as an indication of the child's feelings about or perceptions of the parent, not as an index of the parents' behaviors, then the instrument may still be useful as an aid to evaluating the child's preference and the child's current "cognitive set" for relating to the parent in question. (p. 213)

The *format* employed in a divorce custody assessment also may limit, and perhaps invalidate, the findings of the evaluation. For example, perhaps the most commonly cited problem with child custody evaluations is the tendency of some psychologists to assess only one or some of the parties in question. It has been suggested (Group for the Advancement of Psychiatry, 1981) that clinicians should not agree to participate in a custody evaluation unless they are given access to *all* relevant parties (i.e., both parents, the child, and any other concerned persons). Further, some propose that a psychological or psychiatric consultant should enter the case only when it is agreed that he or she is to serve as an *amicus curiae*, or "friend of the court," whose role is to provide data consistent with the court's purpose in serving the best interests of the child (Derdeyn, 1975; Fredericks, 1976; Melton et al., 1987). This is in contrast to the more typical arrangement whereby professionals are retained by one "side" (i.e., one parent) in the adversary process. The wisdom of agreeing to perform an evaluation while working for one parent or another is questionable on several grounds. First, as impartial as psychologists may attempt to be, employment by one side in an adversarial dispute risks blurring the primary obligation of the psychologist to serve the child's, rather than the parent's, best interests. Second, having contact with only one side in such a case clearly deprives the psychologist of the range of meaningful data necessary to address many questions relevant to a divorce custody case. Third, employment by one side promotes the perception of psychological experts, by the public and by the legal profession, as "hired guns." As chapter 2 (Scott & Emery) above underscores, the adversary process has significant drawbacks in the custody context. The inevitable "battle of the experts" that occurs in adversarial expert testimony not only may be counterproductive to the well-being of the parties in custody cases, but may also impair the public image of psychology.

We recognize that it is not always possible to arrange to enter a custody case as *amicus* and to obtain access to all parties involved. Therefore psychologists must be particularly cautious when reporting findings of an evaluation of one or some of the relevant parties. For example, in no circumstances should psychologists *ever* provide evaluative statements or opinions concerning parties not directly assessed. Whereas it is not inappropriate for psychologists to report what an examinee says about another who is not present (e.g., "Mr. Smith stated that he believed his wife is not able to maintain adequate discipline with the children"), such statements must be recognized merely as one person's perception of another. Psychologists must clarify to the court that whereas they may be reporting such perceptions and statements, the statements remain "hearsay" and no judgment can be made about their veracity, nor can the psychological functioning or behavior of the unseen party be assessed with them. The same restraint is necessary when psychologists infer from children's interviews or test responses that children have certain feelings about or perceptions of their parents. Psychologists must never even speculate to the court that the parents actually possess the particular psychological attributes or have engaged in particular behaviors suggested by the testing without performing a direct assessment of the parents in question. The children's responses must be identified as suggestive only of the children's psychological experiences of the parents.

There is perhaps one exception to the caveat not to make substantive recommendations concerning parties not directly evaluated. Psychologists may recommend, on the basis of an evaluation of one or more parties, that a mental health expert or the court investigate some matter raised in an evaluation relating to a party not seen. Thus, if a mother alleges that the father is an alcoholic, a psychologist who has access only to the mother may recommend to the court that it evaluate the veracity of the mother's report and ascertain whether, if the father is alcoholic, this condition affects his parenting in any manner.

The question of *who* is evaluated is but one dimension of the larger issue of the *comprehensiveness* of the evaluation. Typically, comprehensive custody evaluations will require more than direct observations, interviews, test and measure administrations, and other "intraoffice" sources of information. Failure to investigate a child's or parent's functioning in contexts outside the psychologist's office (e. g., at school or work or in the community) constitutes a common error. For example, we are aware of one case wherein a psychologist failed to obtain court and mental health records concerning one parent. The records would have revealed that the parent had been investigated by the Department of Social Services on numerous occasions in recent years for behaviors such as attempting suicide while his toddler was in his care, leaving the child unattended for extended periods, and driving while intoxicated with the child in the car. This information was not obtained, reviewed, or reported by the psychologist, who concluded that the father was an exemplary prospective custodian based on projective test findings alone. This case illustrates the potentially serious ramifications of psychologists' failure to obtain available and crucial data about extraoffice functioning, as well as demonstrating a clearly inappropriate use of projective tests. Projective measures have not been shown to have the requisite psychometric properties to render them reliable or valid for predicting custodial functioning.

Principles in the Conduct of a
Divorce Custody Evaluation

In the previous section we outlined several of the conceptual and procedural problems characterizing the involvement of some
psychologists in divorce custody cases. In this section we shall attempt to explicate basic principles that characterize a model divorce
custody evaluation, relying heavily on the conceptualizations of psycholegal assessment elaborated elsewhere by one of us (Grisso, 1986).

In general, in a divorce custody case the court is concerned with the
capacities of each of the prospective custodians (together with the resources available to each of them) to provide a home for the child in
question and to promote that child's well-being. We shall refer to this
concept as "parenting capacity." This conceptualization suggests that
perhaps three primary elements should be the focus of a child custody
evaluation: parents' functional abilities, explanations for deficits in parents' functioning, and an interactive comparison between the parents'
abilities and the child's needs (Grisso, 1986).

The first element in this model involves a description of the *functional abilities, behaviors,* or *capacities* of the parents. The functional
abilities of primary concern are those that are recognized (in psychology and in law) as important for child rearing and meeting the needs of
children. They are not synonymous with general intellectual abilities,
personality traits, or diagnostic conditions. Instead, the abilities to be
described are more specifically associated with the role of caretaker of
a child: for example, ability to discipline, ability to maintain consistency
in one's response to a child, and so forth. Precisely *which* abilities, behaviors, and capacities of any parent do promote the well-being of children is not always known. However, legal standards, such as one's
state statute or precedent in case law, together with the guidance of
model statutes or uniform code proposals, will serve to identify those
dimensions of functioning that have been highlighted by the law thus
far. Although such standards may be broad and vague at times and
rather narrow and limited at others, they should constitute the first
building block of the assessment. In our search for criterion-valid psycholegal assessment methods, we must always maintain as clear a
concept as the law permits of what criteria are relevant to the law in
each instance. Once one has identified the general or specific parame-

ters of the legal criteria to be the focus of the evaluation, one may expand or delineate more specifically the range of abilities, behaviors, and capacities to be assessed with the aid of psychological theory and research. Thus, since the Uniform Marriage and Divorce Act suggests that interactions and interrelationships of the child and parent can be considered, psychological theory and research may provide guidance on which aspects of parent-child interactions and relationships are pertinent to the parents' ability to promote the child's well-being.

Second, we recommend that evaluators obtain data with which to provide *causal explanations* for any functional deficits observed. In child custody questions, as in many "legal competencies" in criminal and civil law, it may be important for the examiner to go beyond describing parental strengths and deficits relative to specific child-rearing abilities, in that the law often calls for reasons for any behavioral deficits (Grisso, 1986). The law's interest in reasons for disabilities is related to its recognition that inadequate functioning may be manifested because of temporary or "situational" deficits or may represent more "typical" or chronic conditions. For example, a parent may manifest poor understanding of a child's physical needs because of mere lack of information or because of lack of interest and motivation. In the first instance, the parent's deficit may be easily remedied by instruction; thus it seems unfair for this deficit to weigh heavily in the balance when deciding the parent's appropriateness as a custodian. In the second instance, however, remediation of the deficit may be less likely, and the deficit may become more significant in the court's deliberations.

The third element in the custody evaluation, a description of the *person-situation interaction,* is especially important. Having evaluated the parent's functional abilities and deficits, the examiner now compares those characteristics with the demands that will be placed upon this parent when caring for the *specific* child in question. This comparison attempts to characterize the degree of "congruency or incongruency" between the extent of the parent's abilities and the needs of the child. This comparison, of course, requires a careful assessment of the special needs of the child. This perspective emphasizes that the law perceives no absolute level of parenting abilities as dispositive of the custody question. A parent may be capable of meeting the needs of some children but less capable of meeting the needs of others, depending upon differences among the children and their needs. For example, the ability to provide a nutritionally adequate diet for a child may constitute an essential element of parenting capacity. In a psychological assessment, one of us (Weithorn) observed that a moderately mentally retarded woman was able to provide such a diet for her child with the coaching of an occasional visit from a public health nurse. If, however, that child had been suffering from phenylketonuria, diabetes, or some other physiological disorder requiring a strict dietary management, it is possible that this mother's parenting skills might have been stretched (particularly if she was required to read labels, since she was not able to read). The Uniform Marriage and Divorce Act (1979), to some extent, emphasizes the importance of a person-context interaction approach in its exhortation that: "The court shall not consider conduct of a proposed custodian that does not affect his relationship to the child." Implicit here clearly is the notion that not all areas of functioning are relevant to parenting in general and the parenting of a specific child in particular. Relevance in each particular instance should be demonstrated before it is considered in a custody adjudication.

Grisso's model also delineates two features of a divorce custody determination that are *not* the province of the mental health professional: the *judgmental and dispositional* aspects of custody decisions. Whereas the psychological consultant may offer an opinion about the functioning of the parents relative to the needs of the child, the consultant must refrain from offering a judgment as to whether any observed "person-context incongruency is of a sufficient magnitude" to label a parent "incompetent" or less suitable than another parent. Most typical and dangerous in divorce custody evaluations is the practice of passing judgment on the relative importance of the parent-child incongruencies of one parent compared with those of the other. In so doing one may be comparing the importance, for example, of one parent's difficulty in expressing affection with the other parent's difficulty in maintaining discipline, as if to suggest that the field of psychology can determine which aspects of child rearing are more important to healthy development. As noted above, such judgments are not justified by our knowledge in psychology and should not be couched in psychological terminology that implies scientific grounding (Mnookin, 1975). Further, the question of how much incongruency is enough to warrant a decision, or how the parent-child incongruencies of two possible placements compare, is "an interpretation of justice, in light of the instant circumstances and the dispositional consequences which will accrue for both the individual(s) and society. This interpretation invariably constitutes a legal, moral or social judgment, no matter how it is made" (Grisso, 1986, p. 27).

Thus the role of the psychological consultant is prescribed to some extent by this model. The following objectives of a divorce custody assessment are enumerated by Grisso (1986):

(1) The principal objective will be the description of each examinee's functional abilities that are related conceptually to the legally-defined parenting capacities;

(2) Explanations for any relevant functional deficits will be provided where possible within the limits of our clinical methods;

(3) A complete assessment will compare the parents' abilities and deficits to the unique demands for child rearing represented by the needs of the specific child in question;

(4) The examiner will refrain from reaching conclusions about: (i) sufficiency or insufficiency of parent-child congruencies or incongruencies and (ii) comparative (between two parents) nature and magnitude of the parent-child congruencies or incongruencies. Such judgments are the province of the court.

Roles and Procedures in Divorce Custody Evaluations: Recommendations

Clearly, there are several roles a psychologist might play when providing divorce custody evaluations to the courts. We believe that psychologists as clinical evaluators and behavioral scientists have much to contribute to the disposition of some divorce custody cases, and we shall delineate here what we consider to be the parameters of that expertise.

Roles

Delineation of Emphases of Psychological Inquiry

Above we suggested that whereas legal standards and guidelines define the basic criteria and areas of inquiry to be considered by the court in a divorce custody adjudication, psychological theory and research can elucidate which specific areas of human functioning and relationships are pertinent to those parameters. Therefore, among the first contributions psychologists can make is the delineation of those specific realms of individual and interpersonal behavior, and those capacities, attitudes, thoughts, or feelings, that may bear on the court's ultimate decision. The psychologist's investigation must necessarily be broad and comprehensive (Melton et al., 1987) because the judge's mandate is inquiry into all those aspects of functioning and relationships that may bear on a child's best interests, and because our many theories and data bases suggest a multiplicity of relevant considerations. The identification of appropriate areas of inquiry should lead directly to the assessment techniques selected.

Investigation and Description

Psychologists possess special expertise as data gatherers. Their skills as clinicians and scientists equip them to serve as astute observers of human behavior and interaction. Psychological training should provide them with tools to investigate matters relating to attitudes, thoughts, feelings, behaviors, and relationships in a way distinct from that of a layperson or legal professional. Therefore we believe that psychologists can perform a more thorough (in terms of depth and breadth) investigation of many matters relevant to a divorce custody adjudication than might be available without such consultation. Litwack, Gerber, and Fenster (1979) refer to this function as "discovery," whereby the psychologist investigates and reports to the court those aspects of human behavior and interaction relevant to the adjudication.

The skills we believe psychologists can bring to bear on the investigation of custody cases are those of interviewer; observer; structurer and organizer of observed interactions (e.g., family interactions); administrant and interpreter of specialized assessment techniques; and conceptual organizer and interpreter of disparate and diverse supplementary data sources (e.g., school, medical, employment, social service, or court records). We emphasize that not only do psychologists obtain the relevant information, but they impose a conceptual structure and organization upon it so that it will have meaning to the legal inquiry. Psychologists are able to attend selectively to those strands of data that are meaningful to the proceedings and to recognize relationships or disparities that may exist among the various sources and types of data. For example, psychologists can play a unique role in questions of joint versus single-parent custody. Psychologists can draw from rather lengthy (and typically multiple) interviews with each parent, with the child, and with other family members or data sources, and from any conjoint interviews, those data that bear on coparenting. Hours of interviews and observation and pages of documents may have been available to address the many subjects relevant to the custody questions in general. However, the special skills of psychologists can isolate and organize those data from diverse sources that bear on each limited issue. In general, psychologists consulting as evaluators in a divorce custody case should describe the data relative to functional abilities and environmental demands pertinent conceptually and specifically to parenting capacity in the particular case.

Evaluation

We noted above that psychologists have a specific role in evaluating the functional parenting abilities of caretakers and the special needs of children. Psychologists' strength is in elaborating those aspects of functioning of each party that bear on the *unique* needs of the child. If a child's behavioral disorder is manifest as aggression and discipline problems, one can carefully assess each parent's capacity to provide intervention and discipline that is helpful in controlling and remedying the problems. If a child has a developmental disorder and special education professionals recommend that parents provide several additional hours of habilitation training at home each day, one can assess the capacity, willingness, and availability of each parent to provide such training. If joint custody is an option the court is considering, then assessment of coparenting abilities becomes critical.

Clearly, evaluative roles require psychologists to reach judgments as to the levels of capacity represented by the behavior of the parties with respect to the situation. This does not mean that psychologists should also reach judgments as to whether those levels of capacity are sufficient or insufficient to lead to a custodial placement or whether the overall levels of capacity of one party are superior or inferior to those of another. It does mean, however, that psychologists must explicate the aspects of functioning observed and evaluated in a manner that permits fact finders to apply that data and yet to draw their own conclusions on the ultimate legal issues. Thus evaluation reports and oral testimony must separate fact from opinion and present the factual basis for a psychologist's opinions (Melton et al., 1987).

Communication of Facts, Observations, and Opinions

Evaluation reports and oral testimony must separate for the court *facts, observations,* and *opinions* and must present the basis for the psychologist's opinions (Melton, Weithorn, & Slobogin, 1984). *Facts* are matters about which there is no dispute. In a clinical report, the matters that typically can be viewed as factual are that individuals made particular statements in the clinical interviews, that documents (e.g., a school report) contained certain pieces of data, or that certain events occurred (e.g., the psychologist interviewed the parents for X hours each on X days in her office).

The veracity of the content of statements or data cannot be ascertained by the psychologist. But the fact that one person said something about another person, or the fact that a child's teacher evaluated the child in a particular manner for school records, can be reported. Much of the facts about which a psychologist, as an expert witness, can testify are technically considered "hearsay" evidence. As such, they are admissible only because the expert uses such data as the basis for an expert opinion. Therefore caution is recommended in choosing which facts to present in the courtroom, in that one should limit factual data to that which actually served as the basis for the opinions.

All factually related statements in a clinical report or testimony must be attributed to their sources. Therefore a report should *never* contain a lone statement such as "Johnny does poorly in school." Rather, the report should state the facts available to the psychologist on this matter (e.g., "Mrs. Jones, Johnny's teacher, stated that he is a poor student," or "Johnny received two F's and two C's on his 1984–1985 report card"). As will be noted below, the psychologist may then, in the opinion section of the report, draw conclusions from these data about Johnny's school performance.

Observations are those aspects of individual or interpersonal behavior that psychologists, or their clinical team members, personally have had the opportunity to view or hear. The observations section of a report or testimony should refrain from making judgmental or evaluative statements and must focus on a straightforward reporting of observations. Thus a conclusion that "Johnny was apparently depressed during the interview" is inappropriate for this section of the report. Rather, a description of the relevant observed behaviors (e.g., sad facial expression, psychomotor retardation) is most useful. If to the psychologist these and other behaviors together with other relevant data suggest depression, any conclusions about that judgment should wait for the opinion section and should be accompanied by a report on the various sources and types of data that support such a conclusion.

In another example, Mr. and Mrs. Smith, in separate interviews, may make repeated statements that denigrate each other's parenting capacity. In a conjoint interview, the psychologist may observe Mr. and Mrs. Smith arguing about central as well as minor aspects of child rearing. In a written report or oral testimony the psychologist may highlight these facts and observations to support the conclusion that Mr. and Mrs. Smith do not appear able, at this time, to engage in a low-conflict, cooperative, and mutually respectful coparenting relationship. This *opinion* is a judgment that the psychologist must support with multiple examples from factual and observational material. Psychologists not only must separate facts from opinions in their evaluations but also must draw for the court the connections about which facts lead to, and therefore support, their opinions. The court can thus decide to accept or reject the opinions in a fully informed manner.

Presentation of Relevant Scientific Data

Psychologists, as behavioral scientists knowledgeable about research findings, also can inform the court about the state of our data base as it relates to the questions of inquiry. For example, based on the Felner and Terre literature reviews (chap. 4 above), one might conclude that continued exposure to parental conflict may lead to poorer psychological adjustment in children than might upbringing in a single-parent home. Clearly, the data base is incomplete and has methodological problems. However, specific studies, and their strengths and limitations, could be reviewed briefly for the court, together with the expert's analysis of the direction and strength of the findings, if joint custody is under consideration by the court.

Application of the relevant scientific data base to particular sets of clinical data characterizes the most appropriate model for psychological testimony in custody cases. Thus in cases where the courts are considering joint custody, psychologists may present their opinions about the level of parental conflict and cooperation manifested in an assessed parenting dyad (accompanied by the facts that led to this opinion). However, rather than terminating the testimony there, it would be useful to the court to have information about research on the effect of parental conflict and cooperation on the well-being of children. With this foundation, psychologists may then be in a position to offer an opinion on how the scientific data base relates to the particular facts in this case. That is, psychologists may infer that the continued exposure to the level of parental conflict and the absence of parental cooperation evidenced in the family might lead to (or promote the maintenance of existing) adjustment difficulties in the child (Felner & Terre, chap. 4 above). If psychologists take the courts through their inferential steps in reaching such conclusions, the courts can decide to accept or reject this analysis at any step of the way. As noted earlier, however, psychologists should not take the argument the final step and recommend against joint custody. That final translation of the psychological data into a legal disposition remains the province of the courts.

We have indicated here one example of how a predictive inference may be appropriate in a custody case. Not only are the inferences based on an analysis of general scientific knowledge in psychology and the data gathered in the particular case, but the court is apprised of the analytic process and the scientific and clinical data used in that process. We recommend against predictive inferences that are not based on scientific data or do not illuminate for the fact finder the steps leading to the opinion.

Procedures of a Model Custody Divorce Evaluation

Whom to Evaluate

The model custody evaluation includes direct assessment of all those parties whose functioning is relevant to the case at hand. Typically this includes all prospective custodians, the child whose custody is in question, and any other individuals whose relationships with the prospective custodians and the child will have an effect upon the child's well-being (e.g., the intended new spouse of a parent, a grandparent who may share child-rearing responsibilities with a prospective custodian). Such procedures allow psychologists to investigate the functioning of each party as it relates to the needs of the child. Since interactions and relationships of each parent and associated parties and the child are of apparent interest to the law, it is recommended that direct observation of such interactions be included in the evaluation.

If a psychologist can convince the parties to allow him or her to enter the case as *amicus* and to permit access to all relevant persons, the conditions for a model divorce custody evaluation may exist. If the parties do not agree to this recommendation, the psychologist is immediately limited in certain areas of inquiry and opinions. For example, if the psychologist does not see both parents, it will not be possible to evaluate directly the feasibility of coparenting in joint custody. If the psychologist is unable to evaluate the child in interaction with the parents, there is no opportunity to speak directly to parent-child interactions. Clearly the distillations of others about parties not evaluated may be useful, but they are inferior to the psychologist's trained, and one hopes objective, eyes and ears. Although we recommend against psychologists making comparative and dispositional judgments in a divorce custody case in any event, doing so with access to only some of the parties constitutes more than simply poor professional practice: it manifests blatantly incompetent and unethical psychological assessment procedures.

Without access to all the parties, a psychologist may still make some limited contributions to the proceedings. For example, the psychologist may provide a thorough assessment of the psychological functioning of the child or one parent. It is important to note, however, that without evaluating both the child and a prospective custodian, the psychologist is handicapped in identifying the functional abilities required by the specific situation together with the levels of functioning demonstrated as they relate to that situation. Thus a psychologist who sees the mother only may be able to make certain statements about the mother's general psychological skills, abilities, and behaviors. However, without an assessment of the child, the psychologist is in the dark about the specific capacities called for in parenting that child and about the quality and dimensions of the parent-child relationship and interactions. Thus the contribution to the court proceeding is limited indeed.

Nevertheless, there are rare exceptions to this general rule. A psychologist mentioned to us a case in which a father stated that he would agree to sole custody by the mother if he was assured that she did not suffer from any psychological disorder (A. Bodin, personal communication, August 1983). The father indicated that he would not contest custody if his wife was found to be psychologically healthy. Reportedly, the mother agreed to this inquiry. This is an example of an unusual instance wherein a limited inquiry about one dimension of a party's functioning may be sufficient to address the question of interest.

Sources of Data

In the thorough divorce custody evaluation necessitated by the broad scope of judicial inquiry, multiple sources of data are necessary. Primary, of course, are direct interviews and observation of the various parties interacting with each other. As noted above, standardized psychological tests or assessment tools may be used in a custody evaluation if these measures meet adequate general psychometric standards *and* are valid for describing functional parenting abilities, assisting in forming causal explanations for functional deficits, and suggesting the special needs of children.

Psychologists also must gather relevant evidence from other parties or agencies that have information about the child or the prospective custodians and custodial placements. Typically parties approached in a divorce custody case include the child's teacher/school and pediatrician. Relevant educational and medical records should be reviewed. However, in any specific custody case, many other sources of data may be investigated; for example, reports of relatives, friends, neighbors, employers of parents, and mental health or other specialized professionals who have knowledge of the parties or placements. In addition, sometimes it is relevant to obtain records or documents from police, courts, or public agencies (e. g., Department of Social Services). In approaching all these sources, of course, psychologists must obtain in advance the consent of persons legally empowered to give such consent. Attorneys can provide guidance as to the specific legal requirements for consent. However, psychologists also should be aware that even where there is no legal requirement, ethical imperatives necessitate that the parties' permission be obtained before invasions into private matters.

Assessment Strategies

It is beyond the scope of this review to recommend specifically those assessment techniques that should be used in a model divorce custody evaluation. In fact there is a range of strategies and assessment methods, drawing from a diversity of theoretical orientations and evaluation styles, that can lead to data relevant to divorce custody cases. As noted above, however, probably of greatest use are direct interviews and direct observation of the parties in question, individually and in interaction with one another, and standardized psychological tests and formal assessment devices that have demonstrated validity for the question at hand. Data about functioning outside the psychologist's office can best be obtained from the parties, together with those supplementary data sources listed above. Clearly, of course, any assessment strategies and measures selected should be linked conceptually to the variables that are the focus of the inquiry. It is unfortunate that at times psychologists simply select a test or assessment "battery" without carefully examining whether the measures chosen will in fact provide data directly relevant to the inquiry.

Whatever the constellation of assessment strategies chosen, they should represent a range and diversity of methods. There is no substitute in a clinical assessment for convergent validity demonstrated by multiple assessment methods. Therefore one should not limit an assessment to interview, observation, testing, *or* background sources but should incorporate as many meaningful examples of each method as is feasible. If data collected from these multiple techniques converge, then the psychologist can offer opinions with greater clinical certainty. If, however, the inferences one might draw from the data are discrepant, the clinician must seriously question the validity of any of the disparate findings. In a forensic case, where the consequences for the parties are so serious, conclusions unsubstantiated by multiple methods of assessment have no place. In the case of conflicting data, the psychologist's conclusions either should reflect the impossibility of drawing conclusions in the given instance or should relate to the possible implications of the discrepancies. We suggest that *any clinical opinion or inference should be supported by two or more data sources.* The validity check made possible by use of multiple assessment strategies allows the psychologist greater insight into the strengths and limitations of any given clinical data set.

Conclusions

At the outset of this chapter, we pointed out that psychological evaluations and testimony in divorce custody cases have been the subject of much criticism. Criticisms have typically focused upon the "overreaching" (Melton et al., 1987) that often characterizes such consultation: offering conclusions on matters of law; exceeding the boundaries of one's scientific or clinical data base when presenting testimony; and using inappropriate and irrelevant assessment strategies.

A most serious problem in psychological testimony in custody cases is psychologists' failure to inform courts of the limitations of their evaluations. This shortcoming may result from the temptation to speak with authority, the pressures of the adversarial system, or psychologists' failure to appreciate that they are "overreaching." Whatever the reason, failure to use caution in one's statements violates ethical principles and notions of what constitutes competent psychological practice. As will be reviewed in greater detail in chapter 6 (Weithorn), the need to exercise caution and restraint is particularly great when the psychologist's findings may be used to affect the lives of others (APA, 1981; Grisso, 1984). The potential consequences of psychological testimony in a custody case, where one parent may lose custodial rights and the course of a child's future upbringing is determined, are dramatic. Few would disagree that the parties in such a context deserve from psychologists the utmost in conscientiousness and humility.

References

American Educational Research Association, American Psychological Association, and National Council on Measurement in Education. (1985). *Standards for educational and psychological testing.* Washington, DC: American Psychological Association.

American Psychological Association. (1981). Ethical principles of psychologists. *American Psychologist, 36,* 633–638.

Atkinson, J. (1984). Criteria for deciding child custody in the trial and appellate courts. *Family Law Quarterly, 17,* 1–42.

Bonnie, R. J., & Slobogin, C. (1980). The role of mental health professionals in the criminal process: The case for informed speculation. *Virginia Law Review, 66,* 427–522.

Bradbrook, A. (1971). The relevance of psychological and psychometric studies to the future development of the laws governing the settlement of interparental child custody disputes. *Journal of Family Law, 11,* 557–587.

Brownstone, H. (1980). The homosexual parent in custody disputes. *Queen's Law Journal, 5,* 119–240.

Clingempeel, W. G., & Reppucci, N. D. (1982). Joint custody after divorce: Major issues and goals for research. *Psychological Bulletin, 91,* 102–127.

Derdeyn, A. (1975). Child custody consultation. *American Journal of Orthopsychiatry, 45,* 791–801.

Ellsworth, P., & Levy, R. (1969). Legislative reform of child custody adjudication: An effort to rely on social science data in formulating legal policies. *Law and Society Review, 4,* 167–233.

Foster, H., & Freed, D. (1964). Child custody. *New York University Law Review, 39,* 423–443.

Fredericks, M. (1976). Custody battles: Mental health professionals in the courtroom. In G. P. Koocher (Ed.), *Children's rights and the mental health professions* (pp. 41–52). New York: Wiley.

Grisso, T. (1984). *The interpretation of clinical data in legal assessment: Ethical issues.* Paper presented at the American Psychological Association Convention, Toronto, Canada.

Grisso, T. (1986). *Evaluating competencies: Forensic assessments and instruments.* New York: Plenum.

Group for the Advancement of Psychiatry, Committee on the Family (1981). *Divorce, child custody and the family.* San Francisco: Jossey-Bass.

Hall, J. E., & Hare-Mustin, R. T. (1983). Sanctions and the diversity of ethical complaints against psychologists. *American Psychologist, 38,* 714–729.

180   Psychological Expertise

Halleck, S. (1980). *Law in the practice of psychiatry: A handbook for clinicians.* New York: Plenum.

Lawrence, S. (1981). *Manual for the Lawrence Psychological-Forensic Examination.* San Bernardino, CA: Author.

Litwack, T., Gerber, G., & Fenster, A. (1979). The proper role of psychology in child custody disputes. *Journal of Family Law, 18,* 269–300.

Lowery, C. (1981). Child custody decisions in divorce proceedings: A survey of judges. *Professional Psychology, 12,* 492–498.

Melton, G. B., Petrila, J., Poythress, N. G., & Slobogin, C. (1987). *Psychological evaluations for the court: A handbook for mental health professionals and lawyers.* New York: Guilford Press.

Melton, G. B., Weithorn, L. A., & Slobogin, C. (1984). *Community mental health centers and the courts.* Lincoln: University of Nebraska Press.

Mnookin, R. H. (1975). Child custody adjudication: Judicial function in the face of indeterminancy. *Law and Contemporary Problems, 39,* 226–293.

Monahan, J. (Ed.). (1980). *Who is the client?* Washington, DC: American Psychological Association.

Morse, S. (1978a). Crazy behavior, morals, and science: An analysis of mental health law. *Southern California Law Review, 51,* 527–654.

Morse, S. (1978b). Law and mental health professionals: The limits of expertise. *Professional Psychology, 9,* 389–399.

Morse, S. (1982). Failed explanations and criminal responsibility: Experts and the unconscious. *Virginia Law Review, 68,* 971–1084.

Morse, S. (1983). Mental health law: Governmental regulation of disordered persons and the role of the professional psychologist. In B. D. Sales (Ed.), *The professional psychologist's handbook* (pp. 339–422). New York: Plenum.

Ochroch, R. (1982). *Ethical pitfalls in child custody evaluations.* Paper presented at the American Psychological Association Convention, Washington, DC.

Okpaku, S. (1976). Psychology: Impediment or aid in child custody cases? *Rutgers Law Review, 29,* 1117–1153.

O'Leary, K. D. (Ed.). (in press). *Assessment of marital discord.* Hillsdale, NJ: Lawrence Erlbaum.

Oster, A. (1965). Custody proceedings: A study of vague and indefinite standards. *Journal of Family Law, 5,* 21–38.

Reppucci, N. D. (1984). The wisdom of Solomon: Issues in child custody determination. In N. D. Reppucci, L. A. Weithorn, E. P. Mulvey, & J. Monahan (Eds.), *Children, mental health and the law* (pp. 59–78). Beverly Hills, CA: Sage.

Schaefer, E. (1965). Children's reports of parental behavior: An inventory. *Child Development, 36,* 417–423.

Uniform Marriage and Divorce Act. (1979). *Uniform Laws Annotated,* 9A.

Watson, A. (1969). The children of Armageddon: Problems of custody following divorce. *Syracuse Law Review, 21,* 55–86.

Woody, R. (1977). Psychologists in child custody. In B. D. Sales (Ed.), *Psychology in the legal process* (pp. 249–267). New York: Spectrum.

Woody, R. (1978). *Getting custody: Winning the last battle of the marital war.* New York: Macmillan.

6.

Psychological Consultation in Divorce Custody Litigation: Ethical Considerations

Lois A. Weithorn

Complaints against psychologists who consult in child custody litigation are heavily represented in the caseload of the American Psychological Association's (APA) Ethics Committee (Hall & Hare-Mustin, 1983; Mills, 1984; Ethics Committee, 1985). Among the possible explanations for the frequency of ethical problems characterizing psychological consultation in divorce custody litigation are the following:

1. The indeterminacy of the "best interests" standard (Mnookin, 1975; Whobrey, Sales, & Lou, chap. 3 in this volume), and the pressures of the adversary system (Scott & Emery, chap. 2 above) may entice, and perhaps coerce, psychologists to exceed the limitations of psychological data in custody cases.

2. Because special competencies and knowledge are required for consultation in custody cases, many otherwise capable psychologists may be ill equipped to provide adequate and appropriate psychological services to the court.

3. Many psychologists may not appreciate that the serious consequences following from custody adjudications require that psycholo-

gists consulting to the courts use extreme caution and unusually stringent criteria when interpreting their data.

4. The nature of contractual relationships with parties in the dispute may not always be clear, and psychologists may be requested or pressured to undertake dual roles in particular cases.

5. Psychologists may be unfamiliar with the rather complex considerations relative to whether and when confidentiality between psychologist and client(s) is operative.

6. There are no formal professional standards for child custody consultation. This void leaves many psychologists without guidance from professional groups concerning appropriate conduct in most aspects of child custody consultation.

All these factors probably contribute to the likelihood that a psychologist will commit a professional or ethical blunder in the process of divorce custody consultation. Ochroch (1982) distilled the threat of ethical difficulties in custody consultation succinctly when she referred to "ethical pitfalls" of child custody evaluations. In fact, one might go so far as to characterize divorce custody litigation as a potential minefield for psychologists from the standpoint of ethics.

Ultimately, what constitutes ethical practice is a matter to be determined both by the professional associations and by each psychologist's personal values and standards of conduct. However, this chapter is an attempt, in conjunction with its companion chapter, chapter 5 (Weithorn & Grisso), to highlight some of the ethical issues confronting psychologists who venture to aid the courts in child custody litigation. The first section of this chapter, Recognition of the Limits of Psychology, reviews some of the issues already discussed in chapter 5. At the risk of some redundancy, I have chosen to discuss these issues here as well because of their centrality to responsible court consultation. The following treatment of the issues is an attempt to expand and conceptualize further the related notions introduced in chapter 5.

Recognition of the Limits of Psychology

A primary focus of this book is the review of the state of psychological knowledge and assessment technology relevant to divorce custody questions. Several writers (Grisso, 1986; Hall & Hare-Mustin, 1983; Melton, Petrila, Poythress, & Slobogin, 1987; Ochroch, 1982; Weithorn & Grisso, chap. 5 above) suggest that one of the more common problems characterizing psychologists' involvement in custody cases is the tendency to exceed the boundaries of their knowledge and expertise. Not only do psychologists often go beyond the limits of their data base, but they also often encroach upon the province of the court by offering opinions on matters of law (Grisso, 1986; Melton et al., 1987; Weithorn & Grisso, chap. 5 above).

The Limitations of Psychological Knowledge and Techniques

The Preamble of Principle 4 of the American Psychological Association's *Ethical Principles of Psychologists* (1981a) includes the following caveat: "In public statements providing psychological information or professional opinions . . . psychologists base their statements on scientifically acceptable psychological findings and techniques with full recognition of the limits and uncertainties of such evidence." This section of the *Ethical Principles* appears to require that psychologists use caution when making any statements that are psychological in nature or that are presented to others as derived from psychological expertise. Psychological reports and oral testimony in a child custody case clearly fall under this principle, since they are public statements made by one representing oneself as an expert in psychology.

The APA *Ethical Principles* provide additional guidelines for psychologists regarding appropriate presentation of clinical assessment data: "In reporting assessment results, psychologists indicate any reservations that exist regarding validity or reliability because of the circumstances of the assessment. . . . Psychologists strive to ensure that the results of assessments and their interpretations are not misused by others" (Principle 8c). As is implicit in this principle, psychologists have a responsibility beyond awareness of the data on reliability and validity that exist *generally* for any given measure. They also must consider the applicability of the measure for the *particular criteria* of the assessment. Thus, carefully developed and standardized instruments for the measurement of intellectual functioning or for the diagnosis of mental disorders do not necessarily serve as valid measures of parenting skills (Grisso, 1986). As Weithorn and Grisso (chap. 5

above) point out, the *Standards for Educational and Psychological Testing* (American Educational Research Association [AERA], American Psychological Association [APA] and National Council on Measurement in Education [NCME], 1985) require that evidence for validity of a test be specific to the purpose for which the test is to be used (Standard 6.3). In that the APA *Ethical Principles* (1981a) direct psychologists to abide by all association guidelines and standards, these testing standards are binding.

Ensuring that assessment results are not misused by others, as required by Principle 8c, includes emphasizing to the court the uncertainties that exist in any reported data. In general, Weithorn and Grisso (chap. 5 above) cite as limitations to any custody assessment: failure to see all the relevant parties, failure to investigate all or particular relevant aspects of functioning or relationships, failure to validate the findings obtained from one assessment method with those from another, and use of methods and measures that have not been validated for the specific purposes of the assessment. Practices such as making evaluative or conclusory statements about persons or relationships not observed directly, in the absence of important sources of data, or on the basis of irrelevant or inappropriate data are blatantly unethical (Hall & Hare-Mustin, 1983; Ochroch, 1982; Weithorn & Grisso, chap. 5 above).

The APA *Ethical Principles* also describe the way *research* findings must be presented. Principle 1a, which is directed primarily at psychologists' presentation of their own scientific findings, clearly is also relevant to psychologists' reporting of the findings of other investigators. Psychologists are instructed never to "suppress disconfirming data" and to "provide thorough discussions of the limitations of their data, especially where their work touches on social policy . . . and acknowledge the existence of alternative hypotheses and explanations for their findings."

Testimony on Matters of Law

In chapter 1 above, Wyer, Gaylord, and Grove emphasize that the "best interests standard" guiding most child custody adjudications permits judges substantial discretion in deciding each case. The standard is not characterized by legal presumptions that favor one fit parent over another. Therefore judges are forced to make case-by-case determinations as to which prospective placement offers the child the best opportunities for well-being and positive growth. Although judges may base their decisions on psychological information and opinion, ultimately the decision is a legal one, requiring an application of societal values and child-rearing preferences to each particular case (Weithorn & Grisso, chap. 5 above).

The Task Force on the Role of Psychology in the Criminal Justice System has emphasized that it is not within the competence of psychologists to offer conclusions on matters of law (Monahan, 1980). The Task Force points out that matters of law necessarily encompass "social and value" statements. In an example from criminal law, the Task Force states that an opinion by a psychologist as to the probability that a defendant might commit criminal acts in the future is a *psychological* statement, whereas a statement by a psychologist that the defendant is "too dangerous to be released" is a conclusion on a *matter of law*. The conclusion necessarily requires the psychologist to impose "his or her values as to the degree of risk society should bear in releasing the individual" (Monahan, 1980, p. 9). If we extend this contrast to an example from divorce custody cases, we might conclude that, with sound data, a psychologist may appropriately offer an opinion as to the impact upon a particular "only" child of being placed in a reconstituted family with six stepsiblings. By contrast, offering an opinion on the legal question whether the child *should* be placed in that home is beyond psychology's competence. The final judicial conclusion as to the child's placement must be based upon a consideration not only of psychological and nonpsychological facts, but upon a balancing of the legal and social implications of the adjudication. Psychologists are neither trained nor empowered by society to perform such analyses: "[O]ften it is not that the psychologist volunteers such conclusive statements, but that the courts, in an attempt to evade their responsibility to deal with difficult issues, pressure psychologists to answer legal questions for them" (Monahan, 1980, p. 9). It is particularly understandable that the courts might defer to psychologists in custody matters, where judges are faced with a "Solomon-like" choice in determining how to divide a child between two adequate parents (Hall & Hare-Mustin, 1983; Reppucci, 1984). However, even pressure from the court does not relieve the psychologist of the ethical responsibility enunciated in the APA *Ethical Principles* (1981a). The Preamble to Principle 2, which we will review in greater detail below, requires that psychologists perform only in a manner "for which they are qualified by training and experience." Offering conclusions on matters of law is not in the realm of psychological competence.

Levels of Psychological "Evidence"

Grisso (1984) points out that, depending upon the decisionmaking context, psychologists may allow different levels of psychological "evidence" to guide their clinical actions. For example, a staff psychologist in a psychiatric hospital may use more stringent decision rules when determining whether a "dangerous" patient is ready to be discharged than when deciding whether library visits or recreational therapy will be a more therapeutic addition to that patient's schedule. Clearly, the potential consequences of a "wrong" decision in the first instance seem more serious. Grisso (1984) analyzes the dimensions that may guide us when deciding how stringent must be our standards for assessments. He recommends that we evaluate the *potential harm* that may result eventually from the decision; the *finality* of the decision; the *information control* we possess in the specific situation; and the degree to which the subject of the assessment has any choice about what will happen to him or her as a result of the evaluation (i.e., *client autonomy*).

In a forensic case, the findings of psychologists, while not dispositive, may influence the court's ultimate decision. Imposition of the death penalty, loss of liberty, loss of large sums of money, or loss of the custody of a child may result from such testimony. The *potential harm* of a "wrong" decision may be great. Based in part on assessment of such potential consequences, the law applies different levels of evidentiary certainty in the form of "standards of proof" in different types of cases. The *finality* of the decision also is significant in a forensic case. Some decisions are immutable once carried out (e.g., execution or sterilization), while others are extremely difficult to change (e.g., imprisonment, custody adjudication), and may have caused harm in the interim. *Information control* is poor when psychologists present their findings to nonpsychologists in a legal or other adversarial context (Weithorn, in press). Nonpsychologists may fail to appreciate the limitations of clinical or scientific work. Further, it is consistent with the responsibilities of attorneys to highlight selectively those data most favorable to their clients. Finally, in most forensic cases the parties assessed have little *autonomy* or control over whether they accept or reject the findings of the court. True, parties can appeal the court's adjudication if they have grounds and resources for an appeal, but that is often the extent of their power. Short of an appeal, kidnapping is perhaps the only way a parent adjudicated as noncustodial can reject a court's determination. Obviously such action is illegal in many jurisdictions and may lead to even greater restrictions of the parent-child relationships by the court. For these reasons, Grisso (1984) suggests that we use the *most stringent criteria* possible—that we be particularly conservative—when judging the reliability and validity of assessment measures and drawing conclusions in forensic cases.

McKenna (1984) and Weithorn (in press) raise similar questions in relation to scientific testimony presented in the courtroom: (1) How certain must we be of our scientific findings before we are willing to testify about them? What is the importance of "consensus" within the field, and how much agreement constitutes consensus? (2) What magnitude of effect is required before psychological data are proper grist for expert testimony? (3) How generalizable must laboratory findings be given the real-world situation posed by the case at hand?

Although there are no answers as to precisely *where* we should draw lines (i.e., How high should be the reliability coefficient for a psychological test, or what should be the level of significance for a statistical finding?), the APA *Ethical Principles* (1981a), consistent with Grisso's (1984) position, state that the criteria should be *higher* when questions of social policy are involved or where one's actions may affect the lives of others. Relative to the presentation of research data, Principle 1a cautions psychologists to be particularly careful to permit thorough discussions of the limitations of their data where their "work touches on social policy." And, importantly, Principle 1f states that "[Psychologists] bear a heavy social responsibility because their recommendations and professional actions may alter the lives of others."

Competence

It is incumbent upon psychologists who become involved in child custody cases to assess their competence to perform the required tasks. The Preamble to Principle 2 of the APA's *Ethical Principles* underscores that "psychologists recognize the boundaries of their competence and the limitations of their techniques. They only provide services and only use techniques for which they are qualified by training and experience." However, it is not always clear what constitutes competence for those who participate as experts in child custody, or any forensic case. This section will attempt to provide some clarification and suggestions. At the minimum, conformity to those guidelines listed above relative to the "recognition of the limits of psychology," familiarity with applicable legal standards and procedures, and adequate didactic and experiential training appear to be necessary.

Familiarity with Applicable Legal Standards and Procedures

Writers have commented that a common failing of psychologists providing child custody consultation is a lack of familiarity with applicable legal standards and procedures (Hall & Hare-Mustin, 1983; Keith-Spiegel & Koocher, 1985; Ochroch, 1982). The Task Force on the Role of Psychology in the Criminal Justice System (Monahan, 1980) stipulates that "Psychologists who work in the criminal justice system, as elsewhere, have an ethical obligation to educate themselves in the concepts and operations of the system in which they work" (p. 8). In custody litigation as well, psychologists must ascertain the substantive laws governing divorce custody adjudications in their state. If they cannot gain access to this information directly (from legal research, relevant articles, or workshops on local law), consultation with knowledgeable attorneys is typically an adequate substitute. Familiarity with the relevant law goes beyond knowledge of substantive law, however. Psychologists must apprise themselves of applicable legal procedures as well. For example, psychologists must inform all prospective evaluees at the outset of their professional contacts of the parameters and limitations that define the psychologist's role vis-à-vis the evaluees, other parties in the case, and the court. Psychologists cannot properly inform about these matters if they are not themselves cognizant of the facts.

Expertise

At one level, performance of a custody evaluation requires the same basic training and experience for the conduct of *any* clinical assessment. That is, one must be skilled in the administration and interpretation of measures and techniques to be used and well versed in psychometric issues relating to use of measurement instruments. In addition, one must have completed adequate training and developed a suitable level of skill in evaluating those populations (e.g., children, adults, mentally retarded persons) who might be the subject of the evaluation. Clearly, a clinician whose training and experience have been exclusively adult focused should not venture to conduct a clinical assessment of a child or to offer any statements about what conditions appear to promote or impede a child's optimal functioning. In a similar vein, clinicians who have not worked previously with mentally retarded or psychotic persons should not permit the court-related context be their training ground; they must not participate in any assessment functions for which they do not arrive as experts.

Expertise typically is developed through a curriculum of didactic and practicum training, followed by supervised experience. The *Standards for Providers of Psychological Services* (APA, 1977) and their companion Specialty Guidelines (APA, 1981b) identify some requirements for specialty training. The APA clarifies that formal training in an accredited degree program is the only acceptable route to expertise in certain primary areas (e.g., clinical psychology). It is not clear, however, for which subspecialties it is possible to obtain acceptable expertise through other avenues such as postgraduate training.

The Division of Child, Youth, and Family Services of the APA, in its recommendations for minimal training criteria in work with children and families (Task Force, 1983), implies that one cannot obtain the basic expertise for work with children outside a formal graduate program. To qualify one to work with families and children, for example, it suggests, *at the minimum,* coursework and experience in areas such as child development and life-span developmental psychology; psychopathology (child and adult); mental retardation and developmental disabilities; specialized child assessment techniques; child psychotherapy and behavior change; parent, family, and school intervention; specialized clinical practica in child, parent, and family therapy; research methods in child psychology; ethics and legal issues related to children, youth, and families; and subspeciality work within psychology relating to children, youth, and families. Clearly, this curriculum constitutes a "major" or "minor" emphasis in a graduate training program and could not be obtained easily or practically as continuing education. By contrast, postgraduate acquisition of expertise in forensic psychology generally, and in child custody consultation specifically, may be possible if one has the requisite graduate training in child clinical psychology, for example.

The Task Force on the Role of Psychology in the Criminal Justice System states: "'Competence' is not so much a characteristic of the psychologist, in the sense of having the appropriate degrees or license, but rather an interaction between the abilities of the psychologist and the demands of a given setting. A psychologist may be competent in one setting and incompetent in others" (Monahan, 1980, p. 8). Not only do the demands of a child custody evaluation include basic skills in relevant areas of psychology (e.g., child and life-span development; child, adult, and family assessment; child and adult psychopathology), but psychologists also must have other, more specialized expertise.

If a psychologist is competent to perform the more basic clinical tasks required for psychological assessment of children and families, it is possible that certain combinations of postgraduate training (e.g., continuing education, specialized workshops, supervised clinical experience, and familiarity with the relevant scholarly and professional literature) can qualify that psychologist to participate competently in forensic assessment. This conclusion is drawn from research conducted by Melton, Weithorn, and Slobogin (1984). The investigators demonstrated that community mental health professionals (i.e., psychologists, psychiatrists, and social workers) who participated in a specialized forensic assessment training program were able to provide forensic assessment services considered to be of high quality on a number of evaluative indexes. The training program included didactic and practicum components. Although the emphasis of this training program was adult forensic assessment, child and family forensic assessment probably would lend itself as well to such training.

Precisely how much formal versus informal, or didactic versus supervised practical, training one needs to become competent will depend upon the skill level and sophistication of the psychologists seeking training. It is possible, of course, that, regardless of the extent of a psychologist's training, he or she may perform incompetently or irresponsibly. Other psychologists, by contrast, may find that their unique constellation of previous skills and experiences equips them to move relatively quickly into competent forensic assessment work. It is unfortunate that not all specialized forensic workshops and training programs are of high quality. Thus it is incumbent upon a psychologist to evaluate carefully any such programs by examining the qualifications of the instructors, the content of the workshop, and the nature of the practical experiences offered. Though workshops offered privately often are of high quality, one is probably most certain of quality when selecting training programs sponsored by organizations with known reputations (e.g., APA, or American Psychology Law Society) or educational institutions (e.g., universities).

One brief workshop (e.g., one or two days) and supervision on a handful of cases rarely is adequate training in any area of forensic psychology, including child custody. Further, psychologists should never simply venture into the legal arena without having observed custody assessments or participated as a secondary evaluator or team member. The stakes are too high in a forensic case for psychologists to try their wings without previous exposure to such clinical work. And any first and early attempts as the primary clinician custody cases clearly should be carefully supervised by a clinician with the necessary expertise.

Loyalties and Conflicts

Scott and Emery (chap. 2 above) delineate some of the problematic aspects of the adversary system in child custody cases. Unquestionably, this system presents new challenges to psychologists, who must define their roles vis-à-vis the parties (Weithorn, 1984).

That one's roles, and therefore loyalties, be clear to all the participating parties is required by the APA *Ethical Principles* (1981a, Principle 6) and recommended by the Task Force on the Role of Psychology in the Criminal Justice System (Monahan, 1980). Again, the wisdom of the Task Force relative to the criminal justice system is directly applicable to child custody cases:

> No question arises more frequently . . . than "Who is the client?" . . . When psychologists do try seriously to articulate who their client is—where their loyalties are to be given—. . . they sometimes appear to be under the impression that they are constrained to a multiple-choice answer. . . . It appears to us that there is no need for psychologists to impale themselves on the horns of this dilemma, since "Who is the client?" is not a multiple-choice question. It requires an essay answer. (Monahan, 1980, p. 5)

In a child custody case there is no question whose interests the law has designated as paramount: the child's. Therefore, regardless of who has requested psychological consultation or who is paying the bills, it is still the well-being of the child that is to prevail. Clearly, therefore, the child becomes a "client" in answer to the inquiry "Who is the client?" But other parties may also be clients.

Any other party who is the focus of the psychologist's evaluation also becomes a "client" in response to that inquiry. This means that relative to those other persons, psychologists must ensure that they have abided by all relevant ethical guidelines, including those on informed consent for assessment, confidentiality, dual roles, fees, and so on (APA, 1981a). In addition, the court, as the agent of society, becomes the psychologist's client, in that psychologists agree to assist the fact finder in the search for truth. Thus, as adjuncts to the fact-finding process, psychologists must internalize the court's concern for objectivity, fairness, and the well-being of the child.

Advocacy Versus Objectivity/Impartiality

Weithorn and Grisso (chap. 5 above) suggest that the ideal manner for psychological consultation in custody litigation is as *amicus curiae,* or court-appointed neutral expert. As a "friend of the court," one performs one's evaluative functions free from actual or apparent allegiance to any party in the adversary process. One has, in the eyes of all parties, made a commitment to the shared goals of the court and society: promoting the well-being of the child. If the psychologist is an advocate for anyone, the psychologist is an advocate for the child. The advocacy function is served through the psychologist's investigation and reporting of psychological matters, disclosure of which will aid the court in reaching an informed decision. As noted by Weithorn and Grisso (chap. 5 above) and others (Grisso, 1986; Melton et al., 1987; Ochroch, 1982; Weithorn, 1985) advocacy for the child does *not* include pressing for a particular outcome in the case. The ultimate balancing of facts and opinions is the responsibility of the court, whereas providing information to aid that decision is a role of the psychologist. In discussing ethical quandaries in the presentation of scientific or clinical data in the courtroom, many commentators (Anderten, Stalcup, & Grisso, 1980; Grisso, 1984; McKenna, 1984; Saks, 1984; Weithorn, 1984) underscore the potential role conflicts inherent in such testimony. Terms such as "advocacy" and "objectivity/impartiality" are often polarized. As Anderten et al. (1980) point out, psychologists really do not have a choice regarding objectivity if they wish not to violate the *Ethical Principles*. The commitment to objectivity is so basic to psychological research and practice as not to be negotiable. Purposeful slanting of data reporting to aid the cause of one party in a legal dispute is blatantly unethical. Psychologists' obligation is to discover and report the truth, whether in the form of scientific or clinical findings. (And, as noted above, when the truth is elusive or unclear, as it typically is, it is one's obligation to so report.)

Advocacy by psychologists is ethically permissible only where it requires no diminution in objectivity or impartiality. By contrast, the responsibility of the attorneys for the opposing parties is to use whatever strategies and techniques are available to further their clients' case. This responsibility may lead attorneys to vigorously "press the merits of those evidentiary facts that, no matter how sparse, support the client's claim" (Anderten et al., 1980, p. 766). Attorneys may therefore seek to suppress some information not helpful to their clients' cases and to exaggerate other information that they perceive as helpful. Thus, a first problem encountered by psychologists who enter a case employed by one party is that if their findings are not consistent with what the lawyers desire, they may be rejected for another, more "friendly" expert. A second problem encountered is that, in working for "one side," psychologists' objectivity may be threatened, not because of a purposeful decision by the psychologist to distort findings, but through a type of socialization or contamination process. As Anderten et al. (1980) note:

> In the legal arena, since the attorney decides what is "helpful" to the client, the attorney is essentially the gatekeeper of psychological data used in the courtroom. Psychologists who anticipate this state of affairs and probably most do, consciously or unconsciously—may be drawn away from an objective approach to their assessment task or data collection for any number of reasons. (p. 766)

It is possible for psychologists to become slowly compromised by the "us/them" mentality that pervades each side of an adversarial legal dispute; to become tainted by having only half the data pertinent to the case; or to be influenced in some way by financial remuneration. An insidious process may occur through which psychologists gradually lose their objectivity and unwittingly become partial as advocates for one parent. Although this result is not necessary, it is more likely to occur when one enters the case in the employ of one of the two opposing parties. This phenomenon, together with the reality that psychologists on opposing sides have access to different data, may explain the often dramatic result that psychological experts employed by opposing sides in a legal case typically reach different clinical conclusions, each position "helpful" to its "side."

Thus, whereas it is not unethical, per se, to become involved in a custody case under the employ of one parent or the other, it is unethical if: (1) one permits that alliance to compromise one's objectivity and impartiality in the investigation, interpretation, and reporting of findings; or (2) one extends beyond the limitations of a necessarily incomplete evaluation (which typically characterizes such arrangements) by making statements, drawing inferences, or offering conclusions about parties and relationships not assessed directly (Weithorn & Grisso, chap. 5 above).

Dual Relationships and Conflicts of Interest

Psychologists are ethically bound to "make every effort to avoid dual relationships that could impair their professional judgment" (APA, 1981a, Principle 6a). A psychologist who interacts with an individual in one professional role (e.g., as therapist, evaluator, teacher, researcher, consultant) and also becomes involved with that same party in some other role, professional or personal, is involved in a dual relationship. Not all dual relationships are unethical. Only those that are viewed as creating a conflict of interests for the psychologist, blurring judgment, or risking some harm to the other parties are problematic. A psychologist who enters a custody case having a previous or current professional or personal relationship with one of the parties clearly does face a conflict of interests. For example, a psychologist may have served as the father's therapist for three years. Now the father's lawyer asks him to conduct a custody evaluation. Therapists typically perceive themselves as their clients' advocates; that is, their work is typically geared toward promoting the best interests of their clients in a partnership of trust and collaboration. If suddenly thrust into the adversary process, could the psychologist shift to the role of neutral evaluator? Could and should the psychologist attempt to view both parties in the case impartially? Not only is it unlikely that the psychologist could, after three years of individual therapy with a client, become impartial toward that client and the spouse with whom that client is in bitter conflict, but if he or she could, it might have devastating effects upon the therapeutic relationship. Finally, even if the therapist is able to take on a neutral role, and even if the therapeutic relationship could withstand the process, it is unlikely that the mother would be comfortable with the arrangement. The reasonable "perception" of impartiality by another in this type of situation is sufficient cause for psychologists to disqualify themselves.

A psychologist who has served as a party's therapist may, however, testify solely in that capacity. It may aid the court to learn about the therapy and the therapist's evaluative perspectives. If the client requests the testimony, it is the psychologist's responsibility in this instance to review for the client what may be said to the court and to share any concerns the psychologist may have about whether such testimony may be damaging to the client. In so doing, the psychologist obtains the informed consent of the client for the testimony. However, once on the stand, the psychologist must be truthful and objective. In our section on confidentiality below, we discuss the ethical dilemma posed by the subpoena by a party other than the client.

Another not uncommon, and very unfortunate, type of dual relationship is that of a divorce mediator who undertakes (voluntarily or through court coercion) to present data to the court regarding the parties in a failed mediation process (Bishop, 1984; Emery & Wyer, 1985; Note, 1984). Besides the obvious problems with confidentiality (to be reviewed below), this type of dual relationship undercuts the integrity and efficacy of the mediation process. Couples who are aware that their behavior and statements may end up in the courtroom will be less likely to participate fully and honestly in the mediation process (Bishop, 1984; Emery & Wyer, 1985; Note, 1984). If the clients are not aware at the outset that the mediator may subsequently testify, then their autonomy has been violated in that they have entered into an arrangement without a full appreciation of the limits of confidentiality. This dual relationship also is problematic in that the types of data collected about the couple during the mediation sessions are not likely to permit criterion-valid testimony. It would be rare and perhaps impossible for a mediator to conduct the type of multimethod and ecologically valid assessment described by Weithorn and Grisso (chap. 5 above) concurrent with mediation. Thus, providing testimony in such circumstances would also constitute unethical behavior in that it would provide rather narrow, and probably misleading, data to the court.

Informed Consent: Clarification of Roles, Procedures, and Fees

In nonadversarial circumstances, psychologists must inform clients of "the nature and direction of their loyalties" and must "inform consumers as to the purpose and nature of an evaluative . . . procedure" (APA, 1981a, Principle 6—Preamble). It is incumbent upon psychologists not to relax this responsibility in circumstances where the stakes are particularly high. They must ensure that each party is aware of the psychologist's loyalties: who has requested the psychologist's services, who will be paying the fees, whether the psychologist is representing one side in the adversary process or has been appointed by the court or hired by the child's guardian *ad litem*.

Psychologists must inform clients about the specifics of the assessment instruments and techniques and must report the findings to the examinees while guarding the confidentiality of one party against disclosures to another party (APA, 1981a; Anderten, et al., 1980). It is critical that the client be informed of the disposition of the data collected. Will it go only to the client's attorney, at which point the attorney will decide to use the report only if favorable? Or will it be submitted to the court in any event? It is an unfortunate characteristic of court evaluations that parties may consent to them reluctantly. That is, a party may prefer not to have personal information publicized within the courtroom. However, that party may recognize that if cooperation with the court's procedures relative to psychological evaluations is refused, the court may interpret such refusal in a manner damaging to that party's case. Thus the ethical imperative that psychologists inform clients of their "freedom of choice with regard to participation" (APA, 1981a) is rather hollow in this instance. Although clients do, theoretically, have the right to refuse, it is likely that they will consent whether they wish to take part or not. However, informing them of the limits of confidentiality (see below) does permit them to choose what they wish to disclose or not disclose to the psychologist, a right they retain.

It is beyond the scope of this chapter to discuss the specifics of fee setting. However, it is essential that psychologists clarify in advance, with the parties in the case, what the fees are and who is responsible for them. This is particularly relevant when psychologists evaluate parties on both sides of the dispute. To what extent will the court, as opposed to the parties in the case, be responsible for paying the psychologist? Obviously it is best to clarify any misconceptions at the outset. For example, it may come as a big surprise to an evaluating psychologist, and to parties acquiescing to a psychologist's evaluation at the request of the adversary, that the adversary does not intend to pay for those portions of the evaluation that focus exclusively on parties other than himself or herself. Principle 6d of the *Ethical Principles* (APA, 1981a) places the onus on the psychologist to ensure that financial arrangements are clearly understood by clients in advance.

Confidentiality

Psychologists are bound by an ethical duty to maintain in confidence information gathered about individuals in the course of professional psychological work (APA, 1981a, Principle 5; Shah, 1970). There are exceptions to this general rule, which will be reviewed below. First, let us distinguish between *confidentiality* and *privileged communication*. Confidentiality is an ethical obligation of psychologists and many other professionals (Shah, 1969; Vickery, 1982). It is prescribed by professional associations' codes of ethics (e.g., APA, 1981a), is inherent in more basic principles of biomedical (e.g., Beauchamp & Childress, 1983), scientific (e.g., Beauchamp, Faden, Wallace, & Walters, 1982), or psychological (e.g., Keith-Spiegel & Koocher, 1985) ethics, and at times derives from the confiding party's reliance on a reasonable expectation of secrecy, as promised by the professional (Vickery, 1982). The ethical duty not to disclose professionally obtained information about others is not, however, always required or protected by law.

The term privileged communication refers to those confidences the law protects from disclosure in legal proceedings (Shah, 1969). The concept of privilege represents a deviation from the general legal notion that the public has a right to whatever evidence might be available for a court proceeding (Developments in the Law, 1985). As such, privileges "expressly subordinate the goal of truth seeking to other societal interests" (Developments in the Law, 1985, p. 1454). One might claim that the children, who arguably have the greatest interest in a correct custody adjudication, have a right to full disclosure of relevant information about parents' capacities to provide for their best interests and that privilege is less relevant in the child custody context. It is likely that guardians *ad litem* will attempt to promote disclosures about parental psychological functioning "in the children's interests." However, respect for the social benefits of protecting psychologist-client confidentiality (i.e., promoting mental health by fostering the success of psychological interventions), and respect for privacy in general have been found by many legislatures to outweigh the traditional public interest in full disclosure (Developments in the Law, 1985). In a state where communications between psychologist and client are regarded as privileged in a manner parallel to those between attorney and client, disclosure cannot be coerced by a court of law in most instances (see, e.g., *Pennsylvania Consolidated Statutes Annotated,* 1982). Most states have some type of privilege protection for the psychologist-client relationship, but the extent of and exceptions to the privilege vary across states (Developments in the Law, 1985; Shah, 1969). The general categories of exceptions to the psychologists' ethical duty not to disclose confidential information will be discussed below; they relate to waiver of confidentiality or privilege by the client; voluntary breaches in confidentiality by the therapist, lacking a waiver by the client, for the protection of a child whose well-being will be seriously endangered by maintenance of confidentiality; and compelled testimony following subpoena.

Prospective Evaluations

If there is one clear caveat relative to confidentiality in child custody cases, it is that the psychologist who commences a *prospective* custody evaluation—that is, conducts the evaluation specifically for the purposes of litigation—must ensure that the parties are aware of the limits of confidentiality that may characterize the professional relationship. The parties must understand that, in consenting to the evaluation in most instances, they are consenting to disclosure of the evaluation's findings in the context of the forthcoming litigation. As such, they are waiving whatever ethical and legal protection of secrecy might otherwise have characterized their contacts with a psychologist.

A prospective situation that often proves troublesome, however, is when the psychologist is conducting divorce mediation. The Family Law Section of the American Bar Association, in its Standards of Practice for Family Mediators, indicates that it is unethical for a mediator to disclose *voluntarily* information obtained through the mediation process without the prior consent of both parties (Bishop, 1984; Lande, 1984). As noted above, assurances of confidentiality are critical to the success of mediation. However, psychologists must not promise absolute protection from disclosure if the law will not support these promises. In many states a third party may, through subpoena, trigger a violation of these ostensibly private discussions by requiring the psychologist's testimony in court. Most states do not provide explicit protection for divorce mediators (Emery & Wyer, 1985; Note, 1984), and it is not clear whether the general protection of the psychologist-client privilege in particular states extends to divorce mediation. And even if the privilege does so extend, as noted below, sometimes it is not absolute and does not prevent the court from ordering disclosure of certain types of relevant information. The Family Law Section suggests that the parties to divorce mediation sign a written agreement not to require the mediator to disclose statements made in the course of mediation (Bishop, 1984). However, it is unclear whether such an agreement will be given legal effect by the judges adjudicating custody cases (Note, 1984). The primary result of the document may be to bind the parties morally, to the extent that such obligations are effective. Again, beyond promising not to disclose voluntarily the contents of mediation, and encouraging the parties not to trigger an involuntary disclosure themselves, a psychologist can best protect the parties in mediation by informing them, at the outset of mediation, about the possible limitations on confidentiality in mediation in their state.

Disclosure of Information Gathered in Previous Clinical Contacts

Waiver by Client of Confidentiality or Privilege

If a psychologist has provided services to a client in an individual therapeutic or evaluative relationship and the individual gives permission for the disclosure of personal information, the psychologist can, and typically must, disclose the information as requested. Confidentiality and privilege are controlled by the client, not the psychologist, and therefore if the client waives these rights one must abide by such disclosure requests (Developments in the Law, 1985). A psychologist may, of course, counsel a client against disclosure if it seems counter to the client's best interests. Although psychologists may at times be displeased with disclosing such information, their ethical and legal obligation is relatively clear. By contrast, the situation becomes a great deal more complicated when the clinical information was derived from family or couples therapy. A psychologist faces special dilemmas when asked by one spouse to disclose confidential information about clinical contacts in which both spouses participated together (Hall & Hare-Mustin, 1983; Ochroch, 1982). From an ethical and legal standpoint, it is typically not problematic for the psychologist to reveal only that information that concerns the individual waiving confidentiality. If the other spouse does not *also* give permission for a courtroom disclosure, ethical principles may require a continued guarding of information about that spouse—consistent, however, with exceptions, as noted below, relative to clear dangers and subpoenas. It may be difficult, of course, for a psychologist to sort out what elements of information about the couple "belong" to each spouse or to the couple as a unit. Guidance from colleagues with expertise in ethics may help a psychologist select the content appropriate for the testimony.

Although it may be debatable precisely where to draw the line between released and protected information in the situation above, the critical point is that the psychologist recognize that voluntary waiver of confidentiality and privilege by one spouse may not authorize disclosure of information about the nonwaiving spouse. It may be argued, however, that there is a lessened expectation of privacy in family therapy, as contrasted with individual therapy, and that therefore it is less problematic to divulge information about family therapy in the absence of consent from all of the parties. However, it is key that the psychologist and, one hopes, any ruling judge not *presume* that there is such a diminished expectation but rather, inquire into the actual expectations of the parties. A therapist who has given the parties assurance of such protection will be ethically obligated not to breach that promise voluntarily. One court held that despite the presence of others in group therapy, communications gathered by the therapist remain privileged because the presence of the others is necessary to the treatment (Developments in the Law, 1985). It is possible that a similar argument can be made for family therapy. A recent trend is the recognition of a legal obligation to maintain in confidence communications that would not have been provided without an assurance of secrecy (Vickery, 1982).

The situation becomes even more complicated when the child whose custody is in question participated in the family therapy. In most instances the legal privilege will not be under the minor child's control. A guardian *ad litem* may be able to assert the child's right to waive the privilege; however, to what extent does this waiver bear on information about the parents? Do the parents, separately or together, retain, as they ordinarily would, any privilege derived from their custody of the child? These are complex questions, and a thorough review of the relevant case law is beyond the scope of this chapter. In general, however, precedents in various jurisdictions may differ, and particular judges may exercise broad discretion in making appropriate rulings. The primary caveat here is that psychologists must be apprised of the complexity of these issues and should not voluntarily disclose any information without first consulting an impartial and knowledgeable attorney.

Voluntary Disclosure by Psychologists in the Absence of Client Waiver

The APA *Ethical Principles* (1981a), case law (e.g., *Tarasoff v. Regents of the University of California,* 1976), and most child abuse reporting statutes cite an exception to the confidentiality of the psychologist-client relationship. In those "unusual circumstances" in which not to breach confidentiality "would result in a clear danger to the person or to others," a psychologist may reveal personal information gathered in the course of a professional relationship (APA, 1981a). Thus, if one learns that a client is likely to attempt suicide or may harm his or her child, one is permitted to violate confidentiality. The *Ethical Principles* make the breach *permissible,* whereas in some instances the legal standards *require* the information disclosure for the protection of others.

In child custody cases this exception relates primarily to the possibility that psychologists may uncover information about a child or about contesting parents that is essential for protecting the health and well-being of the child. If the information relates to suspected child abuse or neglect, psychologists are required by law to disclose their suspicions to the authorities designated by their state; this type of situation presents no new ethical problems beyond those typically encountered in balancing confidentiality against the protection of the child (Keith-Spiegel & Koocher, 1985). The report of the investigation of the child protection authorities will undoubtedly be introduced in court, independent of any further action by the psychologist, by the guardian *ad litem* or one of the parents' attorneys.

The more difficult scenarios are those where the psychologist's concern does not rise to the level of suspected abuse or neglect warranting disclosure to child-protection authorities. Rather, a psychologist who has seen a parent or family in therapy fears that one parent's conduct may be damaging to the child's well-being, but in more subtle ways than would be relevant from the standpoint of child protection laws. For example, a therapist may be concerned about a parent's unwillingness to follow through with therapeutic treatment for a child with suicidal tendencies. Or a therapist may feel that one parent's overinvolvement in the child's personal life is directly related to the child's serious, and perhaps one day life-threatening, drug problems. Yet does disclosure of such information really fall within the "clear danger" exception? In both instances the feared danger has not materialized. Whereas at one end of the spectrum we would agree that concern about a less than optimal parent-child relationship does not justify violation of confidentiality, the possibility of a child's death probably does. But how certain a possibility must it be? How certain must one be of one's clinical judgment? There are no clear answers. This situation presents a classic insoluble ethical dilemma: there are two competing and mutually exclusive courses of conduct, both of which may be required ethically. Disclosing voluntarily, and over the objections of one's client, confidential communications by that client in the absence of a clear and imminent danger to another is unethical; however, failing to act to protect the life of a child may also be unethical. It is suggested here that in the event such a quandary presents itself, the psychologist consult with colleagues about the clinical questions, with a knowledgeable and impartial attorney about the legal issues, and with a psychologist with expertise in ethics.

Compelled Disclosure Through Subpoena

Finally, the third possible exception to the client's right of confidentiality is when a court subpoenas otherwise protected information. In this instance there may be a conflict between the ethical requirement for confidentiality and the state laws on privilege. Different states provide varying protection for the communications in the psychologist-client relationship. For example, Pennsylvania (*Pennsylvania Consoli-*

dated Statutes Annotated, 1982) likens the psychologist-client privilege to that of attorney-client. Therefore a psychologist cannot be required to testify in court about most confidential communications. By contrast, the *Virginia Code* (1984) stipulates that where the mental or physical conduct of a practitioner's client is the issue before a court, the court may exercise "sound discretion" in determining whether disclosure of otherwise privileged information is "necessary to the proper administration of justice." If the judge determines that the information is essential to the court, disclosure may be required. Thus the substance of one's therapy contacts with a client may be subpoenaed in Virginia, but typically not in Pennsylvania, by the judge in a divorce custody adjudication. The APA *Ethical Principles* do not prescribe an appropriate solution if one's clinical data are subpoenaed. The *Principles* do suggest that psychologists make known to the appropriate legal authorities their commitment to the *Ethical Principles* and work toward a resolution of the conflict (APA, 1981a). It is quite possible that the court will not be persuaded by psychologists' reliance on the *Principles,* leaving psychologists with a true ethical dilemma. They must then decide whether to refuse disclosure, which clearly may place them at some personal risk (of being held in contempt of court), or to provide the subpoenaed information, thus violating confidentiality and their clients' wishes. While there is no correct solution to this conflict, some steps may be taken to reduce the likelihood of the final "showdown." One's client's attorney can challenge the subpoena on the grounds that the disclosed information may not be relevant to the proceedings. In general, when faced with such a dilemma it is advisable to discuss this matter with the client and then, with the client's permission, with the client's attorney. Consultation with one's own attorney may also be helpful.

In general, psychologists who are treating clients and foresee impending litigation wherein records might be subpoenaed should, in most circumstances, discuss this matter with the clients as early as it is foreseen. Whereas it may not be possible to affect the subpoena of information already obtained, it may be possible to avoid generating future damaging information if that is the agreed-upon choice of the client and therapist. Unquestionably though, this problem may interfere with ongoing therapy. However, unless to proceed in this manner would present a clear danger to the client, it is advisable that the decision whether to generate new information that may be subpoenaed be left to the client, in consultation with the therapist, and not be made exclusively by the therapist.

Conclusions

At the outset of this chapter, I referred to psychological participation in divorce custody litigation as a minefield. Serious blunders that may be detrimental to the parties or the child in a custody dispute are, unfortunately, all too easy to make.

1. The context and the proceedings' consequences require psychologists to exercise exemplary restraint and caution in their testimony. Yet the actors in the dispute may try to persuade or pressure the psychologist to abandon this posture.

2. Ironically, psychologists who refrain from invading the province of the law and refuse to make conclusory statements about the child's best interests may find themselves rejected as experts by many attorneys and, sadly, by some judges.

3. Psychologists may find it difficult to ascertain what types of training are necessary for the performance of competent custody evaluations.

4. The best attempts at objectivity and impartiality may be unable to withstand the often subtle, but sometimes brutal, battering that occurs when one tries to be neutral while in the employ of one "side" of a custody dispute. Yet if one attempts to enter the case as a "friend of the court" one may find the parties resistant.

5. The ethical dilemmas relating to confidentiality arising in some divorce custody cases present challenges that often defy a problem-free resolution.

And yet despite the plethora of ethical pitfalls that characterize any divorce custody evaluation under the best of conditions, psychologists are not relieved from the responsibility to uphold the highest standards of their profession. That is, pressures from others, taxing dilemmas, and lack of commonly accepted standards for the conduct of such evaluations do not constitute mitigating circumstances excusing ethical blunders or abuses in custody cases. To the contrary, they require psychologists to exercise even higher levels of responsibility, because the danger of harm to others, to the profession of psychology, and to the system of justice is so great in likelihood and magnitude. The Preamble to Principle 1 of the APA *Ethical Principles of Psychologists* (1981a), Responsibility, distills this onus: "In providing services, psychologists maintain the highest standards of their profession. They accept responsibility for the consequences of their acts and make every effort to ensure that their services are used appropriately."

One may wonder why any intelligent psychologist would choose to participate as an expert in divorce custody litigation, given the dangers and conflicts inherent in such involvement. It may be money, masochism, the desire to promote the well-being of children caught in the throes of divorce, fascination with and challenge by the legal and psychological issues defining the dispute, or other reasons. It is likely that psychologists' motivations for participating in these cases are diverse. Perhaps, however, the most troubling impetus for such participation is the eager innocence of a novice in forensic assessment who walks blindly into the minefield. The purpose of this chapter and this book is to reduce the likelihood that those who choose to enter this area are uninformed about its dangers.

References

American Educational Research Association, American Psychological Association, and National Council on Measurement in Education. (1985). *Standards for educational and psychological testing.* Washington, DC: American Psychological Association.

American Psychological Association. (1977). *Standards for providers of psychological services.* Washington, DC: Author.

American Psychological Association. (1981a). *Ethical principles of psychologists:* Washington, DC: Author.

American Psychological Association. (1981b). Speciality guidelines for the delivery of services for clinical psychologists, counseling psychologists, industrial organizational psychologists and school psychologists. *American Psychologist, 36,* 640–681.

Anderten, P., Stalcup, V., & Grisso, T. (1980). On being ethical in legal places. *Professional Psychology, 11,* 764–773.

Beauchamp, T. L., & Childress, J. F. (1983). *Principles of biomedical ethics.* (2nd ed.). New York: Oxford University Press.

Beauchamp, T. L., Faden, R. R., Wallace, R. J., Jr., & Walters, L. (Eds.). (1982). *Ethical issues in social science research.* Baltimore, MD: Johns Hopkins University Press.

Bishop, T. A. (1984). Mediation standards: An ethical safety net. *Mediation Quarterly, 1984*(4), 5–18.

Developments in the Law. (1985). Privileged communications. *Harvard Law Review, 98,* 1450–1666.

Emery, R. E., & Wyer, M. M. (1985). *Mediating disputes related to divorce.* Unpublished manuscript. Available from the authors, University of Virginia.

Ethics Committee, American Psychological Association. (1985). *Annual report of American Psychological Association Ethics Committee.* Washington, DC: American Psychological Association.

Grisso, T. (1984). *The interpretation of clinical data in legal assessment: Ethical issues.* Paper presented at the American Psychological Association Convention, Toronto, Canada.

Grisso, T. (1986). *Evaluating competencies: Forensic assessments and instruments.* New York: Plenum.

Hall, J. E., & Hare-Mustin, R. T. (1983). Sanctions and the diversity of ethical complaints against psychologists. *American Psychologist, 38,* 714–729.

Keith-Spiegel, P., & Koocher, G. P. (1985). *Ethics in psychology.* New York: Random House.

Lande, J. (1984). Mediation paradigm and professional identities. *Mediation Quarterly, 1984*(4), 19–48.

McKenna, J. (1984). *Ethical standards and presentation of scientific findings in the courtroom.* Paper presented at the American Psychological Association Convention, Toronto, Canada.

Melton, G. B., Petrila, J., Poythress, N. G., Jr., & Slobogin, C. (1987). *Psychological evaluations for the court: A handbook for mental health professionals and lawyers.* New York: Guilford Press.

Melton, G. B., Weithorn, L. A., & Slobogin, C. (1984). *Community mental health centers and the courts.* Lincoln: University of Nebraska Press.

Mills, D. H. (1984). Ethics education and adjudication within psychology. *American Psychologist, 39,* 669–675.

Mnookin, R. H. (1975). Child-custody adjudication: Judicial functions in the face of indeterminacy. *Law and Contemporary Problems, 39,* 226–293.

Monahan, J. (Ed.). (1980). *Who is the client? The ethics of psychological intervention in the criminal justice system.* Washington, DC: American Psychological Association.

Note. (1984). Protecting confidentiality in mediation. *Harvard Law Review, 98,* 441–459.

Ochroch, R. (1982). *Ethical pitfalls in child custody evaluations.* Paper presented at the American Psychological Association Convention, Washington, DC.

Pennsylvania Consolidated Statutes Annotated, 42, Section 5944 (Purdon 1982).

Reppucci, N. D. (1984). The wisdom of Solomon: Issues in child custody determinations. In N. D. Reppucci L. A. Weithorn, E. P. Mulvey, & J. Monahan (Eds.), *Children, mental health, and the law* (pp. 59–78). Beverly Hills, CA: Sage.

Saks, M. J. (1984). *Role conflict and ethical dilemmas: Research psychologists as expert witnesses.* Paper presented at the American Psychological Association Convention, Toronto, Canada.

Shah, S. T. (1969). Privileged communications, confidentiality, and privacy: Privileged communications. *Professional Psychology, 1,* 56–69.

Shah, S. T. (1970). Privileged communications, confidentiality, and privacy: Confidentiality. *Professional Psychology, 2,* 159–164.

Tarasoff v. Regents of University of California, 529 P.2d 553 (Cal. 1974), *vacated, reheard en banc, and aff'd,* 131 Cal. Rptr. 14, 551 P.2d 334 (1976).

Task Force on Training for Division of Child, Youth, and Family Services of the American Psychological Association. (1983). *Recommended minimal training criteria for psychologists working with children, youth, and families.* Unpublished report.

Vickery, A. B. (1982). Breach of confidence: An emerging tort. *Columbia Law Review, 82,* 1426–1468.

Virginia Code Annotated. Section 8.01–399 (1984).

Weithorn, L. A. (1984). *Responsibilities, roles, and clinical testimony: "Who is the client?" revisited.* Paper presented at the American Psychological Association Convention, Toronto, Canada.

Weithorn, L. A. (1985). *Ethical issues in child custody cases.* Paper presented at the 1985 American Psychological Association Convention, Los Angeles, CA.

Weithorn, L. A. (in press). Professional responsibility in the dissemination of psychological research in legal contexts. In G. B. Melton, (Ed.), *Reforming the law: Impact of child development research.* New York: Guilford Press.

The Contributors

Robert E. Emery, PhD, is associate professor of psychology at the university of Virginia. His primary interests include family conflict, children of divorce, childhood psychopathology, family interaction, and divorce mediation. He is currently directing a study empirically comparing the effects of mediated and litigated child custody determinations on children of divorce.

Robert D. Felner, PhD, is professor of psychology at the University of Illinois at Urbana-Champaign. His research interests include stress and coping in children and families, life transitions, children of divorce and child custody, factors influencing differential vulnerability of high-risk children, and primary prevention. Among his recent publications is *Preventive Psychology,* written with Jason, Moritsugu, and Farber.

Shelley J. Gaylord, JD, is a partner in the firm of Gaylord, Shuett & Norton and serves as an adjunct instructor in the Women's Studies Department of the University of Wisconsin, where she teaches Women and the Law. She devotes a significant proportion of her law practice to family law and has testified several times before the Wisconsin state legislature, most recently on questions relating to joint custody.

Thomas Grisso, PhD, is a professor of psychology and associate professor of psychology and law at St. Louis University. Much of his research and writing has pertained to children's competency to make decisions in delinquency proceedings and in treatment situations. His recent book, *Evaluating Competencies: Forensic Assessments and Instruments,* offers a model and methods for performing forensic evaluations, including evaluation of parents in child custody cases.

Elizabeth T. Grove, JD, is an associate with the firm of Cummings & Lockwood in Stamford, Connecticut. She graduated from the University of Virginia Law School in 1983 and has a special interest in family and juvenile law.

Mimi Lou, PhD, is director of research, Center on Deafness, at the University of California at San Francisco. She is a developmental psychologist with a primary interest in the intersection of cognitive and social development. Her present research focuses on the deaf population, including examinations of the relationships among cognitive, social, and linguistic development and investigations of the early attachment formed between deaf infants and their parents.

Linda Whobrey Rohman, JD, is currently serving a two-year clerkship on the staff of the United States Eighth Circuit Court of Appeals in St. Louis, Missouri. She also is a doctoral candidate in the Psychology in the Law–Psychology Program at the University of Nebraska and is majoring in law and applied social psychology. Her research interests and publications include witness credibility law, child custody law, and alternate methods of dispute resolution by the judiciary.

Bruce D. Sales, JD, PhD, is professor of psychology, sociology, and law at the University of Arizona. He has published extensively in law and psychology. He has been elected or appointed to numerous editorial boards (e.g., editor of *Law and Human Behavior,* and *Perspectives in Law and Psychology*) and numerous American Psychological Association (APA) boards and committees (e.g., the Policy and Planning Board, Committee on Legal Issues). At present he is president of the American Psychology–Law Society (Division 41 of APA).

Elizabeth S. Scott, JD, is director of the Center for the Study of Children and the Law and teaches at the Law School at the University of Virginia. Her primary area of interest is the application of social science to the development of legal policies relating to children and families. Current scholarly interests include joint custody, judicial perspectives on children's participation in divorce custody decisions, and sterilization of the retarded. Among her recent publications is an article, coauthored with Andre Derdeyn, entitled *Rethinking Joint Custody.*

Lisa Terre, MA, is a doctoral student in clinical/community psychology at Auburn University. Her research interests include joint custody, family transitions, and the health consequences of life stress.

Lois A. Weithorn, PhD, is assistant professor of psychology at the University of Virginia. Her research is in the area of psychological functioning and legal competencies, with studies examining the capacities of children and hospitalized psychiatric patients to consent to treatment. She is interested in a range of issues relating to children and the law, mental health and the law, and ethics in psychology. Among her publications is *Children, Mental Health, and the Law,* edited with N. Dickon Reppucci, Edward Mulvey, and John Monahan. She has served on the Ethics Committee of the American Psychological Association (APA) and has chaired ethics committees in several APA divisions. She is currently on leave from her position at the University of Virginia to study law at Stanford University.

Melissa M. Wyer is a doctoral candidate in research clinical psychology at the University of Virginia. Her scholarly interests include social policy and psychology, and social development. Her current research focuses on divorce mediation.

Table of Cases

Subject Index

Author Index